QUANTU
COMPANI

QUANTUM COMPANIES

100 COMPANIES THAT WILL CHANGE THE FACE OF TOMORROW'S BUSINESS

A. DAVID SILVER

PETERSON'S/PACESETTER BOOKS
PRINCETON, NEW JERSEY

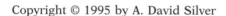

Peterson's/Pacesetter Books is a trademark of Peterson's Guides, Inc.

Library of Congress Cataloging-in-Publication Data

Silver, A. David (Aaron David), 1941–
    Quantum companies: 100 companies that will change the face of tomorrow's business / A. David Silver.
        p. cm.
     Includes index.
     ISBN: 1–56079–373–2
     1. Corporations—United States—Finance—Directories.   2. Market share—United States.   I. Title.
     HG4907.S46 1994
     338.7′4′02573—dc20   94–33198
                                           CIP

Interior Design by Greg Wozney Design, Inc.

Printed in the United States of America

10 9 8 7 6 5 4 3

CONTENTS

INTRODUCTION

Quantum Companies is going to introduce you to a world of sustainable wealth creation inhabited by 100 of the most exciting companies of the year 2000. These are companies that, by virtue of their particular product or service and market, are poised to take a quantum leap in profitability.

Within these pages are the stories of companies that should be of interest to you because they are a harbinger of *how* the business world is shaping up for the next century and *what* the growth industries are going to be. These are companies that are becoming winners in their markets, and so present many exciting possibilities for you to become a winner too. First, if you are an investor—big or small—I offer this opportunity: If you simply throw a dart at a board with the names of the Quantum Companies on it and invest in the one (or more) hit, it is highly probable that you will make ten times your investment in five years, or five times in three years—a compound return on investment of approximately 60 percent per year.

Second, consider the fact that the small business sector is where employment is happening. Then, consider this: If you take a job with one of the Quantum Companies, it is highly probable that you will become wealthy in approximately five years—through the company's stock options.

Third, as a consumer whose expectations of quality and superior customer service are high, you will find the products and services offered by any one of the Quantum Companies so satisfying that you will tell others about it, thus saving the company advertising expenses, which are quite low in any event. The product or service that you buy or rent from one or more Quantum Company will make you or your company a part of the Global Village, where everyone acts cooperatively and strategically to enhance their profits and preserve the planet.

And finally, if your company fits strategically with one of the Quantum Companies and you merge with it for stock, the stock you receive will probably increase at the rate of 60 percent per year.

Who Are the Quantum Companies?

There are 80 public and 20 private Quantum Companies. Of the public companies, only six are not yet revenue-producing. Twenty-five of the companies are in computer software; 24 in health-care delivery; 11 in connectivity hardware; and the balance are in education, law, cosmetics, pharmaceuticals, insurance, trucking, environmental services, building materials, apparel, natural foods, retail, metals, telephony, home automation, and services.

The word *sustainable* was important to me in selecting the 100 Quantum Companies. I looked back several years to determine that each of the companies' Gross Profit Margins (GPM) were increasing. This particular financial ratio says tons about the level of need for a company's product or service (its continuous problem-solving ability), that the market will pay more for it as newer models are introduced, and that management is careful about vendors' costs and does not permit them to rise.

The 10 Quantum Companies that demonstrated the largest increase in GPM from 1991 to 1994 (annualized) are listed in Exhibit 1. These

---

Exhibit 1
Quantum Companies with Largest Percentage GPM Rise 1991–94

	Percentage Increase
FORE Systems	+84.0
Swift Transportation	64.7
Quorum Health	59.7
Megahertz	49.8
Molten Metal	33.3
Three-Five Systems	32.6
Just For Feet	31.5
Harmony Brook	34.8
Orbital Science	28.4
Ascend Communications	22.9

---

companies cross several industry boundaries, including software, trucking, health care, metals, environmental services, connectivity hardware, retail, and telephony. This means, of course, that there are what I characterize as big problems—or opportunities if you prefer—in all sectors; that people—consumers, clients, customers—will pay handsomely for solutions; and that careful, focused management—the entrepreneurs and the people who work for them—is in the driver's seat across the board.

A rising GPM does not necessarily mean that selling, general, and administrative expenses (SG&A) are under control. Notwithstanding, I ran the ratio of SG&A Expenses/Sales for all of the companies under consideration and excluded those who could not control their overhead.

A heavy investment of cash flow in research and development (R&D) is applauded. That can lead to higher levels of future growth.

None of the companies in Exhibit 1 has the highest ratio of Net Profits Before Taxes to Revenues, generally known as the Operating Ratio, which means that quite a lot of their GPM growth is being deployed in selling costs, R&D, and overhead.

The 10 Quantum Companies with the highest annualized 1994 Operating Ratios are listed in Exhibit 2. Corel Corp., located in Ottawa,

---

Exhibit 2
Quantum Companies with Highest Operating Ratios

	Percentage Net Profits/ Revenues—1994
Parametric Technology	43.3%
Corel	42.2
Landstar	34.5
Zebra Technologies	32.6
Mitek Surgical	28.9
Newbridge Networks	27.4
Xilinx	26.3
Frontier Insurance	25.5
Bay Networks	25.1
Informix	23.8

Canada, comes out high on several of my tests. Corel's sales—just over $100 million—are derived from its graphics software "CorelDRAW," newsletter-publishing software under the Ventura label, and other useful and popular connectivity software. Corel acquired Ventura from XEROX Corp. in 1993 for $8 million when it was selling 1,000 copies a month; now Corel is selling 20,000 copies a month. Corel's founder and CEO, Michael Cowpland, co-founded Mitel Corp. in 1973; yet despite Mitel's enormous success, he left when there were too many management meetings. You will hear this theme again and again from other Quantum Company CEOs.

Cowpland's co-founder at Mitel was Terry Matthews, who went on to launch Newbridge Networks Corp., in Kanata, Canada, another Quantum Company. Cowpland and Matthews are co-founding a video telephone company in their spare time, a category in which I have selected two infant, privately held Quantum Companies: InVision Systems Corp. and Workstation Technologies, Inc. (Perhaps I should select the Cowpland/Matthews entrant on track record alone.)

The third highest Operating Ratio is that of Landstar Systems Inc., which makes its home in Shelton, Connecticut. Landstar is an unusual trucking company whose drivers are primarily small businesspeople who own and operate their own rigs. Landstar is an entrepreneurial factory and training ground with a bottom line that proves that giving people a piece of the action pays off. Frontier Insurance, Inc., in Rockhill, New York, appears on a few lists. This rapidly growing company insures risks that other insurers back away from. For example, they sell malpractice insurance to physicians in New York and Florida who have been damaged in their communities by litigation and have been rendered noninsurable.

Corel leads in the efficiency ratio category—Net Profits per Employee—with an amazing ratio of $144,352 per employee. Most companies do not have revenues per employee that high. Corel's ratio is twice that of Microsoft, the king of software. Exhibit 3 presents the top

---

Exhibit 3
Net Profits per Employee—1994

	Net Profits
Corel	$144,352
Parametric Technology	98,200
Xilinx	97,875
Transmedia Network	90,000
Frontier Insurance	83,452
Zebra Technologies	82,266
Xircom	81,964
Mitel Surgical	76,857
Progressive Corp.	59,793
Newbridge Networks	41,476

---

10 in this important category. Parametric Technology, in Waltham, Massachusetts, also appears on a couple of top 10 lists. The company is one of the most fascinating toolmakers of our day. Its solids modeling software enables manufacturers of products from cars to faucets to design and develop new products and bring them to market in one-tenth the time they ordinarily take for the task.

The rate at which a company's revenues grow is testament to the perceived need for its product or service and its ability to get its product or service into the market on a sustained, continuous basis through one or more channels. The leaders in the category of rate of revenue growth from 1991 to 1994 (annualized) are listed in Exhibit 4.

These companies are in software, connectivity hardware, health care, and environmental services. FORE Systems, in Waitendale, Pennsylvania, is run by four former Carnegie Mellon professors who developed some unique connectivity software. Education Alternatives, in Minneapolis, Minnesota, manages public schools. Located in Marietta, Georgia, Healthdyne Technologies manufactures a monitoring device that mitigates death during sleep (e.g., it is used to protect against Sudden Infant Death Syndrome). Ascend Communications, also a developer of connectivity hardware, offers a unique product that permits global digital video transmission. DNX is the leader in organ transplantation using transgenic animal organs.

Exhibit 4
Quantum Companies Percentage Increase in Revenues 1991–94

	Percentage Increase Sales
FORE Systems	+2253.7
Education Alternatives	1266.2
Healthdyne Technologies	1160.0
Ascend Communications	769.3
DNX	697.3
Ensys	636.3
Quorum Health	634.1
Bay Networks	557.3
Heart Technology	514.0
PARCPlace Systems	492.6

The stock market, which is made up of many brilliant analysts and astute investors, does not put its highest Price/Earnings (P/E) ratios on the highest-rated Quantum Companies, but rather on its own favorites. In some instances, the stock market materially underestimates the future earnings of several Quantum Companies. As I believe that the stock prices of the Quantum Companies will increase approximately tenfold in five years, those with the highest P/E ratios today will increase less than that and those with the lowest P/E ratios today will exceed my prediction. The Quantum Companies with the lowest and highest P/E ratios appear in Exhibit 5. Clearly, the stock market will correct its opinions of many of the Quantum Companies whose future earnings growth is either over- or underestimated by the yardsticks being used in the mid-1994.

The Making of the Quantum Companies List

Identifying the 100 most exciting companies of the next quarter century was a process of gathering and eliminating. First I asked the hemisphere's venture capital investors to provide me with their top recommendations. To that pool of names I added some company lists compiled by business journals. I then culled substantially every new-issue prospectus of the last three years. The result? Four hundred potential Quantum Companies. To make the first cut, I used the following equation:

$$V = P \times S \times E$$

where:

    V = valuation or wealth
    P = the size of the problem that the company is attempting to solve
    S = the elegance of its solution
    E = the quality of its entrepreneurial team

Exhibit 5
Lowest and Highest P/E Ratios[1] Among Quantum Companies

LOWEST P/E RATIOS

	P/E Ratio
Hauser Chemical Research	6.0
Megahertz	10.0
Asanté Technology	14.0
Roper Industries	14.0
Quorum Health	14.0
Quantum Health	15.0
Cirrus Logic	16.0
Frontier Insurance	17.0
Healthdyne Technologies	17.0
Sunrise Medical	17.0

HIGHEST P/E RATIOS

	P/E Ratio
FORE Systems	123.0
Davidson Associates	85.0
Wholesome & Hearty Foods	60.0
Envirotest	59.0
Synopsys	55.0
Orbital Sciences	52.0
Wall Data	50.0
QualCom	50.0
Ascend Communications	48.0
PARCPlace Systems	47.0

[1] P/E ratios are on trailing earnings measured in August 1994. Names in italics indicate that the company is on at least one top 10 list.

I assigned values to P, S, and E, and when they are multiplied by one another, they produce a numeric value for V. This is the First Law of Entrepreneurship: Many selling sites (a large P factor) times a proprietary product or nonduplicable delivery system (a large S factor) times an experienced entrepreneurial team, perhaps one that has launched another successful company (a large E factor), will always produce a high valuation for the company's investors, founders, and employee stockholders. Conversely, should one of the factors—P, S, or E—suddenly develop a value of zero, V will crash to zero in a millisecond. Zero, when multiplied by any whole number, becomes zero. Thus, the sudden elimination of an opportunity by a competing technology, or the failure of the market to accept a new product or service, or the resignation by the management team when the auditors find misbookings, will send the V factor into the toilet.

The second sifter that I put the Quantum Company prospects into was the DEJ Factor Test. DEJ stands for Demonstrable Economic Justification. There are eight DEJ Factors, which are described below. If a company has all eight, the new product or service has more than a 90 percent probability of success, and customers will pay up front or with an order, thus minimizing capital requirements. With seven out of eight, the probability of success is between 80 and 90 percent, but the capital requirements are several million dollars. With six out of eight, the probability of success is about two-thirds, but the capital requirements are in the tens of millions of dollars. Below six out of eight, forget the idea. Each of the 100 Quantum Companies was founded with at least seven DEJ Factors.

DEJ Factor	Ask	What Will It Cost?
1. Existence of Qualified Buyers	Are the consumers to whom this product or service is marketed aware that they have a need for it?	Advertising needed to find buyers.
2. Large Number of Buyers	Are there lots of consumers who need this product or service?	Competitive pressure on price if there are too few customers.
3. Homogeneity of Buyers	Will the market accept a standardized product or service, or must it be customized?	Manufacturing, tooling, and die costs to customize each product.
4. Existence of Competent Sellers	Is the product or service so complex to explain that customers will need 90 days or more to test it?	Salespersons' salaries and expenses if "brilliance" needed to make sales.
5. Lack of Institutional Barriers to Entry	Is there a requirement for governmental or industry association approval before the product or service can be marketed?	Working capital that burns while approval is awaited.
6. Easy Promotability by Word of Mouth	Can the product's or service's merits be described by consumers via word of mouth?	Advertising if lacking word-of-mouth promotability.
7. Invisibility of the Inside of the Company	Is there a need to reveal profit margins to the public?	Competitive pressure on price once profit margins are publicly known.
8. Optimum Price/Cost Relationship	Is the selling price at least five times the cost of the goods sold?	Restrictions on the number of marketing channels if profit margins are too low.

These two tests—the First Law of Entrepreneurship and the DEJ Factor Test—were used to weed the list down to about 150. To make the final cut, each company was tested for:

- A rising Gross Profit Margin.
- Significant growth in revenues.

- SG&A/Expenses Sales Ratio increasing more slowly than revenue growth.
- A high and increasing Net Profits per Employee ratio.
- A high and increasing Operating Ratio.
- A relatively low debt-to-equity ratio.
- Considerable amount of cash on hand.
- No outside investments by management in companies selling services back to the company.
- Conservative accounting entries selected over aggressive alternatives.
- A thorough reading of footnotes showed no, or relatively few, egregious issues such as unwarranted gifts to management, changes in auditors, internecine litigation, product recalls, or other red flags.

Finally, the Quantum Companies include companies that either improve the ecosystem, our health, or the environment in some direct or meaningful way, or at least do not destroy it further.

I am absolutely certain that I have failed to include some outstanding companies. There are certain industries that I didn't even consider, because of their intense lack of social utility, such as real estate development and casinos. I admit to stretching my criteria in a few instances where the company otherwise qualified, except for a small down-tick in its GPM, a high debt-to-worth ratio while "pipe" is being laid, or an investment in a company that sells services to the Quantum Company.

The question of the relative worth of this list of 100 Quantum Companies to the Global Village cannot be determined for at least five, and, more realistically, 10 years. Quite a bit can happen in that time period. But the forces driving these, and other rapidly emerging companies, are in place and turning the crank of entrepreneurship. These forces of change are powerful and ineluctable, like ocean waves. In fact, there are 26 such waves that the Quantum Companies are riding. You can read about them in Part One. Just turn the page.

PART ONE

26
CHANGE-MAKING
WAVES

ASSETS

We do not live in the age of asset accumulation, at least not those of us who live in developed countries. But that represents only one-third of the planet's 6 billion inhabitants. The other two-thirds need and want roads, dams, reservoirs, factories, cars, trucks, buses, hospitals, telephones, TVs, and affordable, hygienic housing. We are suppliers to that need.

If your company builds things like factories, buildings, manufacturing equipment, oil and gas compressors, construction equipment, and transportation equipment, you must get to China. There are 1.2 billion people in China and with democracy bursting out like forsythia in April, the "new republicans" want all the consumer products that we have in developed countries. You can get to China by forming strategic alliances with companies in Singapore, Malaysia, Hong Kong, and Thailand that have Chinese ownership, speak Cantonese Chinese, and can sponsor your company in the mainland. Infrastructure building is also a necessity in the new democracies of Eastern Europe and Russia, but they lack hard currency. To do business there, you will need a trading partner skilled at bartering mink, vodka, gold, and other assets that these companies use in place of currency.

Quantum Company Roper Industries is selling compressors in the Russian oil and gas fields. All of the Quantum connectivity hardware companies are selling systems in South East Asia and Europe. And some of the more interesting companies who have important roles to play when infrastructures are involved are surety bond underwriters. Who will insure the completion of construction jobs in China, Russia, and the Ukraine? Will surety bond underwriters such as Quantum Company Frontier Insurance take the plunge?

True, we no longer accumulate assets in North America and Western Europe, but we can provide assets and service assets in the Far East and in Eastern Europe. Figuring out if you are a *transaction* company or a *content* company isn't all that difficult, but the new century will reward the transactors more.

BURGLARIES

Burglaries, arson, theft of personal property, and other crimes against property will decline as home alarm systems become more efficient and less expensive. And the word alarm will be replaced with a more user-friendly word, such as monitoring. At this moment you can install a home-monitoring system for about $2,000; it can be accessed from your portable or cellular telephone. The system can call you and say "There is a break-in," or "There is a fire." Or you can query it from anywhere with questions about doors, windows, temperature, or if grandma took her heart pill. You can change the temperature, turn on the VCR, start the microwave, or backwash your swimming pool filter with a verbal command from your cellular or portable phone or the modem on your PC. Quantum Company Sentinel Systems, Inc., in Hampton, Virginia, is in the home-monitoring business.

Within two years, you will be able to connect your home-monitoring system to your portable digital video conferencing PC that fits into your purse or jacket pocket. Then you can watch grandma take her heart pill. Advances in integrated circuit design by Quantum Companies Atmel and Cirrus Logic will bring prices down. Watch venture capital funds flock to the home-monitoring and central alarm systems companies.

CONNECTIVITY

Companies, government agencies, and associations with multiterminal computer installations hooked up to mainframe and midsize computers are asking themselves if they should continue paying IBM or DEC annual service fees of $1 million, or instead make a one-time $300,000 outlay of cash to buy a client/server computer and so link all of their computers to a local area network (LAN). Most client/server networks run on industry-standard software known as UNIX, for which IBM and DEC are not providers.

Client/server shipments in 1993 were $4.7 billion and are expected to double by 1988, according to International Data Corp. The Quantum Companies that are capturing this important niche are Asanté Technologies, Ascend Communications, Chipcom, Computer Network Technology, NetFRAME, and the pioneer of networking, 3Com.

The point of being on a network is to communicate with other members of the organization online, in real time, and to leave E-mail messages if the person isn't in. Many LANs hook into wide area networks (WANs) for branch-to-branch connectivity and to allow the organization to connect online with vendors, customers, and others.

The senior managers of IBM and DEC listened to their sales departments—and so missed the client/server market. Their share of the computer market will fall to less than 10 percent in the aggregate over the next five to 10 years because they are mainframe and minicomputer dependent. The future of the computer business, which is many times larger than any other market you can think of—approximately $160 billion in 1993 hardware and software shipments—belongs to those companies with a *connectivity* product, service, or channel.

We are riding a rocket of miniaturization, where every month that goes by, we learn to do more with less. While hardware requires uniformity of product to pay for a centralized form of information management, faxes, UNIX software, E-mail, LANs, WANs, and eventually mobile wireless digital video conferencing create a wide diversity of economic units, more of them hardware dependent.

DIY

DIY, or do-it-yourself, is a form of retailing that shifts costs to the customer. When DIY first appeared in the 1960s the stores were barely more than four walls with a ceiling and floor, and the products were primarily those requiring assemblage, such as furniture. Today DIY has evolved. The stores are brightly lit warehouse-size buildings with products arranged on inexpensive rack-type shelving, clearly marked, and very inexpensive, with relatively few salesclerks. To minimize shrinkage, small items are lashed together into packages too large to slip under one's raincoat. The consumer is left on his or her own.

The DIY concept is wide-ranging. Take, for instance, the listening room. In the 1950s, record stores set up small booths in which customers tried out records before buying them. Today, the listening room is returning to musical recording megastores. Blockbuster's music stores have listening centers. Circuit City, which has succeeded with the DIY retailing in consumer electronics, is entering the used car retailing business with its CarMax chain, the ultimate DIY product.

Quantum Company Just For Feet, Inc., in Birmingham, Alabama, is employing the DIY retailing concept with athletic shoes. It builds its stores with half-court basketball courts and encourages its customers to shoot some hoops wearing their prospective new shoes before purchasing. Needless to say, the customer walks out of the store 30 minutes later with more shoes than he intended to buy. Nike is copying Just For Feet at its Niketown retail stores.

DIY is popping up in the exquisitely operated Home Depot, which will cut bathroom tile and construct to order window and door frames, among other services, enabling home owners to use DIY products in his or her home without calling in carpenters and plumbers. Tweaking the DIY concept by calling it "cause marketing," The Body Shop (West Sussex, United Kingdom)—a Quantum Company retailer—encourages its customers to bring back their bottles for refill and avoid using wrapping paper, in order to help save the planet.

EDUCATION

The next great market to adapt the PC is education. *Every* child who attends a school will become computer literate by age six. Children will interact with their teachers via palmtop computers, letting them know when they don't understand something. Tests will be given and scored via computer. If a teacher is not available to teach a subject requested by students, say Chinese, a CD-ROM player, or distance-learning program provided over a dedicated satellite node, will become the teacher and the students will interact with it through their palmtops.

Of course, the teachers union will fight these changes. But schools will be opening at plant sites, operated by private companies in competition with public schools. Elizabeth Coker, founder and CEO of Minco Labs, Inc., an electronic components manufacturer in Austin, Texas, opened an on-premises elementary school simultaneously with the launch of the company a few years ago. Quantum Company Work/Family Directions, Inc., in Boston, Massachusetts, assists corporations in educating their employees' children. When these students get higher SAT scores than public school students, and when their dropout rates move toward zero, the unions will have no choice but to let the computer make the classroom more interactive.

Among the leaders in this revolution are Quantum Companies Better Education, Inc., in Yorktown, Virginia, and Education Alternatives, Inc., in Minneapolis, Minnesota. Software companies serving the school market, such as Quantum Company Davidson Associates, will move into the Fortune 500 as well, because of the high level of social utility of its educational software.

FACILITIES MANAGEMENT

Call it privatization or uncoupling bureaucratic bloat, if you prefer, but call the facilities-management business profitable for sure. Its most successful version invented by Ross Perot in 1968, when he founded Electronic Data Systems Corp. (EDS), the format has been replicated by money managers, risk managers, and asset managers over time, but the essentials remain the same: A lean and efficient entrepreneurial company persuades a bureaucratic organization that it can operate one of its divisions at 80 percent (pick a number) of its current annual budget, and not raise costs for five years. The small company is awarded the contract, after much gnashing of teeth and snarling of lip, and it takes the division's employees onto its operating statement and puts the division's equipment onto its balance sheet. It hacks away at union-driven costs and manages the facility at 70 percent of the budget, pocketing a profit of 10 percent before overhead. A second contract is even more profitable, as the company provides some of the services to its second client using personnel and assets assumed in the first contract. The third contract is even more profitable, as overhead is spread even further; and so forth.

Among the Quantum Companies are several facilities-management contractors, including Corrections Corp. of America, a Nashville, Tennessee, prisons manager; Cambridge Technology Partners, in Cambridge, Massachusetts, which manages the re-engineering of organizations when they upgrade information systems to local and wide area networks; Work/Family Directions, Inc., in Boston, Massachusetts, which manages human resources activities for large corporations; Envirotest, in Tucson, Arizona, which manages the automobile emissions testing operation for several states; and Education Alternatives, Inc., which manages public schools under contract. The stock market has always been enamored of fac-man companies. Perot's EDS went public at an initial public offering P/E ratio of 115.0x, a legendary multiple. Corrections Corp. sports a P/E ratio of 42.0x, and Envirotest has a lofty 59.0x in mid-1994.

Governments facing budget deficits have few options, but one they will increasingly turn to is the facilities-management contractor to operate its agencies. In France, the government sells her highways to fac-man companies that get their money back via erecting tollgates.

GOVERNMENT TOLLGATES

The validity of government is its ability to raise money. With further hikes of our income taxes verboten, look for governments to erect "tollgates" along the fastest-growing markets. In mid-1994, the Feds sold licenses to send messages through the air for more than $600 million. E-mail may soon require a "postage stamp" equivalent to generate revenues for the federal government.

And what about city governments? While new growth companies are opening up in small, rural communities to enable their workers to live in the mountains and at lake shores, cities are losing their tax bases at an accelerated rate. To remain valid, to operate courts, fire departments, schools, and police forces, managers of cities will privatize as many agencies as they can and look for new highways to plunk tollgates on to. The most likely candidate is the telephone pole. City governments will begin charging taxes (or tolls) to telephone, cable, and computer companies who send voice, data, or video signals over wires hung on their poles. (Actually, the poles are on city-owned land; thus, the toll will go from the communications carrier to the utility to the city.) The lowly, once-forgotten telephone poll will become city government's most valuable tollgate in the next quarter century.

Telecommunications rates will rise, even if we live outside the city, to pay for municipal services to urban dwellers and urban workers.

Guiding government agencies through the thicket of new highway signs in the Global Village are Quantum Companies Tresp Associates in Alexandria, Virginia, and Research Management Consultants, Inc., in Camarillo, California.

HOSPITALS

The number of hospitals in the United States will shrink from about 5,000 to 2,500 as many of their expensive services are taken over by entrepreneurial companies organized to provide less expensive but highly effective health care in smaller clinics, patients' homes, and through company doctor programs. If you consider procedures in hospitals as transactions and drugs and devices as content, then the major cost reductions and savings will come in transactions. The number of physicians, particularly specialists, will also decline as the profitability of their practices attenuates.

The force downsizing the health-care transaction market is and will continue to be health insurance. The surviving hospitals will be the large ones, many of them aggregated into chains, or university-related with research and teaching capabilities: big enough to establish negotiating parity with the insurers.

Dionex, Health Management Associates, Homecare Management, Quantum Health, Quorum Health, and Vivra—all Quantum Companies— will profit by being atavistic and opportunistic in this shrinking environment.

INCENTIVES

Incentives will replace advertising as the primary expense in generating consumer product and service sales. Already the frequent flyer programs offered by the airlines have been copied with frequent traveler programs by the hotels, frequent filler programs by oil companies, frequent reader programs by bookstores, and frequent shopper programs by supermarket chains.

National Health Corporation, in Grand Prairie, Texas, one of the Quantum Companies, is an association-based health insurance company that offers membership in a club for $20 a month along with health insurance for approximately $80 a month. Policyholders— club members— are entitled to 12 percent discounts on all airline tickets and 50 percent discounts on hotel rates, car rental fees, at a myriad of fine shops, at Lenscrafters and Foot Locker, and for pharmaceuticals and food. The incentive to use the health insurance policy wisely is compelling because the discounts pay for the cost of the premium and sometimes more than that. Another incentive company is Transmedia Networks, Inc., in New York City. This Quantum Company offers a 30 percent discount at fine restaurants to diners who join its club.

America is a nation of joiners. We love clubs, contests, groups, and associations. We accumulate plastic cards addictively. Thus when we are offered discounts, or free trips, or money back, we join and play the game. The pull is more powerful than advertising, which for the most part has strayed from its original purpose of product identification. With more of us shopping via Internet, direct mail, or home shopping networks where the product is highly visible and clearly described, advertising is redundant. Stores Automated Systems, Inc., in Bristol, Pennsylvania, has built a customer E-mail system into the checkout cash register. Catalina Marketing Corp., in St. Petersburg, Florida, has mastered electronic coupon delivery and redemption management for supermarkets and consumer goods producers. Incentives will influence our purchases—and the number of advertising agencies will be cut in half as a result.

JOINT VENTURES

We expect certain symbolic relationships in our very American institutions. For example, televised championship wrestling has six matches. The first match establishes the thesis of the event: the cleaner cut, usually blond and non-evil wrestler wins; virtue triumphs. In matches two through five, we experience the antithesis and evil triumphs over those not fully American. In the sixth match, a synthesis forms and a patriotic, virtuous American (e.g., Sgt. Slaughter) wins. The audience for wrestling mistrusts the Horatio Alger ideology of upward mobility within a free market economy and trusts lived experience, where hard work and ability are seldom rewarded, except in the end where the "American Dream" triumphs over unscrupulous behavior.

And so it is with the stock market. A start-up biotechnology or pharmaceutical company cannot achieve an initial public offering at a valuation in excess of $100 million unless it has a strategic alliance with a major pharmaceutical company. The market expects and must have a mentor and customer for every upstart that it applauds with wealth before revenues.

There have been approximately 500 strategic alliances in the pharmaceutical industry in the last five years between large companies, which have distribution systems in place, and entrepreneurial companies, which have better research and development capabilities. Transaction marries content. The former pump capital into the latter and take back the right to market the product under a license agreement, plus a small amount of equity. If the new product can be developed, tested, and approved by the government tollgate, the FDA, before the entrepreneurial company runs out of money, then the alliance succeeds. If the entrepreneurial company runs out of money, the large one can acquire it cheaply by buying it out of bankruptcy.

The race to be one of the first companies to produce mobile wireless video communication products has led to dozens of joint ventures between software providers and PC manufacturers, cable operators and telephone companies, and digital video conferencing companies and semiconductor manufacturers. No one goes off into the jungle alone anymore.

KNOWLEDGE-BASED COMPANIES

In complexity there is intense profitability. The heightened cash flow comes from designing a network to explain the uses and applications of the product to customers, prospects, and journalists. The *users group* was invented by Hewlett-Packard in the mid-1970s as a meeting place for its customers to meet vendors of peripherals and software and discuss how they might learn and grow as computer users. The knowledge content of the product exceeded the value of the product without the knowledge. Now connectivity hardware, telecommunications, and software producers are generating cash flow through knowledge channels that often exceed cash flow from product sales. Knowledge-based companies are able to generate more than a dozen cash flow channels to push through their new products. Some of these channels are:

- product sale
- sale of information (newsletter) about the product
- sale of aftersale services
- sale of user group membership or club membership with benefits accruing to owners of the product
- share of proceeds with joint-venture partners (called affinity partners) whose products are marketed to the users group members
- sale of ad space in the users group magazine
- sale of booth space at the users group expositions
- sale of ads in magazine published for exposition attendees
- sale of affinity services to club members—such as telephone calling cards' list-rental of members names to companies that want to meet an upscale group of potential customers
- sale of credit or insurance products to members via strategic alliances

Every consumer product manufacturer will attempt to make its product seem knowledge-based. Nike pushes self-esteem in every pair of its shoes. Tasters Choice offers romance as part of its coffee. Note how many product-specific magazines have recently been published. Coffee producers, gym shoe makers, and automobile companies are attempting to aggregate their consumers into clubs, even though their products lack a knowledge base.

LITIGATION

Following health insurance, legal expenses are the next largest overhead item on the operating statements of American business. The lawyers have had it their way much too long. Their unleveled playing field exists because politicians are mostly lawyers, and they create laws of obfuscated tautology so when they are voted out of office they can make a decent living explaining the laws they created.

But the PC and its ability to access legal libraries via modems at relatively little cost will enable every company and intelligent individual to become pro se in many legal disputes. There are approximately 350,000 pro se litigants presently networking with one another and sharing pleadings and other information to improve one another's skills. This number will grow tenfold as the content of bringing or defending a lawsuit becomes inexpensive in a CD-ROM configuration. Information America, Inc., in Atlanta, Georgia—a Quantum Company—is bringing the information highway of the courtroom to the people by simplifying the transaction.

Also in the legal services arena is Quantum Company Decision Quest, Inc., in Los Angeles, which enables the arguing sides to inexpensively play-act their dispute in front of a jury. It uses the behavioral sciences and rapid database analysis to predict the outcome of jury trials. With these cost-saving forces moving into the arena once monopolized by lawyers, their numbers will decline from 750,000 to 400,000–500,000, and one-tenth of U.S. law schools will shutter their windows or begin publishing on CD-ROM for the emerging pro se market.

MOBILE WIRELESS COMMUNICATIONS

The Dick Tracy watch is less than two years away. It will probably not be a wristwatch initially, but rather a palmtop PC with voice, data, and video communication capabilities. The initial products will be developed by entrepreneurial companies. InVision Systems Corp., in Vienna, Virginia, has carved a niche for itself with a $1,500 system that operates on local and wide are networks. Its R&D team is working on a wireless system. One candidate that seems to be ahead of the pack is Voyant, Inc., in Fremont, California, a Quantum Company. It has the financial backing of Cable & Wireless, its chip maker Cirrus Logic (a Quantum Company), and its venture capitalist, Nazem & Co. Voyant is in a race with Workstation Technologies, Inc., in Irvine, California, and Innovasys, Inc., in St. Louis, Missouri, to bring digital video conferencing to the palmtop computer. Each one has its own unique strength.

Cellular phone companies are racing in the same direction. Quantum Company Qualcom could be one of the leaders in mobile wireless communications. It intends to introduce code division multiple access (CDMA) in 1995, a bandwidth multiplier. CDMA expands one channel to more than 30, then reassembles it at the receiving end. If it works, the cellular phone can have the power of the PC and the Dick Tracy watch will be in the handset of our cellular and portable phones.

The inevitable result will be continuously less expensive remote voice, data, and video communications capabilities. We can get together to review designs, memorandums, blueprints, and magnetic resonance imaging printouts without traveling to a specific destination. Movies on demand? We will be ordering the movie of our choice on to our laptops for less than $20 by 1996.

NEW DEMOCRACIES

Although some of the citizens of the new democracies of Eastern Europe have been confusing democracy for anarchy, most particularly in the former Yugoslavia, things will normalize and people will get back to the business of living rather than dying. Some warlords want to see themselves on CNN and once they have achieved that, their totalitarian spirit diminishes and they seek wealth and give up power. Connectivity hardware companies such as Chipcom, Bay Networks, and Xircom, Quantums all, are busily selling into the new democracies.

Hundreds of government agencies in Eastern Europe will have to be privatized to raise capital for the governments and make their currency worth something. This will provide jobs for U.S. management consultants, investment bankers, accountants, management training companies, marketing consultants, and the like. Important systems such as courts and banks must be created. Consultants will be hired to create infrastructure models and write codes of laws.

Once there is more currency floating, then the people can be paid more and they will spend it on essential assets—cars, homes, televisions, telephones, furniture, and clothing. The process will take a decade or more, but in the end the markets of Eastern Europe will be important to U.S. assets producers. Like him or not, President Ronald Reagan opened many new markets for U.S. companies and consultants to sell into. An early opportunistic Quantum Company is Roper Industries, Inc., in Bogart, Georgia, which is selling oil and gas compressors in Russia.

ORGAN TRANSPLANTATION

Organs on demand by 2020. The use of seat belts and air bags has sharply reduced the number of traffic fatalities—and so shrunk the supply of organ donors. The flip side of this scenario is that enhanced longevity of our population has increased the demand for organs. There are approximately 31,600 people on waiting lists for organs in the United States, and only 16,000 new transplants performed each year. So acute is the demand that criminals are doping tourists and cutting out a kidney which they can sell on the black market for upwards of $150,000.

In addition to the problem of an insufficiency of organs, the rejection rate is still high. With the introduction of Cyclosporine in 1986, a threefold increase in the number of successful transplants occurred. FK-506, a new immunosuppressant drug believed to be superior to Cyclosporine, is expected to be available in 1995. Identify a breakthrough area—and you'll find a Quantum Company. Homecare Management, Inc., in Ronkonkoma, New York, provides Cyclosporine therapy to transplant patients. DNX, Inc., in Princeton, New Jersey, is attempting to develop transplantable organs from hogs. Both companies are Quantum Companies because they are addressing this enormous problem rapidly, carefully, and with elegant solutions.

And here's the flip side again: Life Resuscitation Technologies, Inc., in Chicago, Illinois, has patented a Brain Cooling Device, enabling paramedics who arrive on the scene within six and one-half minutes following the onset of cardiac arrest, to keep the victim alive for up to 50 minutes. This means either more lives saved or more oxygenated organs to donate.

PCs

For Macintosh users, Asanté Technologies, Inc., in San Jose, California, will link you onto an interactive network. If you are traveling and need to see your faxes, E-mail messages, and voice mail messages, you can slip a Fax/Modem card made by Megahertz Holding Corp. (Salt Lake City, Utah), into your laptop computer. These and other Quantum Companies give connectivity to the PC. They are the infrastructure of the information superhighway.

The information superhighway will link PCs rather than television sets, for the simple and obvious reason that the PC is a tool that we interact with and the T.V. is a tool that we sit and look at. Families with PCs will join the information superhighway, and those without will go through life on rutted, dirt roads at much slower speeds.

The Internet is typical of what markets for computer users will look like in the future. The Internet is already as important to small businesses as an 800 number and overnight courier services. Mom-and-pop stores with unique products can become billion-dollar retailers in a couple of years by advertising on the Internet. (It happened to Dell Computer pre-Internet with its 800 number and the ability to deliver overnight.)

As of mid-April 1994, there were 14,154 commercial domains (business users) on the Internet, up from 6,545 a year earlier. Approximately 1,500 new commercial domains are added each month, of which 70 percent are small companies. There are 2.2 million PCs on 32,400 computer networks accessible in 135 countries hooked into the Internet. That's 25 million people and the number is growing by 10 percent per month.

This fantastic growth in PC networking makes several statements. First, PC users want to connect with others and with libraries and databases. Second, networks of PC users are in fact markets in which products are paid for up front, i.e., on a trust basis. Third, PC networks flatten the power structure of large organizations, because information becomes available to all. The implications of these three statements are far-reaching and include a diminution in the importance of warehousing, commercial banking, advertising, and the necessity for living in large cities.

QUORUMS

Some of the greatest business successes have been achieved by entrepreneurial companies that have acquired a large number of small companies in highly fractionated industries. These are known as consolidators, but I prefer to think of them as quorums, because it takes a minimum number of them to make a meaningful company.

Previous successes in the consolidation business have occurred in the funeral home, pawnshop, and waste removal industries. Some of these highly profitable quorum companies are described in the following table:

Valuation Comparisons of Consolidators

	Sector	FY End	Mkt. Cap. ($MM)	EPS 1994 E	P/E 1994 E
Ameri. Med. Response	Ambulance	Dec.	$ 370	$ .95	29.1x
Cash America	Pawnshops	Dec.	251	.60	14.8x
EZ Corp.	Pawnshops	Sept.	156	.80	16.3x
Hanger Orthopedic	Health Care	Dec.	161	1.20	16.1x
Ins. Auto Auctions	Salvage	Dec.	348	1.05	35.2x
Loewen Group	Funeral Homes	Dec.	926	.97	26.2x
Novacare	Health Care	Jun.	674	1.15	11.8x
Rehab Clinic	Health Care	Dec.	184	.86	24.4x
Rural Metro	Ambulance/Fire	Jun.	121	.70	27.9x
Sanifil Inc.	Waste	Dec.	304	1.05	19.4x
Service Corp.	Funeral Homes	Dec.	2,108	1.35	18.6x
Stewart Enterprises	Funeral Homes	Oct.	529	1.30	21.5x

The acquirers look for somewhat troubled companies to buy, where they can make improvements that will enhance cash flow, and where they can point to the trouble as a reason for paying less than the buyer expects or desires.

There are quite a few quorums among the Quantum Companies, as one might expect. American Medical Response, in Boston, Massachusetts, was founded in 1992 and has annualized revenues of $189 million and annualized Net Profits Before Taxes of $16 million in 1994. Its business is acquiring and operating ambulance companies. In just two and one-half years, it has become an exit strategy of choice for owners of mom-and-pop ambulance companies.

Hospital acquirers include Quorum Health Group and Health Management Associates. And the principal consolidator of companies that manufacture products for the disabled is Sunrise Medical, in Torrance, California.

REAL ESTATE

Real estate values in large cities will decline as new companies find that they can do nicely in the mountains, by the lakes and streams, and at the seashore. Real estate developers will reverse engineer their skills over the next 25 years and replace commercial buildings and warehouses with ice skating rinks, golf and tennis courts, zoos, outdoor theaters, amusement parks, and open spaces that lure people back to the cities.

Seniors will return to or continue living in cities as country roads become too full of 18-wheelers carrying material and components between factories and from loading docks to retailers, and high-speed executives driving over the speed limit in Range Rovers while working their cellular phones and faxes simultaneously. As a result, they will demand accident-proof bathrooms and kitchens, safe stairways and hallways, and crime-free neighborhoods. They will be the first market for video/voice-activated home-monitoring systems. (See the description of Quantum Company Sentinel Systems, Inc., in Hampton, Virginia.)

Country property values will move up sharply as entrepreneurial companies seek locations that make the appropriate SNAC (Sensitive New Age Company) statement: "We're environmentally conscious and fully mobile, wireless and interconnected." Ensys Environmental Products, Inc., in Morrisville, North Carolina, and Molten Metal Technology, Inc., in Waltham, Massachusetts, among other Quantum Companies, are recapturing once-contaminated real estate for us to put homes and businesses into.

SOUTH EAST ASIA

The United States' most important trading partner will become, collectively, the countries of South East Asia: Singapore, Hong Kong, Taiwan, Malaysia, Vietnam, Indonesia, and—coming on rapidly because of their inexpensive labor—China, India, and the Philippines. These countries have relatively youthful populations eager for American consumer products that they see on television, and equally eager to sell their products into the U.S. market.

Surprisingly, many mature U.S. companies chose to ignore South East Asia, while setting their sights on the new democracies of Eastern Europe. But Quantum Companies opened their first foreign satellite offices in South East Asia not Europe. NetFRAME, Computer Network Technologies, and Chipcom, three leaders in the PC connectivity business, have South East Asian offices. The road to the huge Chinese market is paved with learning the Chinese culture in the countries that attach to China or sit in the China Sea.

TRANSPORTATION

Several dynamics will work themselves out in the U.S. transportation market in the next quarter century. Large, nationwide airlines, such as American, Delta, TWA, and United, will lose a large number of business travelers who will have their meetings by hooking up on digital video conferencing networks. These carriers will file for protection, or enter informal reorganization agreements, spin off some unnecessary assets, cut costs, and re-emerge in the image of low-cost Southwest Airlines.

Growth in the transportation industry will come from short-haul trucking companies that will be mobile warehouses: picking up product shipped in from Mexican and South East Asian plants and delivering it to retailers. Fixed-base warehouses are a thing of the past. Sub-contracting the manufacture of all components and adding labor and technical know-how puts a premium on short-haul trucking companies. Consumers are ordering products via home shopping, catalogs, videologs, and on the Internet—and expecting next day delivery. The demand for efficiently managed short-haul truckers, supplied by Quantum Companies Swift Transportation Co., in Sparks, Nevada, and Landstar Systems, Inc., in Shelton, Connecticut, will become enormous.

UNWANTED TREASURES

My grandfather used to call people who turned money into trash "chemists." He is not alive to give a colorful name to people who reverse the process. But I call them Quantum entrepreneurs. One of the most impressive is William N. Haney III, founder and CEO of Molten Metal Technology Inc., in Waltham, Massachusetts, whose company destroys hazardous materials in a bath of molten metal while recovering the dissolved materials' basic elements in the form of gases, metals, and other inorganics that can be used in industry. A stock market favorite, Molten Metals' market capitalization in mid-1994 is $518 million on revenues of $8 million.

Another Quantum Company in the business of turning waste into wealth is Phenix Composites, Inc., in St. Peter, Minnesota. The company manufactures a unique building material from used newspapers and soybeans. The material, which it calls Environ, looks like granite, is three times the strength of white oak, and is worked and shaped like lumber.

Zia Metallurgical Processes, Inc., in Dallas, Texas, is a Quantum Company because it has developed a means of producing steel in a manner that does not require deep mining ore or relying on scrap metal. Its process is inexpensive and environmentally friendly—perfect for the United States and developing countries.

VIDEO CONFERENCING

See it now. The hottest vehicle on the connectivity superhighway is video conferencing. Eight years ago, video meetings stimulated a mere $1 million worth of interest. Last year businesses bought almost $500 million worth of video conferencing systems. Conservative estimates have purchases exceeding $2 billion by 1997, as more companies employ video meetings to join workers in distant offices, share visual information among different company locations, even "bring in" customers from outlying areas—and so lower travel and expense costs. The popularity of video conferencing surged when miniaturization —and the corresponding price reduction—arrived in earnest last year, largely through desktop products that harness a PC to serve as a videophone. Quantum Company C-Cube Microsystems, Inc., in Milpitos, California, thought digital video conferencing might be a neat idea back in 1988. It began developing digital compression products—encoders, decoders, and codecs—to permit high-quality, full-motion video to be transmitted over telephone lines through the air and be brought up to the CRT on PCs.

Just as digital desktop publishing equipment unleashed thousands of new text-publishing companies, so the new digital desktop video-publishing systems will unleash thousands of filmmakers. The video business will increasingly resemble not the current film business, in which output is 100 or so movies a year, but the book business, in which some 55,000 new hardcover titles are published annually in the United States.

When digital video teleconferencing becomes wireless, and you and I can converse and see each other over the palmtops that we carry in our pockets and pocketbooks, then we truly can work and live anywhere we wish to and phone in our jobs.

WOMEN ENTREPRENEURS

Up until now it has been one of the best kept secrets in America: Women entrepreneurs are the principal force driving the U.S. economy. In an age of transactions, who is the best at networking, connecting, allying, joint-venturing? Clearly women do that better than men.

Accordingly, most women have started trust-based businesses—those in which the customer pays in advance for a subscription, franchise, party-plan territory, or mail order product. Some of the better known companies launched with customer financing are The Body Shop, Gymboree Corp., Mary Kay Cosmetics, Mothers' Work, and Lillian Vernon Corp.

Because they have very little capital with which to expand their businesses, women entrepreneurs substitute labor for capital. Sweat equity is the time-honored phrase, and it means that everyone works long hours for less pay.

It bears pointing out that women not only hire more employees than do their male counterparts, but they hire predominantly women. Quantum Company Research Management Consultants, Inc. has 225 employees, 60 percent of whom are women. "We have a few men working here," says Lucy Mackall, founder and CEO of Quantum Company Have a Heart, Inc., in Boston, Massachusetts. "But they're mostly in the mail room." More women than men are employed by Quantum Companies.

Women start roughly 1.75 million new businesses a year in the United States. Assuming each one hires five people per new company, that's nearly 9 million new jobs a year, about 6 million of which go to women. Over a five-year period, 20 million women get jobs with entrepreneurial companies and, using historical ratios, about a quarter of them will catch the entrepreneurial fever themselves one day.

It is interesting to note that women entrepreneurs run companies where male skills are not needed or required. Their companies are in the caring and curing fields 36 percent of the time; dressing, beautifying, and feeding people account for 32 percent; computers, electronics, and manufacturing for 19 percent; and entertainment/novelties 13 percent.

Very few women entrepreneurs choose asset-based businesses or capital equipment manufacturing, because they require a heavy infusion of capital. The assets of women-owned companies are information, networks, insight, and trained people who will follow the owners to hell and back. Twenty women-founded, women-run companies are among the Quantum Companies.

X-POS FOR SENIORS

Where will all the seniors go? A generation or two of people who avoided the computer will grow old in the next quarter century, and they will seek relatively passive ways to amuse themselves.

New gene therapies and improved organ transplants will keep them alive well into their 90s, with high-energy levels. They will attend expositions (x-pos for short) in convention centers and hotel conference rooms where product companies will rent booth space for thousands of dollars in order to meet seniors in relaxed atmospheres. Booth renters will include drug manufacturers, medical device producers, mutual fund managers, cruise lines, travel companies, credit card companies, entertainment companies, and consumer products companies.

Since this group of people vote in most elections, politicians will speak at Senior Expos and shake hands at the entrances. Towns that lack convention centers will erect them in order to have a place to hold Senior Expos.

Keeping careful track of this important database will be Quantum Company Acxiom Corp., in Conway, Arkansas, one of the best data gatherers for the direct mail and telemarketing industries.

YOUTH

Young people will have vast choices in their daily lives. They will be educated at the plant or office where their mothers work. They will be educated at home via CD-ROMs bought at a school supplies membership warehouse store. They can choose between a private, commercially run, or a public school, also commercially managed (see Quantum Company Education Alternatives, Inc.). Young people will be able to hook up to the Internet, CompuServe, or other networks and communicate with pen pals in foreign countries. They will be able to call for basketball scores or the movies of their choice, or trade baseball cards via their palmtop PCs. If they see a crime in progress in school or in a playground, they will be able to videotape it and transmit it in real time to a 911-equivalent video mail number.

Companies catering to young people will add educational content to their toys and games or lose serious market share. Quantum Companies serving youth will flourish. The Pleasant Company, which produces and markets historically significant dolls and accompanying books, has caught the pulse of a youth market segment and is running with it. Davidson Associates, Inc. has sold more than 1.5 million copies of *MathBlaster*, one of the most successful packages of all time. Corel Corporation's *CorelDRAW* and *CorelVentura* can put young people rapidly into the newsletter-publishing business. All three of these are Quantum Companies.

ZIMBABWE

There will be an important renaissance in Southern Africa—Zimbabwe, Botswana, and South Africa. With stable governments and a reduced currency exchange risk, these three countries will attract tourists to see the big animals and U.S. companies selling their products to a black population that will begin to earn some serious money.

Zimbabwean and township art and sculpture will become important export products. Their textiles and jewelry will capture an important niche in the American market. Afrocentric items from $200 evening suits to $8 *kente* baseball caps are being imported to the United States by entrepreneurs such as Mohamed Diop, founder of Homeland Fashions, in New York. Like Russian students who paid as much as $100 for a pair of faded Levi's, a lot of African-Americans are willing to pay a premium for African products. No Quantum Companies have entered this market as yet, but there will be some in several years.

Every U.S. manufacturer of office products, electronics, telecommunications, pharmaceuticals, and consumer products will form strategic alliances with black businesspeople in Southern Africa in order to gain a foothold in the second most rapidly growing market after South East Asia. Black entrepreneurs in Southern Africa can hold their own with any businessperson in the world given equal capital and a level playing field. Blacks from other developed countries will go there for training, employment opportunities, and a better life.

Up north, Gaza, which owns the last remaining undeveloped beachfront on the Mediterranean Sea, will be developed as an Atlantic City of the Middle East in an Israeli-Palestinian joint venture.

PART TWO

100
QUANTUM
COMPANIES

ACXIOM CORPORATION

The direct mail marketing industry owes its current growth to the increase in information one can get from a catalog which is in inverse proportion to the product information one can get from a sales clerk, whose favorite response to any question is, "Let me get my manager to answer that." As the computer illiterate and high-school dropout class of young people continue to join the uninformed army of sales clerks, catalog and videolog shopping will become more and more popular.

Direct marketing service companies specialize in marketing consultation, list compilation and management, creative and lettershop services, data-processing services, and product fulfillment. According to the annual statistical and qualitative survey of U.S. businesses using mail order published in *Direct Marketing* (July 1993), direct marketing industry sales in the United States during 1992 totaled approximately $211.1 billion, up from $200.7 billion the previous year. This total represents an overall annual growth in consumer mail order of around 4 percent in current dollar terms, 1 percent higher than the growth in overall retail sales for the same period. Of the $211.1 billion in sales, consumer mail order sales accounted for $108 billion, business mail order sales $54 billion, and charitable mail order $49 billion.

According to a *Direct Market* survey, many companies have turned to database marketing, shifting from prospecting (i.e., finding noncustomers) to customer-based marketing. The survey reports that the scope of database sales is greater than that of mail order sales, since it includes mail order sales plus direct selling and vendors' location selling. Of 6,000,000 U.S. firms, it is estimated that 400,000 maintain databases for finding prospects, compared to approximately 10,000 with significant mail order sales. The growth prospects in database marketing are very large. Acxiom's GPM increased 31.7 percent from 1991 to 1994.

The products and services offered by the Acxiom Corp. are designed to assist its direct mail customers achieve a higher rate of return on their lists by selectively targeting their marketing efforts to individuals who are most likely to respond. Acxiom is in the "list massage" business. The company provides computer-based targeted marketing support for direct marketers, which consists of planning and project design, list cleaning, list enhancement, list order fulfillment, database services, fulfillment services, and response analysis. Rather than focusing solely on direct marketing programs designed to obtain new business prospects for its

ACXIOM CORPORATION

Chief Executive Officer:	Charles D. Morgan Jr.
Principal Location:	301 Industrial Blvd. Conway, AK 72032
Telephone/Fax:	501-336-1000/501-336-3925
Satellite Locations:	Sunderland, England, plus U.S. sales offices
Date Founded:	1969
Description of Business:	Designs, develops, produces, markets, and supports computer systems for the direct mail and telemarketing industry.
# Employees Current:	1,400
# Employees Projected by 6/30/95:	1,300
Sales (Annualized) 1994:	$151,669,000
Gross Profit Margin (GPM):	39.5%
Selling Expenses/Sales:	17.0%
% Sales Increase 1991–94:	+155.2%
% Change GPM 1991–94:	+31.7%
Total Debt/Net Worth:	78.4%
Net Profits Before Taxes:	$13,433,000
Operating Ratio:	8.9%
Net Profits per Employee:	$8,395
Traded On:	NASDAQ/ACXM
Principal Competitors:	Dun & Bradstreet, Equifax, TRW, ADP
# Potential Selling Sites:	Domestic: 400,000 Foreign: 100,000
Problem Company Is Attempting to Solve:	Direct marketing companies are heavily dependent on specific market information and the application of statistics and computer modeling to assist them in predicting market behavior.
Solution Company Is Conveying to Problem:	The company addresses these needs for financial institutions, insurance companies, catalogers, retailers, TV shopping networks, publishers, and membership associations.

customers, the company has begun to build marketing databases that enable its customers to convince their customers to order more and more often. In addition, the company offers integrated data-processing software systems and enhancement services, which provide its customers with rapid access to marketing information.

An integral aspect of Acxiom's traditional business is offering its customers access to extensive customer lists and databases of information. Rather than owning any of the approximately 25,000 lists to which its customers are granted access, the company acts as a link between those who own or manage lists and those who buy or use lists for direct marketing purposes.

Through a national data communications network in the United States, Acxiom provides decision support information for direct marketing organizations. The network is composed of dedicated, leased data communication lines which link approximately 2,392 customer workstations and printers at 177 U.S. sites, computer-to-computer links to customers, and communication to remote data centers located in the United States and England connected to the network's central computer in Conway.

For the past five years, Acxiom has provided outsourcing or facilities management services, whereby they manage a customer's data center and/or provide information systems functions, both on-site at the customer's location and remotely from the company's headquarters. In several of these instances, Acxiom has licensed its software to its customers and has involved its two largest customers, Trans Union Corp. and Allstate Insurance Co., as partial underwriters of and participants in its research and development efforts.

Acxiom is currently pursuing contracts with other insurance companies, whereby they will provide information management services to assist with the insurers' risk management, underwriting, and marketing functions. In February 1994, they entered into a strategic alliance agreement with Fair Isaac and Company, Inc., a leading developer of scoring technology for the insurance and credit industries. Together, the two companies plan to offer risk management information services to the insurance industry.

In September 1993, the company entered into a $2.6 million, three-year data collecting agreement with the Texas Department of Insurance (TDI). Under the agreement, the company is collecting statistics on private passenger automobile insurance, residential property insurance, and various kinds of business insurance, including general liability, commercial property, and commercial casualty. The statistics gathered by Acxiom will be used by TDI for regulating insurance rates and monitoring Texas insurance markets. Acxiom Corp. demonstrates that the "Big Brother Is Watching You" phrase from George Orwell's *1984* is more than good literature. It's good business for the 21st century.

AMERICAN MEDICAL RESPONSE, INC.

A merican Medical Response, Inc. was formed in February 1992 by Paul M. Verrochi to become the most acquisitive company in the ambulance business. That it achieved its goal in a little under two years is testament to the highly fragmented nature of the industry and the prior inability of ambulance company owners to achieve an exit strategy. Of 15,000 or so ambulance services nationwide, nearly half are run by volunteers, one-fourth are municipally operated, and the balance are private or belong to hospitals. A mere fraction of the private companies have annual revenues of more than $300 million, and fewer than a hundred bill more than $15 million a year.

Yet splintered as it is, the ambulance business also is growing 10 percent or more a year, driven by the increased demands of an aging population, greater centralization of medical services, and earlier discharge of patients: A $200 ambulance ride is a bargain if it moves a stabilized patient from a $2,000-a-day, critical-care facility to a $300-a-day clinic bed. On the other hand, higher capital and training costs have left many privately held ambulance companies unable to keep up with demand—a situation that beckons consolidation.

Verrochi learned how to consolidate industries in the 1970s and 1980s when he put together little janitorial and waste-removal companies. Noticing that the ambulance market needed a "scooper," he lined up three acquisition candidates for $10.2 million and 4.1 million shares of its stock, and then sold 36 percent to the public to raise $21.5 million. The stock promptly tripled in value.

Health-care reform may be a timely benefit for ambulance services. For example, high-profit, scheduled ambulance runs between hospitals would probably increase under any managed-care plan because health maintenance organizations demand that patients be transferred in ambulances from emergency rooms to their preferred hospitals. In many big cities, emergency medical service companies are already providing curbside medicine that used to be done at much higher cost in hospital emergency rooms. Now there is talk of dispatching ambulances to poor neighborhoods to give vaccinations and checkups, because emergency medical technicians are trained to administer drugs and even to do some simple invasive procedures. Still another favorable development is the trend toward privatization made necessary by state and local budget squeezes.

AMERICAN MEDICAL RESPONSE, INC.

Chief Executive Officer:	Paul M. Verrochi
Principal Location:	67 Batterymarch St. Boston, MA 02110
Telephone/Fax:	617-261-1600/617-261-1610
Satellite Locations:	10 states throughout the U.S.
Date Founded:	1992
Description of Business:	A consolidator of ambulance companies.
# Employees Current:	4,800
# Employees Projected by 6/30/95:	Company withheld
Sales (Annualized) 1994:	$206,318,000
Gross Profit Margin (GPM):	29.3%
Selling Expenses/Sales:	not available
% Sales Increase 1991–94:	+194.4%
% Change GPM 1991–94:	+5.1%
Total Debt/Net Worth:	27.2%
Net Profits Before Taxes:	$19,314,000
Operating Ratio:	9.4%
Net Profits per Employee:	$4,024
Traded On:	NYSE/EMT
Principal Competitors:	Secom, Laidlaw, Rural Metro, CareLine
# Potential Selling Sites:	Domestic: 6,000 Foreign: 12,000
Problem Company Is Attempting to Solve:	With the high cost of labor and equipment, and low collection rates, running an ambulance company is very difficult.
Solution Company Is Conveying to Problem:	American Medical Response has become the exit strategy of choice for owners of quality ambulance companies.

All in all, Verrochi can figure that the prospects for the ambulance services industry have never been brighter. But only the most efficient ambulance operators will share these bounties. Labor accounts for about 50 percent of an operator's total costs. So using satellites and computers to dispatch ambulances to form the most efficient coverage patterns is more a necessity than an option. Thanks to this technology, American Medical Response can respond in most of its communities to more than 90 percent of the emergency calls it receives in less than eight minutes—and beating competitors to the scene of an emergency is what the ambulance business is all about.

Consolidators like American Medical Response have the ability in most of their markets to act like a tollgate, setting (read "raising") prices as the dominant player typically does. Note that American Medical Response's GPM has risen 5.1 percent since 1991. The stock market likes American Medical Response's future; it gives it a P/E ratio greater than that of 80 percent of the Quantum Companies.

ASANTÉ TECHNOLOGIES, INC.

Desktop computers and their networks are no longer the realm of scientists and hobbyists. More than 5 million people in this country will have subscribed to commercial online services by the end of 1994, up from 3.9 million in 1993.

The Internet, the network that connects online services as well as students, scientists, and government employees, is growing even more quickly, and now counts 20 million computers worldwide—roughly the number of homes viewing one of the most popular TV shows, "60 Minutes."

The number of networking applications are mind-boggling. The 20 million computers that are currently linked to networks are the early adopters; the people who for professional or personal reasons like to be and have to have the first.

That leaves perhaps a billion or so more potential PCs still to be networked. Think of your own office. If you are using an outside payroll processing firm, it would certainly simplify and lower the cost of paychecks if a network permitted them to come over a wide area network (WAN) to your printer, rather than to come by truck or courier. If your company has multiple branches where people are assigned to participate in decision-making processes several times a month or a year, networking can save expensive airline travel by bringing everyone together online. If your company deals with suppliers that quote prices and specs via telephone and fax, how simple it would be to use E-mail, with its speed, low cost, and high degree of accuracy.

Quite literally, the networking products companies are pushing all of us with PCs in our offices to use them interactively with contractors, vendors, branch offices, and customers. These companies, and Asanté Technologies, Inc., possess the energy that propelled Icharus to the sun.

Asanté is smaller than many of its competitors. It has a lower GPM—40.2 percent—than some of its larger competitors, but it is growing. Its Operating Ratio this year is 7.3 percent, not anywhere near as high as many of its competitors, but this ratio is growing as well. Asanté is fighting a patent infringement and trade secrets lawsuit with a competitor, and litigation drains management time.

But Asanté is a scrapper. Located in Silicon Valley, it raised a sparse $2 million in venture capital from an offshore investor, not a local venture capital fund, and $440,000 from Orient Semiconductor Electronics, Ltd., Taiwan, a vendor to Asanté. The company brought in a

ASANTÉ TECHNOLOGIES, INC.

Chief Executive Officer:	Ralph S. Dormitzer
Principal Location:	821 Fox Lane San Jose, CA 95131
Telephone/Fax:	408-435-8388/408-894-9150
Satellite Locations:	none
Date Founded:	1988
Description of Business:	Designs, produces, markets, and supports data networking products, particularly for Macintosh Ethernet adapters.
# Employees Current:	175
# Employees Projected by 6/30/95:	Company withheld
Sales (Annualized) 1994:	$79,282,000
Gross Profit Margin (GPM):	40.2%
Selling Expenses/Sales:	20.7%
% Sales Increase 1991–94:	+426.8%
% Change GPM 1991–94:	+3.3%
Total Debt/Net Worth:	50.6%
Net Profits Before Taxes:	$5,777,000
Operating Ratio:	7.3%
Net Profits per Employee:	$33,011
Traded On:	NASDAQ/ASNT
Principal Competitors:	Cabletron, ChipCom, Hewlett-Packard, Standard Microsystems, 3Com, Bay Networks, Inc.
# Potential Selling Sites:	Domestic: 2 million Foreign: 6 million
Problem Company Is Attempting to Solve:	Apple Computer users like the ease of programming on the Apple, but it is a closed environment system, not one that interacts with the PC-DOS world.
Solution Company Is Conveying to Problem:	Asanté brings connectivity to the Mac environment.

new CEO, Ralph Dormitzer, from Digital Equipment Corp. in mid-1993, *and* changed auditors—an unusual and expensive step.

Accordingly, given this profile of the playground runt, Asanté is merely the unquestioned leader in connectivity in the Apple environment. "Our goal is to be the market leader in providing network connectivity solutions for work group and departmental users," says Dormitzer. To achieve this objective, Asanté has adopted a business strategy incorporating the following key elements:

The company has increased its market share steadily since its founding, and in 1992 accounted for 46 percent of worldwide sales of Ethernet adapters for Macintoshes. It offers a family of full-featured, reliable, and easy-to-use client-access and network system products for Macintosh networks at competitive prices, and it has been early to market its products for Macintosh and PowerBook users. Asanté has developed brand name recognition in the Macintosh community, and "We intend to maintain our leadership position by enhancing current products and by continuing to introduce new products for connecting Macintosh users," says Dormitzer.

Asanté also believes that the characteristics that have enabled its client-access products to become leading sellers in the Macintosh Ethernet connectivity market are similar to the product characteristics required in the broader departmental connectivity market. Accordingly, Asanté has designed its hub products to be competitively priced, integrate seamlessly into networks, and support heterogeneous computing environments.

Asanté also believes that its established distribution channels and its brand name recognition will facilitate the introduction of new products and expansion into new market segments. The company sells its products through distribution channels tailored to the purchasing patterns of its work group and departmental connectivity customers. Its distributors include Ingram, Micro, Merisel, and Tech Data, the leading wholesale distributors of computer products in North America. Many of Asanté's client-access products have regularly been the top sellers in their respective categories for these distributors.

Asanté's ratio of selling expenses to sales is running at 20.7 percent, which is reasonable in the dog-eat-dog networking products market. The stock market has all but ignored this scrappy little company, valuing it at one-half of its revenues and giving it a P/E ratio of 14.0 percent. Asanté is an important competitor in what is becoming a huge industry. As they say in the Southwest, this dog can hunt.

ASCEND COMMUNICATIONS, INC.

The Monkees were the first rock 'n roll music group to be put together by the music producers. They had an excellent career—not at the level of the Beatles or the Stones, but everyone made money. Ascend looks like a packaged deal. The venture capital funds put up $18.2 million for 80 percent ownership at the outset. The management team divided the remaining 20 percent. They came from companies like Softcom, Ungermann-Bass, Micom Systems, Inc., BBN Communications Corp., and Hayes Microcomputer Products, that were aware of problems with digital access to wide area networks, but did not attempt to solve the problems because it would have cut into their sales. The three co-founders came from the Softcom division of Hayes, and within 10 months had raised their capital and were in business.

We could all do much worse than back the companies launched by Kleiner Perkins Caulfield & Byers, the premier venture capital fund in Silicon Valley. It launched Genentech and Tandem Computer in its offices in Menlo Park, after incubating Robert Swanson (Genentech) and James Treybig (Tandem) while they wrote their business plans. James P. Lally, the Kleiner Perkins partner on the Ascend board, is also a NetFRAME director. The other venture capitalists with part of the $18.2 million investment in Ascend sit on the boards of Xircom, Silicon Graphics, SyQuest, and Telebit. The amount of industry knowledge brought to Ascend's management team is extraordinary. Shoptalk at the board meetings is more electric than "Geraldo."

The Ascend product line fills an expanding need. Its bandwidth-on-demand product line is three-deep: Multiband products for videoconferencing access, Pipeline products for remote local area network (LAN) access, and MAX products for voice, video, and data-integrated access. These products support a wide variety of application interfaces, cabling systems, switched digital services, and digital access line types. This wide range of connectivity and interoperability options significantly increases the number of corporate sites that can benefit from bandwidth-on-demand networking. The company's products are distributed and serviced globally, and Ascend maintains marketing and sales relationships with major telecommunications carriers, including contractual relationships with AT&T, British Telecommunications PLC, Sprint, MCI, PictureTel Corp., and VTEL Corp. It also works with 55 value-added resellers, who market and sell its products to end-users.

ASCEND COMMUNICATIONS, INC.

Chief Executive Officer:	Robert J. Ryan
Principal Location:	1275 Harbor Bay Parkway Alameda, CA 94502
Telephone/Fax:	510-769-6001/510-814-2300
Satellite Locations:	none
Date Founded:	1989
Description of Business:	Develops, produces, markets, and supports a broad range of digital wide area network access products.
# Employees Current:	87
# Employees Projected by 6/30/95:	Company withheld
Sales (Annualized) 1994:	$24,279,000
Gross Profit Margin (GPM):	65.9%
Selling Expenses/Sales:	25.4%
% Sales Increase 1991–94:	+769.3%
% Change GPM 1991–94:	+22.9%
Total Debt/Net Worth:	11.0%
Net Profits Before Taxes:	$4,490,000
Operating Ratio:	18.5%
Net Profits per Employee:	$51,609
Traded On:	NASDAQ/ASND
Principal Competitors:	Teleos Communications, Promptus Communications, Newbridge Networks, Premisys Communications
# Potential Selling Sites:	Domestic: 100,000 Foreign: 250,000
Problem Company Is Attempting to Solve:	Standalone network facilities for individual video, data, and voice applications often are managed and administered separately, resulting in higher costs.
Solution Company Is Conveying to Problem:	A new generation of integrated access equipment that permits these applications to share a common set of access lines to connect to digital network services, thereby reducing costs and increasing manageability.

Ascend's manufacturing operations consist primarily of materials planning and procurement, final assembly, burn-in, final system testing, and quality control. It designs all of the hardware subassemblies for its products and uses the services of contract manufacturers to build them to their specifications.

The Multiband family of bandwidth-on-demand controllers provides global bandwidth-on-demand and uses inverse multiplexing, a fundamental enabling technology that aggregates multiple independent switched digital connections to create a single, high-bandwidth end-to-end connection. The Multiband products provide bandwidth at speeds from 56 kbit/s to 4 Mbit/s using switched digital services and support for simultaneous high-speed digital connections, connecting to videoconferencing applications using high-speed serial ports. This product family also incorporates dynamic bandwidth allocation, global connectivity, and comprehensive management capabilities to allow users to create bandwidth-on-demand network solutions for videoconferencing.

The Pipeline family of remote LAN access servers provides remote LAN access for remote offices, telecommuters, and mobile computer users. Pipeline products incorporate standards-based LAN routing and bridging protocols over switched digital services, and include inverse multiplexing functionality to allow users to obtain higher data rates than are available from individual digital access lines and switched digital circuits. Pipeline products equipped with integrated digital modems permit nondigital remote sites to connect to corporate backbone networks using modems.

The MAX family of integrated access servers provides bandwidth-on-demand for voice, video, and data applications over a single common set of digital access lines. The MAX is a modular card and backplane system that allows users to configure each unit according to application and bandwidth requirements. MAX products support up to 8 Mbit/s of bandwidth to the wide area network. The MAX can be configured with Multibandcards, providing up to 38 high-speed inverse multiplexing ports for central site video conferencing, dedicated circuit backup and disaster recovery, dedicated circuit overflow and load balancing, high-speed bulk file transfer, high-quality audio transmission, and other applications. MAX products can also be configured with Pipeline Ethernet cards and digital modem cards to act as a central site remote LAN access server, allowing up to 96 remote users to dial into the corporate backbone network.

Global videoconferencing traffic will run through the MAX family of integrated access servers. Your company may not be video conferencing with plants, vendors, or clients in Europe or Asia, but technological developments from Ascend are inevitably moving you and others in that direction. The stock market loves Ascend's prospects. It puts a 48.0 percent P/E ratio on Ascend's earnings.

ATMEL CORPORATION

George Perlegos, founder and Chief Executive Officer of Atmel Corp., identified an emerging market: integrated circuits that use less battery power for portable computers and cellular telephones. Perlegos, a Greek immigrant, left a doctoral program in electrical engineering at Stanford University in 1978 to join Intel Corp. He became intensely interested in designing better memory chips, and when Intel set its cap for high-speed processing chips, Perlegos quit Intel. That was 1981, the year that Perlegos and others founded Seeq Technology Inc. to design and produce better memory chips. Three years later, after management disagreements, Perlegos left along with some of Seeq's best people to form Atmel. They put in $30,000.

An early decision not to build and own a chip-making foundry mitigated Atmel's need to raise venture capital. It used the excess capacity of its chip-makers until 1989 when it bought a foundry from Honeywell, Inc. for $15 million. Its first customers paid upfront or COD to minimize working capital needs, and obviating equity sales, thus permitting broad employee ownership of stock.

Meanwhile, Atmel poured all available remaining cash into research and development in search of the lowest voltage-consuming chip. It came out with the first three-volt "flash" chip in 1991, upstaging the competitions' 12 volts. Flash chips process information rapidly and retain data even when a computer loses power.

Having identified this burgeoning niche, Intel came after Atmel with guns blazing. Intel is converting its huge Albuquerque plant to a flash chip plant, and Advanced Micro Devices, Inc., another competitor, said it plans to open a $750 million flash chip "fab" (the industry's nickname for chip foundries) in Japan in 1995.

Intel and Advanced Micro, it is generally agreed, have the brains and financial muscle to develop their own three-volt flash chips and give Atmel a run for its money. But Atmel is sitting on approximately $50 million in cash and has a debt to worth ratio of 37.9 percent, which provides it with ample cash and borrowing ability to invest heavily in innovative R&D areas. Construction for a new fab in 1994 will cost the company about $120 million. Atmel also acquired EEPROM assets from Seeq in early 1994, making it the world's largest EEPROM producer. In 1994, the company introduced a single volt chip, an industry first.

Can Perlegos stay ahead of Intel and Advanced Micro? He has never failed in business. And he avoids management meetings. "Meetings are

ATMEL CORPORATION

Chief Executive Officer:	George Perlegos
Principal Location:	2125 O'Nel Dr. San Jose, CA 95131
Telephone/Fax:	408-436-4227/408-436-4200
Satellite Locations:	Colorado Springs, CO
Date Founded:	1984
Description of Business:	Designs, develops, and manufactures high-performance memory and logic chips for telecommunications and other markets.
# Employees Current:	600
# Employees Projected by 6/30/95:	700
Sales (Annualized) 1994:	$257,102,000
Gross Profit Margin (GPM):	45.4%
Selling Expenses/Sales:	13.9%
% Sales Increase 1991–94:	+213.6%
% Change GPM 1991–94:	+10.5%
Total Debt/Net Worth:	37.9%
Net Profits Before Taxes:	$55,203,000
Operating Ratio:	21.5%
Net Profits per Employee:	$49,069
Traded On:	NASDAQ/ATML
Principal Competitors:	Intel, National Semiconductor, Micron
# Potential Selling Sites:	Domestic: 150 Foreign: 450
Problem Company Is Attempting to Solve:	The need for low-cost, efficient PCs and telecommunications devices.
Solution Company Is Conveying to Problem:	The company's flash memories combine the flexibility of EEPROMs with the lower cost of EPROMs. They are used primarily to store operating programs in PCs.

worthless," says Perlegos. "If top management is in meetings, it isn't producing. We have a meeting once a month, and it's with the gloves off. All the complaints are listened to." This man sounds like he runs a pit crew at Indy. And he produces solid results: a GPM of 45.4 percent; a GPM increase of 10.5 percent since 1991; an Operating Ratio of 21.5 percent; and Net Profits per Employee of approximately $50,000. Atmel could be the Intel of the next quarter century.

BAY NETWORKS, INC.

Bay Networks, Inc., formerly Wellfleet Communications, Inc., one of the fastest growing publicly-held companies in the United States in the 1992 to 1994 time period, develops, manufactures, markets, and supports a family of high-performance, multiprotocol internet-working products commonly known as routers. Routers interconnect multiple types of local area networks (LANs) made up of computer equipment of the same or different manufacturers to form an internetworked system. Bay Network's products connect LANs located in a single facility and, through wide area network (WANs) connections, may connect LANs dispersed around the world. The internetworking of these networks enables computer users operating different types of equipment in different locations to communicate, exchange data, and share other computing resources.

Bay Networks, Inc., shocked the networking market in July 1994 when it announced the acquisition of SynOptics Communications, Inc., a competitor twice its size but with two-thirds its market value. SynOptics makes hubs that typically manage communications between a cluster of desktop computers on a single floor of an office building. It leads this market, but an inventory glut in 1994 drove the company's share price down 43 percent. Bay Networks, Inc., which doesn't make hubs and needed a sales force such as SynOptics', scooped up the company for $1.01 billion in stock.

Organizations are increasingly seeking to internetwork their disparate, often incompatible PCs in various locations onto LANs and WANs to share information and computing resources across the organization for applications such as electronic mail, sharing of databases, multisite engineering and product development, transaction processing, and electronic image transfer. Enterprisewide networks facilitate efficient and rapid data communications among connected work groups, departments, and locations, and provide for more effective utilization of information and computer resources. The internetworking of LANs and WANs into enterprisewide networks requires data communications products that efficiently, reliably, and quickly transmit data to appropriate locations on different networks, reconcile incompatible LAN and WAN standards between networks, and provide management for large complex internetworks.

Many of Bay Network's products are based upon a modular, multiprocessor architecture that enables large organizations to config-

BAY NETWORKS, INC

Chief Executive Officer:	Andrew Ludwick
Principal Location:	8 Federal St. Billerica, MA 01821
Telephone/Fax:	508-670-8888/508-436-3436
Satellite Locations:	36 in U.S.; 11 offices abroad
Date Founded:	1985
Description of Business:	A technology leader in internetworking computer systems that connect LANs to WANs.
# Employees Current:	1,152
# Employees Projected by 6/30/95:	1,200
Sales (Annualized) 1994:	$235,858,000
Gross Profit Margin (GPM):	61.1%
Selling Expenses/Sales:	26.2%
% Sales Increase 1991–94:	557.3%
% Change GPM 1991–94:	+8.0%
Total Debt/Net Worth:	30.9%
Net Profits Before Taxes:	$59,310,000
Operating Ratio:	25.1%
Net Profits per Employee:	$51,484
Traded On:	NASDAQ/WFLT
Principal Competitors:	Cisco Systems, 3Com, Cabletron, Lannet
# Potential Selling Sites:	Domestic: 15,000 Foreign: 45,000
Problem Company Is Attempting to Solve:	There are myriad computers and operating systems within an organization that need to cooperate with each other.
Solution Company Is Conveying to Problem:	The company's multiprotocol routers permit disparate computers to interconnect.

ure Bay Network's systems to meet their specific internetworking requirements and to expand these systems without degradation of performance as their networks grow. Based on its familiarity with the market for internetworking products, the company believes that it supports substantially all of the widely used LAN and WAN media interface standards and protocols for large complex internetworks for which specifications are publicly available.

Bay Networks, Inc., has about 20 percent of the router market, which is a $2 billion marketplace, that is growing at 60 percent per year. In 1993, Bay Networks shipped more than 10,000 routers with about 60,000 network connections. It sells direct as well as through value-added reseller systems integrators and through the sales departments of AT&T, Sprint, MCI, Hewlett-Packard, and Cabletron. This is multichannel marketing at its best.

The company's strategy has been to concentrate on high-end LAN "backbones"—the systems that interconnect a company's LAN environments. The Backbone Node sells for around $85,000 per unit.

In acquiring SynOptics, based in Santa Clara, California, Bay Networks gained a lead in the $2.5 billion hub market. Cisco Systems, Inc., is the leading router company with three times Bay Networks' market share. Cisco, Bay Networks primary competitor, is believed to be ahead of Bay Networks in developing next-generation switches that could obsolete routers and hubs. SynOptics is expected to level the playing field with Cisco in switch development.

The company's newest product is the Access Feeder Node, available in both Ethernet and Token Ring configurations. This is Bay Networks' remote access router, designed for users who want to extend their networks to remote sites and small work groups. These routers are designed to be smaller, less expensive ($4,000 a unit), and easier to configure than Bay Networks' higher-end products. Bay Networks has seen significant growth in access products—about 50 percent quarter-to-quarter unit growth. Although this is coming off of small numbers, since the product just started shipping in 1993, it represents an almost tenfold increase in units year after year.

BETTER EDUCATION, INC.

Until recently, technology has been outside the mainstream of classroom teaching. Several forces are converging that are driving technology into the classroom. First, the cost of PCs, CD-ROMs, and software is dropping and is competitive with textbooks. Second, there is a growing consensus that students need to be prepared for the Information Age, in which students change from passive observers to active participants and become more independent and take responsibility for their own learning process. Third, teachers and their powerful unions are finally growing less resistant to computer-based teaching.

Total U.S. expenditures on education increased from $270 billion in 1985 to $450 billion in 1993, or 7.5 percent of GNP. Notwithstanding, the Business Roundtable reported that as many as 60 percent of high-school graduates are not prepared for entry-level jobs. The high-school dropout rate in the United States is 30 percent, ranging as high as 50 percent in the inner cities. Of those who graduate, many are being funneled into college factories and lectured to in halls in which 200 to 500 slumber while their professors lumber on. The boredom factor ends with the interactivity of a computer attached to every student's clipboard.

Better Education, Inc. (BEI) turns a boring high school, college classroom, or lecture hall into an interactive learning center, where every student has the opportunity to answer questions, solve problems, and work with other students. BEI has developed a software communications system known as *Classtalk* that consists of a teacher's computer, a projection display, and a series of small, handheld, palmtop student computers, which are linked to the teacher's computer via a networking system. Student desks in the classroom are wired with special network adapters and plug-in ports for the palmtops, which minimize cost and promote learning interaction among the students.

Using their palmtops students can interrupt a professor when they don't understand what he or she has said, discuss their answers before entering them into their palmtops, and take tests. If one-third of the students in a 500-student lecture hall flash the professor to go back over a subject, or if they get the same wrong answer on a test, then the professor knows to adjust his or her method of teaching.

Moreover, curriculum can be developed in software to operate on *Classtalk*. Early adopters of *Classtalk*, such as Eric Mazur of Harvard University, are developing instructional courseware to operate on *Classtalk*. If his and others' courseware prove superior to trying to make

BETTER EDUCATION, INC.

Chief Executive Officer:	A. Louis Abrahamson
Principal Location:	4822 George Washington Blvd. Yorktown, VA 23692
Telephone/Fax:	804-898-4846/804-898-1897
Satellite Locations:	none
Date Founded:	1990
# Employees Current:	9
# Employees Projected by 6/30/95:	28
Sales (Annualized) 1994:	$2 million
Gross Profit Margin (GPM):	The company is privately-held and not required to disclose its financial statements.
Selling Expenses/Sales:	not available
% Sales Increase 1991–94:	not available
% Change GPM 1991–94:	not available
Total Debt/Net Worth:	not available
Net Profits Before Taxes:	not available
Net Profits per Employee:	not available
Principal Competitors:	Apple Computer Company, Control Data, Elkins Institute
# Potential Selling Sites:	Domestic: 12,000 Foreign: 24,000
Problem Company Is Attempting to Solve:	Large classrooms and lecture halls are not conducive to learning, because they are as impersonal as department stores.
Solution Company Is Conveying to Problem:	BEI has developed an interactive instructional system that enables each individual student to let the teacher know when he or she isn't understanding something.

textbooks meld with networks, *Classtalk* could become the *Windows* of the classroom—the gatekeeper that controls which software is used in high-school and college classrooms.

BEI was founded by A. Louis Abrahamson, an engineer who previously worked on developing the Concorde, the U.S. Space Shuttle, and the Space Station Freedom, and Fred Hartline, who developed the software for *Classtalk* while teaching physics at Christopher Newport College. Following successful beta tests of the product, funded by National Science Foundation grants, Dr. Abrahamson persuaded Michael Tomczyk to join the company as head of marketing. Tomczyk was second in command to Jack Tramiel, the legendary founder of Commodore Computer Corp., the developer of the first home computer.

The *Classtalk* system is installed and running in physics, psychology, and education classrooms at Harvard, Ohio State, Stanford, University of Massachusetts, and Duke, among others. It is priced to sell from $10,000 to $46,000 depending on classroom size, easily affordable by colleges, high schools, the training facilities of corporations, and government agencies.

THE BODY SHOP INTERNATIONAL PLC

The concept of doing *good* by doing *well* is the mission of The Body Shop. The doing well component is evident by these numbers: In 1993 the company earned 15.2 percent on revenues, grew revenues by 16 percent, and profits by 38 percent, while reducing its debt-to-worth ratio to 12 percent. The company's Net Profits per Employee were an elegant $18,156. Its market capitalization is approaching $750 million.

The measurements of doing good are too numerous to mention. A handful of them are worthy of note:

- Its 1992 voter registration drive signed up to 40,000 new voters in the United States.
- It opened its first community-based store in Harlem in 1993 in which one-half of pre-interest, pre-tax profits are invested in other community-based stores and the other half is given to a fund (monitored by local community leaders) for Harlem community projects.
- In 1993, The Body Shop USA's biggest campaign focused attention on people living with HIV and AIDS. Working with groups like the American Red Cross, the San Francisco AIDS Foundation, the Gay Man's Health Crisis, and the National Leadership Coalition on AIDS, the company developed a multifaceted campaign focusing particularly on women and teens, who comprise the fastest-growing risk groups for HIV infection. Using the theme "Protect & Respect," its campaign included a new corporate life-threatening illness policy; training for all employees; educational materials on safer sex and living with HIV and AIDS for distribution in its shops; outreach to local community groups; and funding support for organizations that assist people with HIV and AIDS.

The Body Shop is recreating the language of responsible business. Its basic business is cosmetics, which solve problems relating to beauty and health. CEO Anita Roddick, repackaged them for the soul. Much of The Body Shop's approach seems aimed at making customers feel good rather than look good. Its packaging shuns elaborate cardboard boxes in favor of simple plastic bottles with plain labels. Customers are encouraged to recycle these bottles by bringing them back for refilling. To further set itself apart, the company sells its products in individual

THE BODY SHOP INTERNATIONAL PLC

Chief Executive Officer:	Anita Roddick
Principal Location:	Watersmead, Littlehampton West Sussex, UK BN17 6LS
Telephone/Fax:	44–71–375-8240/44–71375-6057
Satellite Locations:	Wake Forest, NC
Date Founded:	1976
Description of Business:	Develops, produces, and sells cosmetics, and skin and hair products based on natural ingredients.
# Employees Current:	2,456
# Employees Projected by 6/30/95:	2,800
Sales (Annualized) 1994:	$293,100,000
Gross Profit Margin (GPM):	54.2%
Selling Expenses/Sales:	22.0%
% Sales Increase 1991–94:	+202.0%
% Change GPM 1991–94:	+1.0%
Total Debt/Net Worth:	12.0%
Net Profits Before Taxes:	$44,600,000
Operating Ratio:	15.2%
Net Profits per Employee:	$18,156
Traded On:	NMS/UK
Principal Competitors:	Revlon, Procter & Gamble, Estee Lauder, Jovan
# Potential Selling Sites:	Domestic: 75 million Foreign: 200 million
Problem Company Is Attempting to Solve:	The Body Shop helps its customers give back to the planet by buying and using products whose raw materials are farmed and harvested by tribes of poor hunter-gatherers in the underdeveloped regions of the world.
Solution Company Is Conveying to Problem:	The Body Shop promotes human rights, environmental concerns, indigenous rights, and investment in the poorer regions of the world with every sale of its bubble bath and jojoba shampoo.

Body Shop stores rather than in department stores or pharmacies. The company has captured the moral high ground over its competitors, who have only recently begun to see the emergence of cause marketing as an important segment of the cosmetics market.

"The Body Shop did sound a wake-up call," says William P. Lauder, General Manager of Origins.[1] Lauder, the 31-one year-old grandson of the company's founder, Estee Lauder, freely acknowledges that some aspects of Origins' business plan, such as donating a portion of its sales to charity, were inspired by The Body Shop.

The Body Shop, which opened its first store in the United States in 1988, has more than 1,000 retail outlets and it continues to expand aggressively. While cosmetics with natural ingredients have long been available from mom-and-pop stores, Roddick has taken the fad sector mainstream with a simple marketing plan, and has created an entire generation of consumers who will not buy a product unless the jar is returnable for refills and the ingredients have botanical names. Animals may not be used to test The Body Shop's products. Employees will not offer customers shopping bags; Body Shop customers know enough to bring their own. The windows and walls of the stores are plastered with socially conscious posters and calls to protest terrorism, anti-abortion, hunger, torture, and violence against women.

The Body Shop was conceived as a means to make a living. Roddick and her husband, Gordon, presented a business plan to their banker and he loaned them £4,000. They spent six months looking for a small store in Brighton and even longer to locate the product. "This was the hardest thing in the world because I went about it all the wrong way," recalls Roddick.[2] First she tried the big contract manufacturers. She wrote to them, rang them, and visited them with the raw materials she wanted in the products. But they were interested only in large quantities and she had a total of about £700 to invest. She was forced to consult the Yellow Pages for smaller companies. Here she found a local laboratory that liked the concept and had a very good herbalist who preferred natural ingredients.

Everything was done on a shoestring with no concession to aesthetics. Roddick chose plastic "hospital" bottles because they were so cheap. They painted the shop dark green because it covered everything, and filled it with a small range of preparations, all carefully labeled by hand. They hung a handwritten notice saying "OPEN."

The first day, they took in £100, more than enough to cover the projections. Feeling confident that his wife could make a go of the store, Gordon left for an 18-month horseback ride from Buenos Aires to New York. When he returned to the United Kingdom, a chain was emerging. The image was firmly in place, and Roddick has never diluted it.

---

[1] Trish Hall, "Striving to Be Cosmetically Correct," *The New York Times*, May 27, 1993, p. B-1.
[2] Nicky Smith, "Italian Brio + British Phlegm = The Body Shop," *Working Woman*, November 1994, p. 39.

CAMBRIDGE NEUROSCIENCE, INC.

W e raised $14 million in a private placement in this difficult market, which we believe speaks volumes about our company," says Elkan R. Gamzu, President and CEO of Cambridge NeuroScience, Inc. The company's stock had fallen to $6¾ per share following the cacophonous dialogue surrounding the Clinton Health Plan. But with its research and development so near to a bell-ringing triumph, the company sold 2,100,000 shares at one-half its market price pre-Clinton election, and diluted its stock by 20 percent in order to keep the cash flowing. What's driving Cambridge NeuroScience? A drug called CERESTAT. What is this fascinating drug, CERESTAT?

CERESTAT is an ion-channel blocker used for the treatment of stroke and traumatic brain injury (TBI). Approximately 500,000 individuals suffer strokes each year in the United States and an additional 500,000 suffer severe injuries to the head and spine. There currently are no FDA-approved treatments that limit or reduce the brain damage associated with stroke or TBI. CERESTAT has been shown to be effective in multiple animal models of stroke in preventing up to 70 percent of the brain damage observed in untreated control groups.

In an open label study, twenty-five patients who had suffered head injuries in the previous 72 hours received a blood infusion of CERESTAT followed by an infusion of the drug for four hours. The drug was well-tolerated, and no drug-related adverse effects were reported. Mean temperature fell during administration of the drug and returned to baseline within 12 hours. Researchers have sought methods for lowering brain temperature without a concomitant drop in arterial pressure.

Dr. Gamzu says, "Clinical development of CERESTAT is proceeding on schedule and efficacy trials in this patient population are planned for late 1994." In addition, the company is developing other ion-channel blockers for the treatment of Parkinson's disease, neuropathic pain, and brain damage frequently associated with cardiac surgery.

Acute events such as stroke and traumatic injuries to the head and spine often cause a reduction of blood flow (ischemia), and the premature death of nerve cells, resulting in permanent damage to the central nervous system. Nerve cell death following an ischemic event in the brain is triggered by the excessive release of glutamate from damaged nerve terminals, which in turn stimulates the massive entry of calcium into nerve cells through activated ion channels. Ion channels are membrane proteins that control the flow of charged ions, access cell

CAMBRIDGE NEUROSCIENCE, INC.

Chief Executive Officer:	Elkan R. Gamzu
Principal Location:	One Kendall Square Cambridge, MA 02139
Telephone/Fax:	617-225-0600/617-225-2741
Satellite Locations:	none
Date Founded:	1985
Description of Business:	The discovery and development of proprietary pharmaceutical products to treat severe neurological and psychiatric disorders.
# Employees Current:	93
# Employees Projected by 6/30/95:	98
Contract Revenues 1993:	$417,000
Gross Profit Margin (GPM):	not available
Selling Expenses/Sales:	not available
% Sales Increase 1991–94:	not available
% Change GPM 1991–94:	not available
Total Debt/Net Worth:	46.0%
Net Profits Before Taxes:	not available
Net Profits per Employee:	not available
Traded On:	NASDAQ/CNSI
Principal Competitors:	Neurogen, research universities, pharmaceutical companies
# Potential Selling Sites:	Domestic: 5 million per annum Foreign: 10 million per annum
Problem Company Is Attempting to Solve:	Lives are lost and treatment costs soar in the areas of acute neurological disorders, such as stroke and traumatic brain injury, schizophrenia, and neurodegenerative diseases.
Solution Company Is Conveying to Problem:	The company has been granted FDA approval to test CERESTAT on humans. CERESTAT is an effective therapy for stroke and traumatic brain injury.

membranes, and are responsible for generating all the electrical activity of the nervous system. Overloading nerve cells with calcium ions activates a biochemical cascade that results in cell death.

Cambridge NeuroScience believes that drugs that can arrest the biochemical cascade that results in cell death at an early stage offer the greatest potential as treatments for a wide variety of neurological disorders. Accordingly, it has focused its drug development program in this area on the synthesis of molecules, known as ion-channel blockers, which directly block passage of ions across cell membranes. In cerebral ischemia, overstimulation of the N-methyl-D-aspartate (NMDA) ion channel is primarily responsible for flooding nerve cells with calcium ions. Cambridge's first approach to developing an acute treatment for stroke and TBI had been to identify candidates that inhibit calcium entry into nerve cells by blocking glutamate-activated NMDA ion channels. CERESTAT is such a product candidate.

In 1993, CERESTAT received a U.S. patent. Back-up compounds and other similar chemical structures that number over 100 different molecules also received patent protection. Also in 1993, Cambridge completed two Phase I studies of safety, tolerance, and pharmaconetics in 47 healthy volunteers in the United Kingdom. An additional Phase I study in the United Kingdom is almost completed. The initial tests in the United States will be priced at $6,000 per dose.

Although substantially all publicly held, start-up biopharmaceutical companies saw their access to capital dessicated by the Clinton administration. Cambridge was able to raise capital to keep the development of CERESTAT alive.

CAMBRIDGE TECHNOLOGY PARTNERS

How would I define Cambridge Technology Partners (CTP)?" asks Jim Sims, the company's co-founder and CEO. "We are an international professional services organization that partners with clients to assess structure and implement customized information technology solutions with strategic business benefits in unprecedented time frames. CTP enables business and technological transformation within client organizations by leveraging the power of open systems and distributed technology."

Since it was founded in March 1991, CTP has specialized in building leading-edge software applications, each designed for maximum, positive business impact. CTP's development organization is positioned to use high-performance hardware, best-in-class languages, and powerful software tool sets to create new strategic applications in six to eight months—that's in contrast to traditional time frames of 18 to 24 months.

In addition to building individual mission-critical systems, a key component of CTP's strategy is to help the clients evaluate its complete software applications portfolio and prioritize the elements of a longer-term, information technology Open Enterprise Plan. This involves the sophisticated business of integrating new technology with traditional data center computing. CTP is intent on transferring the skills required to be successful in open systems to its client organizations.

CTP's ability to rapidly prototype and successfully deploy robust, production-quality client/server systems for a fixed price comes from a combination of *both technology and organizational know-how*. In the rapidly growing, $40 billion worldwide systems integration and professional services marketplace, this CTP skills combination is appealing to the information technology executive who wants to build a trust-based supplier relationship for the upsetting transition period.

"There is an entirely new focus on transitioning an organization's information technology system," says Sims. "It includes increasing revenues and profits, reducing Sales, General, and Administrative (SG&A) Expense, and/or improving customer service and satisfaction levels. In other words, the information systems mission statement now has a business component. The goal is to improve profitability and ROI."

Further, the costs associated with traditional proprietary systems are not falling as rapidly as will be required to meet the new service and profit objectives. Clearly, the expense associated with open systems technology components is a fraction of the cost of traditional

CAMBRIDGE TECHNOLOGY PARTNERS

Chief Executive Officer:	James Sims
Principal Location:	304 Vassar St. Cambridge, MA 02139
Telephone/Fax:	617-374-9800/617-374-8300
Satellite Locations:	Amsterdam, Bracknell, United Kingdom; Linkoping and Stockholm, Sweden
Date Founded:	1991
Description of Business:	Provides software development and information systems consulting services in the complicated transition to next-generation open and distributed computing.
# Employees Current:	450
# Employees Projected by 6/30/95:	Company withheld
Revenues (Annualized) 1994:	$37,950,549
Gross Profit Margin (GPM):	60.5%
Selling Expenses/Sales:	10.6%
% Sales Increase 1991–94:	+258.0%
% Change GPM 1991–94:	+10.6%
Total Debt/Net Worth:	55.8%
Net Profits Before Taxes:	$6,907,000
Operating Ratio:	$18.2%
Net Profits per Employee:	$15,349
Traded On:	NASDAQ/CATP
Principal Competitors:	Lannet, Innovative Information, BSG, TSC, US Connect, Lan Systems
# Potential Selling Sites:	Domestic: 500 Foreign: 2,500
Problem Company Is Attempting to Solve:	As large users of computers migrate to client/server-based networks they fear the re-engineering process and often become overly dependent on hardware vendors.
Solution Company Is Conveying to Problem:	CTP works back from the business need to the systems solution and then specs the hardware and software according to function.

mainframes and other proprietary midrange systems. However, there is an investment cost associated with the transition to these new, high-performance, flexible systems. While recognizing that the transition will require an initial investment, it is also critical to minimize the pain and expense associated with training the staff to create new applications. *Only by quickly demonstrating and proving the practical results of open systems* can the MIS organization effectively and successfully manage the expectations of users and senior management. This is the role that CTP plays: *transition therapist.*

The core of CTP's business is software development, and the company specializes in building new strategic applications for its customers. One strategic system involves an application designed to run on new hardware platforms—independently of any existing applications. Typically CTP uses UNIX midrange multiuser machines from a supplier such as Hewlett-Packard (H-P) or Sun Microsystems, with an application hosted by a relational database from Oracle or Sybase. CTP has entered into a strategic partnering relationship with H-P, Sun, and others to maximize its profits from these relationships; but it will not compromise its integrity by forcing the wrong tools on its clients.

Once the initial strategic application has been created and successfully deployed, CTP has found that its clients often gain confidence and begin to turn their attention to a broader range of challenging information technology issues: how to integrate whole portfolios of new and legacy applications across a variety of computing platforms, how to identify which of the enterprise's existing computing environments is rapidly becoming obsolete, and how to prioritize new information technology opportunities and create a realistic open architecture that makes sense for the business.

To round out the target services options created by downsizing and open systems, CTP offers a variety of information technology support programs. These include transferring technology skills to the client's information systems personnel and end-users so that they are capable of rapid prototyping and developing applications independently of CTP. CTP can also act as a buffer for the customer by providing ongoing evaluations of new technology. And finally, CTP will license its core application components so that clients can accelerate new application project schedules and benefit from CTP's previous work.[1]

CTP is redesigning the basic ways in which work gets done in an organization. This would have been unthinkable several years ago; after all what is management's function? But in today's business environment, with the process of doing business being information-driven, companies such as CTP are re-engineering the work flow and modifying the behavior of managers.

---

[1] A portion of this description is based on a report prepared by Aberdeen Group, 92 State Street, Boston, MA 02109.

CATALINA MARKETING CORP.

There is the story of the packaged goods salesman for a laundry detergent slashing the boxes of a competitor as he walks down the aisles. But that story is tame compared to tales of fist fights in the diaper aisle. Catalina Marketing is an electronic warrior—and not a one-dimensional one. In addition to the elegant electronic couponing system that it built, Catalina operates and offers other electronic weaponry to its packaged goods clients.

In September 1992, Catalina announced a joint venture with Information Resources, Inc., to leverage the proprietary capabilities of the two companies to provide clients with enchanced decision-making capabilities in the critical areas of timely monitoring of retail out-of-stock conditions, just-in-time product reordering, and day-after sales performance tracking. By March 1994, the program was running in approximately 1,200 stores.

In November 1993, Catalina announced a joint venture with Spectra-Physics Scanning Systems, Inc., named CECS, to utilize Catalina's existing in-store marketing network linked to scanners to electronically clear coupons. (CECS is a majority-owned subsidiary of Catalina Marketing.) When retailers scan and validate coupons, CECS will capture the coupon scan data and supply coupon count and value data to manufacturers for redemption payment. The CECS program is scheduled for testing through 1994 in major retail chains.

Catalina holds a majority interest in three subsidiaries outside the United States. During the later part of fiscal 1993, Catalina Marketing UK Ltd., completed market testing and installed the Catalina Marketing network in 129 retail stores throughout the United Kingdom. At year end, Catalina Marketing de Mexico SA de CV was in the final stage of a six-store pilot program and Catalina Marketing de France, SA had just been formed to begin market testing in France. The company also licenses the use of its software and equipment in two stores of the largest retailer in Belgium.

But like the time-worn battle cry "the war is in the store," there is hand-to-hand combat in the couponing and point-of-sale promotion fields. Free-standing inserts, known as FSIs, have historically dominated coupon distribution. These are four-color booklets with multiple coupons per page, typically inserted into Sunday newspapers. (In my hometown newspaper on a typical Sunday there are 20 pages of news and ads and 100 pages of FSIs.) Three companies that comprise the FSI

CATALINA MARKETING CORP.

Chief Executive Officer:	Tommy D. Greer
Principal Location:	11300 9th St. North St. Petersburg, FL 33716
Telephone/Fax:	813-579-5000/813-570-8507
Satellite Locations:	none
Date Founded:	1984
Description of Business:	Provides cost-effective methods of implementing a targeted consumer marketing strategy based on an electronic company system.
# Employees Current:	403
# Employees Projected by 6/30/95:	450
Revenues 1993:	$91,448,000
Gross Profit Margin (GPM):	61.4%
Selling Expenses/Sales:	28.7%
% Sales Increase 1991–94:	+276.0%
% Change GPM 1991–94:	+16.5%
Total Debt/Net Worth:	89.6%
Net Profits Before Taxes:	$19,261,000
Operating Ratio:	21.0%
Net Profits per Employee:	$54,902
Traded On:	NYSE/POS
Principal Competitors:	Valassis, News America/Product Movers, Sullivan Marketing, NCH Promotional Services (Dun & Bradstreet), CMS, Inc.
# Potential Selling Sites:	Domestic: 200,000 Foreign: 500,000
Problem Company Is Attempting to Solve:	Packaged goods manufacturers are hooked on couponing, but they need an outside organization to manage the unwieldy data.
Solution Company Is Conveying to Problem:	A communications network that delivers coupons to the checkout counters of its client stores electronically and records the use of the coupon.

industry are: Valassis, a large public company; News America/Product Movers, a subsidiary of News Corp. Ltd., and Sullivan Marketing. Sullivan Marketing, whose entry into this business sparked a severe price war, recently agreed to be acquired by Rupert Murdoch's News Corp's units. Despite prices falling by half over the past year, the unit volume of coupons printed has not gone up. This suggests that manufacturers view coupons as having specific tactical uses, rather than being substitutes for general advertising or trade spending.

There are many different reasons for couponing, including trial, new product introductions, price reductions, rewarding loyal customers, building a consumer database, increasing short-term volume, retailer support, etc. The type of coupon a manufacturer decides to use is primarily determined by the marketing objective and the price. Catalina promotes its ability to target "competitive users" more effectively than virtually any other method of couponing. Because the system will only issue a coupon based on known purchase behavior, it is generally regarded as having the best system for this application.

Couponing in a macro sense rewards the loyalty of consumers and is not a good means of prospecting for new customers; that is, unless the couponing system can capture the name, address, and other data on prospects, which Catalina would ultimately like to do. With connectivity software and Catalina's in-store systems, we will soon be acosted by a charming voice at the cereal shelf asking us to put back the Wheaties and pick up the Cheerios along with a dollar bill at the checkout counter.

Catalina has maintained its premium prices in the face of brutal competition. Its GPM of 61.4 percent is up 16.5 percent from 1991. Net Profits per Employee are an effluvial $54,902. And Catalina Marketing has Rick Benicke as a venture capital backer. Benicke is the son of the founder of S & H Green Stamps, the pioneer of in-store promotions.

C-CUBE MICROSYSTEMS, INC.

There are those new and rapidly emerging companies whose entrepreneurial teams appear to have as their goal to systematically abuse their investors in new and imaginative ways. That is never the case with a Don Valentine-backed company. Valentine—the senior partner of Sequoia Capital, in Menlo Park, California, a 20-year-old venture capital management company—was the first venture capitalist to back Apple Computer, Elantec, Inc., a leader in connectivity hardware products, and Sierra Semiconductor, Inc. He frequently plays the role of board chairman until he feels he can safely abandon that responsibility. And so he is with C-Cube Microsystems, Inc., a company that has already rewarded its public investors with an 80 percent increase in its stock price in its first five months of being public.

In C-Cube, Valentine backed a proven entrepreneurial team, including William J. O'Meara (a co-founder of LSI Logic, Inc. who did sufficiently well to invest in one of Sequoia's venture capital funds); Alexander A. Balkauski, a founder of a semiconductor company and director of Sierra Semiconductor; and other Silicon Valley veterans of myriad electronics, systems, and computer-related start-ups. No virgins in this team.

If you believe that video teleconferencing will become one of the major uses of the PC, then C-Cube is a company to watch closely. Here are the reasons:

Video is pervasive in today's society, with televisions, VCRs, or computers in use in the vast majority of homes and businesses in the developed world. Since the 1930s, video images have been transmitted and stored almost exclusively using analog formats. However, digital video provides a number of fundamental benefits over analog video. Unlike analog video, digital video can be compressed, providing significant storage and transmission efficiencies and can be transmitted and reproduced without perceptible image degradation. Digital formats also provide users with the benefits of random access and superior editing capabilities. In the 1980s, the benefits of digital formats led the consumer audio industry to convert from analog long-playing records to digital CDs, resulting in rapid growth in the market for CD players. In the 1990s, the ongoing evolution from analog to digital is transforming the way in which video is transmitted, stored, edited, and viewed.

C-Cube is focused on providing powerful, highly integrated, standards-based, programmable compression solutions that are cost-

C-CUBE MICROSYSTEMS, INC.

Chief Executive Officer:	William J. O'Meara
Principal Location:	1778 McCarthy Blvd. Milpitas, CA 95035
Telephone/Fax:	408-944-6300/408-944-6788
Satellite Locations:	Cambridge, MA; Seven Oaks, Kent, United Kingdom; Yokohama, Japan
Date Founded:	1988
Description of Business:	Provides encoder, decoder and codec products, and digital video compression solutions to permit videos to be transmitted over desktop PCs and direct-broadcast satellite systems.
# Employees Current:	118
# Employees Projected by 6/30/95:	Company withheld
Revenues (Annualized) 1994:	$23,739,000
Gross Profit Margin (GPM):	65.0%
Selling Expenses/Sales:	34.6%
% Sales Increase 1991–94:	+431.0%
% Change GPM 1991–94:	+30.5%
Total Debt/Net Worth:	129.1%
Net Profits Before Taxes:	$(154,000)
Operating Ratio:	deficit
Net Profits per Employee:	deficit
Traded On:	NASDAQ/CUBE
Principal Competitors:	Motorola, SGS-Thompson, Intel, Zoran, LSI Logic, IBM Microelectronics
# Potential Selling Sites:	Domestic: 30 million Foreign: 75 million
Problem Company Is Attempting to Solve:	Video is traditionally transmitted and stored in an analog format, a slower and costly format.
Solution Company Is Conveying to Problem:	Highly integrated, standards-based programmable compression solutions that deliver high-image quality for a broad range of mass-market applications.

effective and deliver high image quality for a broad range of mass-market applications. The company has developed extensive expertise in programmable architectures, algorithms, microcode development, and very large scale integrated (VLSI) circuit design. This expertise has enabled C-Cube to be a leading innovator in the development of video compression.

The company introduced the first single-chip, Joint Photographic Experts Group (JPEG) codec, the first single-chip, Moving Pictures Experts Group (MPEG) decoder for consumer electronics and computer applications, the first single-chip MPEG decoder for communications applications, and the first single-chip MPEG video encoder. These highly complex single-chip solutions are designed to meet both the massive computing requirements of digital video compression and the size and cost constraints of mass-market applications.

C-Cube offers its customers complete, highly integrated compression solutions, including encoders, decoders, codecs, and development systems that are fully compatible. By offering a complete solution, the company provides customers full standards compliance and interoperability at both the compression and decompression stages, and optimizes the interaction of the encoder and decoder, potentially resulting in improvements in image quality and compression efficiency.

The company has designed a set of unique programmable architectures for both its encoder and decoder products, which enable it to respond to the requirements of different markets and system manufacturers without redesigning the core silicon. C-Cube's high-performance programmable architectures are comprised of core silicon augmented by two levels of microcode, one providing functionality that is common across applications and the other providing applications and customer-specific functionality. These architectures allow the company to provide system manufacturers with compression solutions that address their cost, time to market, image quality, and interoperability requirements, while allowing the manufacturers to differentiate their products.

C-Cube's encoder products are based on a proprietary 32-bit video RISC processor, which features a highly specialized instruction set optimized for digital video compression. As a result, their encoder products are able to compress digital video at a rate of 10 to 100 times faster than existing general-purpose processors. In fact, the products are able to compress the same images in real time. Real-time encoding is an essential attribute for compression solutions used in broadcast applications. C-Cube believes that it will be essential for the development of future applications that require both encoder and decoder functionality in real time, such as digital camcorders.

On an abstract level, if digital video conferencing is going to become a major business, C-Cube will be one of the industry's tollgate suppliers. Providers of PCs with video capability very likely will buy their codecs from C-Cube.

CERNER CORPORATION

ounded in 1980, CERNER Corp. is a leading provider of clinical information systems to providers of health care, such as hospitals, clinics, HMOs, and laboratories. Unlike many typical provider information systems, which focus solely on automating patient billing or on automating the operations of a single department, CERNER Corp. collects clinical and financial information from the time of a patient's admission to discharge. This information is then presented in an integrated format that allows health-care professionals and managers to optimize the quality of care provided, while reducing costs.

A few years ago, CERNER's systems would be a yawn, since insurers paid whatever bill the hospital administrators churned out. Not so anymore. Hospital managers actually have to know their costs in the 1990s. And CERNER has one of the systems to help count up the costs.

As indicated by the rapid rise in managed-care enrollment and the clamor for legislative reform, the desire to control rapidly rising health-care costs is at an all-time high. However, unlike other industries, the tools necessary to control costs and allow for intelligent decisions are not fully developed in the health-care industry. Employers, payors, and providers alike are utilizing patterns, pricing trends, and outcomes to determine the appropriate level of medically necessary care and the appropriate price for that care. However, the information infrastructure necessary to obtain the necessary data to control costs on a large scale, for the most part, does not exist outside of advanced managed-care and provider companies. This need—to find costs—is driving growth in the demand for comprehensive, timely, and accurate health-care information systems. CERNER was an early entrant into this sector, and as an industry leader it is well positioned to benefit from the demand to get a handle on costs.

In contrast to many standard industry information systems, which are composed of several nonintegrated components, CERNER's proprietary Healthcare Network Architecture (HNA) represents an integrated, comprehensive information system for health-care providers. With components that help manage the entire spectrum of patient care from admission to discharge, including laboratory work, radiology, pathology, nursing care, and respiratory therapy—as well as components that compile common clinical data and assist in clinical decision support—HNA is able to automate and manage the entire process of patient diagnosis and treatment. HNA's individual components employ a

CERNER CORPORATION

Chief Executive Officer:	Neal Patterson
Principal Location:	2800 Rockcreek Parkway Kansas City, MO 64117-2551
Telephone/Fax:	816-221-1024/816-474-1742
Satellite Locations:	9 U.S.; Germany, Australia, Scotland, Saudi Arabia
Description of Business:	Provides clinical information on patients to health-care providers from the time of patient admission until discharge.
Date Founded:	1980
# Employees Current:	1,000
# Employees Projected by 6/30/95:	1,400
Sales 1993:	$120,572,000
Gross Profit Margin (GPM):	63.6%
Selling Expenses/Sales:	7.4%
% Sales Increase 1991–93:	+56.1%
% Change GPM 1991–93:	+14.7%
Total Debt/Net Worth:	54.3%
Net Profits Before Taxes:	$24,120,000
Operating Ratio:	20%
Net Profits per Employee:	$34,457
Traded On:	NASDAQ/CERN
Principal Competitors:	HBO & Co., SMS, First Data, IBAX, TDS, Meditech, Community Health, Citation
# Potential Selling Sites:	Domestic: 5,000 Foreign: 5,000
Problem Company Is Attempting to Solve:	Hospital and other health-care providers have not known their costs, because they could get paid no matter what they charged. In today's health-care market, hospitals and other providers have to be much more accountable.
Solution Company Is Conveying to Problem:	The company offers patient monitoring systems that account for every patient and all of his or her costs from admission to discharge.

common database, and all data concerning a patient can be made available to any user of the system immediately.

CERNER is experiencing explosive growth. Reflecting the market opportunity and the company's strong market position, revenues and net earnings have grown at a compound annual rate of 33.1 percent and 94.1 percent respectively, since 1990. Furthermore, its backlog has grown from $3.6 million at the end of 1990 to $93.8 million at the end of 1993. The number of installed systems has grown from 396 at the end of 1991 to 496 at the end of 1993.

CERNER is the leader in the standalone laboratory information systems (LIS) market, a niche roughly $100 million in size in the United States. (Sunquest, a private company, is CERNER's closest competition.) And it is an emerging leader in integrated clinical information systems—which allow lab, pharmacy, radiology, and other clinical department systems to send and receive information from one another, and format all relevant data into an electronic medical record.

CERNER's most formidable competitor has been SMS, the industry's largest hospital information systems vendor. With vast resources and a full complement of product offerings, its best-selling product is an IBM-mainframe-based information system called *INVISION*. The very mention of the word "mainframe" creates the sound of billfolds snapping shut. CERNER's systems are less expensive and its utility appears to be cutting edge.

CERNER is taking its act into Germany, Australia, Scotland, and Saudi Arabia. Its GPM is growing while its Selling Expenses/Sales ratio remains under 10 percent, an indication that "word of mouth" is moving lots of product. Management is managing growth elegantly.

CHIPCOM CORPORATION

Chipcom Corp. is on the cusp of slip-sliding away from quantum status. Its GPM has declined in each of the last three years, which indicates difficulties in distinguishing Chipcom's product from its competitors' (could intelligent hubs be commodity products so quickly?), lack of attention to the serious task of squeezing costs out of raw materials, or perhaps problems with Chipcom's sales commission structure, which rewards salespeople at the sales rather than the GPM line. What persuades me that Chipcom has another quarter century of excitement is Rob Held, its replacement CEO in charge. Chipcom is a junkyard dog at a 12-dog kennel of lap dogs and retrievers with one lamb shank.

Held, who earned an undergraduate degree from Yale and an MBA from Harvard, credits his submarine service for one of his most important business lessons: to hold an abiding respect for people's abilities. "You learn from day one that although you're the manager, the troops who work for you have been on the submarine for years and know a lot more than you do. Your job as manager is not being smarter than anybody else. Your job is to lead, organize, and provide direction. It's a job that depends strongly on using the combined knowledge of the people who work for you."

This lesson was put into practice when Held took over the helm at Chipcom in 1988, five years after the Southborough, Massachusetts, company was founded. At that time, it was growing smartly as a broadband backbone supplier, designing long-distance Ethernet networking products for manufacturing plants, universities, and other large institutions. However, with the arrival of technologies such a fiber optics and PC local area networks (LANs), the market began to change. "My role coming into the company was to define the next round of growth," Held says. "The company already was growing 80 percent a year. The question was how to sustain the growth and where to take the company in the future."[1]

As an outsider coming into the networking industry, Held relied heavily on his abilities to organize and redirect established resources and talent. While the arrival of a new CEO customarily means shakeups and dismissals, this was not the case with Held. "I made sure we

---

[1] Joseph E. McKendrick, "Subbin a Network Periscope," *Midrange Systems*, November 9, 1993, Vol. 6, No. 21, A Cardinal Business Media Publication.

CHIPCOM CORPORATION

Chief Executive Officer:	J. Robert Held
Principal Location:	118 Turnpike Rd. Southborough, MA 01772
Telephone/Fax:	508-460-8900/508-460-8990
Satellite Locations:	Major U.S. cities plus Australia, China, France, Germany, Israel, Italy, Malaysia, United Kingdom
Date Founded:	1983
Description of Business:	Designs, manufactures, distributes, and supports intelligent switching hubs and other computer networking products.
# Employees Current:	634
# Employees Projected by 6/30/95:	Company withheld
Revenues (Annualized) 1994:	$150,019,000
Gross Profit Margin (GPM):	57.9%
Selling Expenses/Sales:	30.1%
% Sales Increase 1991–94:	+313.0%
% Change GPM 1991–94:	–4.0%
Total Debt/Net Worth:	24.4%
Net Profits Before Taxes:	$22,698,000
Operating Ratio:	15.1%
Net Profits per Employee:	$35,801
Traded On:	NASDAQ/CHPM
Principal Competitors:	Cabletron, SynOptics, Ungermann-Bass, 3Com, NetWorth
# Potential Selling Sites:	Domestic: 5,000 Foreign: 15,000
Problem Company Is Attempting to Solve:	"A corporate decision to tie all of the PCs into a LAN is an easy over-the-weekend tactical decision," says Held. "Extending that system outside the building requires systematic planning and extensive equipment."
Solution Company Is Conveying to Problem:	To provide the equipment and consulting necessary to install companywide networks.

collected the best ideas of the people inside the company," he says. With that input, Held steered the company toward developing intelligent hubs that perform centralized network management and switching functions, and providing LAN products for facility networks or large interdepartmental installations. "Because Chipcom had a background in backbones, we saw the hub business differently," he adds. Typically, networking vendors come from the LAN level. "I let the employees do the rest. All I did was make sure we had the right conversation that led us in the right direction."

Held's constant energy and sense of adventure are legendary. On occasion, he can be seen riding his bicycle to the office. An avid outdoorsman, Held has been helicopter skiing in British Columbia, where he was dropped out of a helicopter at a high elevation on a mountainside and descended thousands of feet through uncharted slopes. His fascination with network computing is just as passionate. It's a revolution shaking the whole computing industry, he points out. "Network computing is the core of what people talk about as client/server. It's everything that is going to happen in the business through the rest of this decade."

Intelligent hubs provide the flexibility and manageability needed among large networks for these day-to-day changes, as well as for larger changes such as downsizing or expansion. Networking is commonplace in all larger companies. "It's no longer a strange, high-tech niche," Held says. However, "It probably takes three years or more to do it," Held adds. "Many have networks in smaller subunits and are looking at it for a higher level corporate or divisional installation."

The size of the opportunity is huge, and the dozen competitors are in many respects mirror images of each other's spirited competitiveness. Where Chipcom appears to shine is in knowing it is time to consolidate some of the players—and being the consolidator. In February 1994, Chipcom acquired Artel Communications Corp., and bumped its revenues 62 percent to $52 million, only $16 million of which came from Artel. Net profits before taxes and before charging off acquisition costs were $5.1 million.

Chipcom's marketing channels are a fascinating amalgam. Its principal channel is through value-added resellers (VARs), but IBM is licensed to sell Chipcom domestically and the IBM European rollout is just beginning. Forty percent of Chipcom's sales are foreign. Harnessing IBM's sales force was a brilliant stroke on Held's part. With $70 million in the bank, virtually no debt, and a net worth of $125 million, look to Chipcom to make some strategic acquisitions to reduce the number of competitors and keep its quantum status.

CIRRUS LOGIC, INC.

Michael Hackworth was a Senior Vice President of Signetics Co., the semiconductor arm of North American Philips Corp. in 1985 when Suhas Patil called on him. Patil founded Patil Systems, Inc. the year before to develop and market his Storage/Logic Array (S/LA) very large scale integration (VLSI) design software. The company had 11 employees.

"At Signetics it was taking us a year and a half to two years to bring out a VLSI chip, with huge numbers of people involved and a long debug cycle," Hackworth told *Upside* magazine.[1] He thought he might hire Patil to design some chips for Signetics, "But when I got in and met the people and understood what they had, it hit me like a ton of bricks that this could be the basis for a new kind of chip company," says Hackworth.

Upon joining Patil Systems, Hackworth contacted the venture capital firms that had provided them seed capital to raise additional funds. In fact, one of them had assured Hackworth prior to joining Patil that upon his arrival, a fresh $3 million would be invested. The seed round had been at 70 cents per share without a CEO or management team. Hackworth figured he added value—but the VCs told him they would only invest at 50 cents per share.

Unabashed, but certainly awakened to his scary situation, Hackworth began dialing for dollars. Brad Jones of Brentwood Associates took the lead, and others soon followed, providing Cirrus Logic with ample capital to carry out Hackworth's business plan. The name change followed the Brentwood funding.

Hackworth's idea was to take advantage of the firm's proprietary S/LA technology to develop peripheral chips from a systems point of view, attack emerging markets where standards and requirements change rapidly, pursue high-integration solutions, and use outside foundries instead of burdening the company with expensive fabs. None of those components was novel, but together they gave Cirrus a defensible strategy.

Initially, Hackworth says, "we were going to attack the minicomputer market, but just as we were forming the company, the PC market took off. So we just jumped on it and took that same peripheral concept and applied it to the PC market."

---

[1] "Cirrus Takes PC Market By Storm," Bill Arnold, *Upside*, August 1993.

CIRRUS LOGIC, INC.

Chief Executive Officer:	Michael L. Hackworth
Principal Location:	3100 West Warren Ave. Fremont, CA 94538
Telephone/Fax:	510-623-8300/510-226-2240
Satellite Locations:	Austin, TX; San Diego, CA; Plano, TX; Raleigh, NC
Date Founded:	1984
Description of Business:	Develops innovative integrated circuits for applications that include user interface (graphics, audio, and video), communications, data acquisition, and mass storage.
# Employees Current:	1,500
# Employees Projected by 6/30/95:	Company withheld
Sales (Annualized) 1994:	$544,077,000
Gross Profit Margin (GPM):	46.5%
Selling Expenses/Sales:	16.4%
% Sales Increase 1991–94:	+316.3%
% Change GPM 1991–94:	+2.8%
Total Debt/Net Worth:	48.6%
Net Profits Before Taxes:	$54,845,000
Operating Ratio:	10.1%
Net Profits per Employee:	$736,563
Traded On:	NASDAQ/CRUS
Principal Competitors:	Adaptec, Western Digital, Sierra Semiconductor, Teseng Labs, Weitek
# Potential Selling Sites:	Domestic: 100 Foreign: 200
Problem Company Is Attempting to Solve:	The computer is a nonintelligent tool; the intelligence resides in integrated circuits. Someone needs to architect chips to meet the market's needs.
Solution Company Is Conveying to Problem:	The company supplies specialty chips, such as graphics chips, to PC manufacturers.

Now focused, Cirrus first targeted the hard disk drive market because "it represented what we saw as the fastest ramp to volume," Hackworth says. What the company did was jump on the transition from disk controller integrated circuits (ICs) being on cards outside the electromechanical hard disk drive to a ground swell of highly integrated controller chips embedded inside the drive.

Cirrus's next and ultimately successful thrust into the graphics display arena began in 1987 when, in the midst of designing a display graphics controller, IBM announced its new Video Graphics Array (VGA) technology standard. Quickly, Cirrus engineers changed their design, and the company was able to announce available samples of a VGA controller by the next COMDEX trade show several months later.

As a result, Cirrus was the first company to design and ship a fully compatible and highly integrated VGA controller for PCs, initially to board manufacturers and later to PC original equipment manufacturers (OEMs). The company followed in 1989 with a VGA controller for flat-panel liquid crystal displays in the emerging notebook PC market.

Hackworth's vision of the future for Cirrus is a company where computer, communications, and consumer electronics technologies merge and become digital, and the distinctions among them blur. For example, the recent acquisition of Crystal Semiconductor Corp. gives Cirrus analog technology that's becoming important as other Cirrus chips incorporate more of those functions. It acquired Acumos, Inc. to buy a position in the advanced display controller products market. It acquired Pacific Communication Sciences, Inc., to get into the digital wireless communications field. Cirrus makes venture capital investments in applications start-ups in order to sit on the windowsill of many opportunities, all of which need chips. Visualizing the future, building new products that meet demand, and making and integrating appropriate acquisitions is a difficult and complex task. The Cirrus management team seems up to it.

COMPUTER NETWORK TECHNOLOGY CORP.

For many design engineers to create a new product in computer-aided design and computer-aided manufacturing (CAD/CAM), channel extension provides significant operational and cost benefits. Economically, channel extension provides significant economies of scale and administrative benefits. Other benefits of channel extension of graphic applications include: shared access to large engineering design databases by a variety of engineering groups in different facilities, states, or countries; integration of graphics with mainframe database applications; and design simulation algorithms that demand processing and memory capabilities found only in a mainframe.

Today's engineers—those accustomed to working with CAD/CAM—care precious little about the information processing infrastructure beyond the screens of their workstations. Their task is to get the product from blueprint to market fast. So dynamic is the pace of business these days, the engineering function often represents the competitive edge in moving new products to the market faster. In such an environment, engineers need the best CAD/CAM tools and support to meet their deadlines.

The move to outsourcing and moving designers near to customers has physically separated the engineering groups and data centers that support them. The physical separation causes both technical and organizational problems.

Traditionally, CAD/CAM-based engineering groups were located physically proximate to the data center for two main reasons: Most organizations evolved as centralized entities, with administrative and manufacturing facilities under one roof; and physical proximity was critical because limitations in networking technology severely constrained the maximum distances between CPUs and peripherals such as workstations and printers. For example, the IBM 5088/6098 terminals used by CAD/CAM applications must be channel-attached to the host, a configuration that inherently has a 400-foot limitation.

Networking technologies and client/server architectures helped enable the shift of design engineers to customer sites. However, support for distributing mainframe-based graphics design systems did not keep up with this important trend until Computer Network Technology Corp. and its *channel extenders* came along. Channel extension technology gives remote-graphics users high performance while eliminating distance limitations. CNT's Graphics Controller Interface provides an

COMPUTER NETWORK TECHNOLOGY CORP.

Chief Executive Officer:	C. McKenzie (Mac) Lewis III
Principal Location:	6500 Wedgwood Rd. Maple Grove, MN 55311-3640
Telephone/Fax:	612-550-8000/612-550-8800
Satellite Locations:	United Kingdom; France; Germany; Japan
Description of Business:	Designs, develops, and manufactures networking products that link geographically dispersed, dissimilar computing platforms and peripheral devices, enabling them to communicate seamlessly.
Date Founded:	1979
# Employees Current:	400
# Employees Projected by 6/30/95:	500
Sales 1993:	$55,687,318
Gross Profit Margin (GPM):	69%
Selling Expenses/Sales:	24.9%
% Sales Increase 1991–93:	+150.0%
% Change GPM 1991–93:	+6.3%
Total Debt/Net Worth:	36.2%
Net Profits Before Taxes:	$7,901,381
Operating Ratio:	14.2%
Net Profits per Employee:	$24,237
Traded On:	NASDAQ/CMNT
Principal Competitors:	Data Switch Corp., McData Corp., Network Systems Corp.
# Potential Selling Sites:	Domestic: 1,000 Foreign: 2,000
Problem Company Is Attempting to Solve:	Valuable data are stored in mainframes, but engineers working in CAD/CAM models want to be at customer sites. The dilemma can be costly.
Solution Company Is Conveying to Problem:	Network channel extenders break the bonds that once kept mainframe storage tethered to the data center.

effective solution for delivering channel speed response with IBM 5088/6090 Graphics Systems in remote environments by attaching to the mainframe channel at one location and to IBM 5088/6098 Graphics Channel Controllers at other locations. Distance limitations are thereby eliminated. Channel-extended high-speed links allow organizations to locate engineers where they will be most effective and productive.

Moreover, channel extension enables organizations to support multiple engineering groups from a central location. A number of benefits ensue. First, organizations derive considerable economies of scale by eliminating a number of hosts. Second, to the extent that other channel-connected devices share the same CNT Extended Channel Network, further savings are realized. Third, system management tasks such as backup and recovery are simplified by having a consolidated system and common network. Finally, and perhaps most significant, channel extension permits engineers from different work group locations to share resources such as databases, designs, drawings and applications, as well as peripherals such as printers and other devices more efficiently.

CNT's customer list reads like a Who's Who of large manufacturers whose products have a heavy design content: AT&T Technologies, Deere & Company, Daimler-Benz, Mitsubishi Cable Industries, and Shell Oil Company.

Not content with a single product, the company recently acquired Brixton Systems, Inc., Cambridge, Massachusetts. With $4 million in revenues, Brixton makes and sells data communications software for the client/server environment, permitting flexible interconnections of existing networks with Unix-based applications.

COREL CORPORATION

Describe the perfect company. It would produce a unique, proprietary product for a growing market with lots of purchasing power and no regulations. The product's features would be extolled by word of mouth. The management team would be experienced in managing rapid growth. My way of describing the perfect company is one that has the highest quantitative values in the equation $V = P \times S \times E$, where V is valuation, P is the size of the problem, S is the elegance of the solution, and E is the experience of the entrepreneurial team.

Another way to describe the perfect company is to say "Corel Corporation." The problem that it has identified is the desire for people from kindergarteners to business leaders to self-publish and create their own artwork. The solution is the CorelDRAW line and the CorelVentura line of software products. The entrepreneurial team is headed by Michael Cowpland, who built Mitel Corporation into a major telecommunications company a decade ago.

Corel Corporation—a world leader in the development of graphics and Small Computer System Interface (SCSI) software—has one leg in graphics software, another in interface software, and a third in desktop publishing: three of the fastest-growing industries in the world. Originally, the company was engaged primarily in the systems integration business, providing customers with turnkey PC-based desktop publishing systems and local area networks (LANs) by combining various manufacturers' hardware and software products with its proprietary software enhancements.

As a result of its experience in developing software enhancements, Corel began to devote additional resources to developing a separately packaged graphics software program. In January 1989, the company introduced its first version of CorelDRAW. CorelDRAW 2.0 was introduced in November of 1990; CorelDRAW 3 became available in May of 1992. CorelDRAW 4, the most recent upgrade, was launched in May 1993, and CorelDRAW 5 in June 1994.

The company's acquisition of Ventura Publisher and DataBase Publisher in 1993, along with the launch of CorelVentura 4.2, further increased Corel's visibility as a provider of a complete software solution for desktop publishing.

In 1991, Corel launched CorelSCSI, which allowed SCSI users to connect up to seven PC peripherals to a single-host adapter. In May of

COREL CORPORATION

Chief Executive Officer:	Michael Cowpland
Principal Location:	1600 Carling Ave. Ottawa, Ontario, CAN K1Z8R7
Telephone/Fax:	613-728-3733/613-761-9176
Satellite Locations:	none
Date Founded:	1985
Description of Business:	A leading publisher of graphics and small computer interface software.
# Employees Current:	331
# Employees Projected by 6/30/95:	425
Sales (Annualized) 1994:	$113,064,000
Gross Profit Margin (GPM):	76.7%
Selling Expenses/Sales:	36.7%
% Sales Increase 1991–94:	+300.6%
% Change GPM 1991–94:	+7.7%
Total Debt/Net Worth:	8.4%
Net Profits Before Taxes:	$45,806,000
Operating Ratio:	42.2%
Net Profits per Employee:	$144,352
Traded On:	NASDAQ/COSFF TSE/COS
Principal Competitors:	Adobe Systems, Microsoft, Autodesk
# Potential Selling Sites:	Domestic: 150,000 Foreign: 300,000
Problem Company Is Attempting to Solve:	Marshall McLuhan said upon witnessing xerography for the first time, "Now everyone is a publisher." But, publishers need tools.
Solution Company Is Conveying to Problem:	Corel produces software that permits anyone to publish a handsome newsletter with high-quality graphics.

1992, Corel launched a software-only version of CorelSCSI, which has become one of the most popular SCSI software solutions on the market today.

The multivolume Corel Professional Photos on CD-ROM Series has also greatly increased Corel's range of products and visibility. Accessible by both PC and Macintosh users, this premier source of royalty-free stock photography and screen-saver images is helping to revolutionize the digital stock photo industry.

Corel Corporation ships its products through a network of more than 100 distributors in 60 countries. "We are excited about the market's response to CorelDRAW 5," says CEO Cowpland. And well he should be. The company's sales for the first half of 1994 were $65 million versus $35 million for the previous year, on which it earned $17 million before taxes—compared with $7.2 million in the previous year. Stockholders' equity stood at $125 million as of May 31, 1994, and cash and short-term investments were $100 million. With earnings doubling every year and profit margins improving, Corel is one of the most dynamic companies in the PC marketplace. As for its operating efficiency, Net Profits per Employee exceeded $140,000. That's more than twice the ratio for Microsoft or Oracle.

CORRECTIONS CORPORATION
OF AMERICA

Corrections Corporation of America (CCA) was co-founded by John Massey, the only entrepreneur to take three companies to the New York Stock Exchange (Brunswick Corp., Hospital Corp. of America, and Kentucky Fried Chicken). He founded CCA, but it is not yet on the New York Stock Exchange.

CCA is in the facilities-management business: prison management. It is paid 85 percent of the prisoner-per-diem budget of the states that hire it. If it delivers the job for less than the contract price, it makes a profit. Profits had been hard to come by for CCA until 1992, when it broke into the black. Now they are practically doubling on a year-to-year basis.

Net income for the first half of 1994 was $2,532,806, compared with $1,949,912 in the same period of 1993. For the year to date, CCA has earned $.20 per primary and fully diluted share, versus $.17 at the halfway mark of 1993. Revenues for the first six months of 1994 were $52.9 million, 7 percent greater than the $49.3 million reported last year.

"CCA made substantial progress during the second quarter," said CCA co-founder and CEO Doctor R. Grants. "We improved the financial performance at our existing facilities, considerably strengthened our balance sheet, and enhanced our international marketing with our Sodexho alliance.

"CCA's net margin was boosted by expanding capacity at two of our facilities, higher occupancy across the board, and lower interest expense," continued Grants. "At the same time we used the $17.5 million CCA received from the Sodexho transaction to pay off debt and build our cash reserves. Our current ratio is now comfortably above 2:1 and debt-to-equity, including the current portion payable, is now below 1:1. Additionally, the conversion of our preferred stock at the end of June 1994 increased shareholders' equity and eliminates the dividend going forward."

On June 23, 1994, CCA announced it had formed an international joint venture with Paris-based Sodexho, S.A., a French conglomerate that provides contract-management services, to market its prison business worldwide. The company also sold 700,000 shares of common stock at $15 per share and $7 million of 8½ percent subordinated convertible notes to Sodexho. Sodexho plans to achieve and maintain a 20 percent stake in CCA.

"Our company has never been better positioned financially or strategically to take advantage of the opportunities that are before it. We

CORRECTIONS CORPORATION OF AMERICA

Chief Executive Officer:	Doctor R. Crants
Principal Location:	102 Woodmont Blvd. Nashville, TN 37027
Telephone/Fax:	615-292-3100/615-269-8635
Satellite Locations:	none
Date Founded:	1983
Description of Business:	The largest private owner/operator of prisons in the United States.
# Employees Current:	2,600
# Employees Projected by 6/30/95:	2,800
Sales (Annualized) 1994:	$103,396,000
Gross Profit Margin (GPM):	15.8%
Selling Expenses/Sales:	7.7%
% Sales Increase 1991–94:	+152.3%
% Change GPM 1991–94:	+15.3%
Total Debt/Net Worth:	165.7%
Net Profits Before Taxes:	$4,737,000
Operating Ratio:	4.6%
Net Profits per Employee:	$2,078
Traded On:	NASDAQ/CCAX
Principal Competitors:	Wackenhut Corrections Corp., state, federal, municipal agencies
# Potential Selling Sites:	Domestic: 1,200 Foreign: not applicable
Problem Company Is Attempting to Solve:	Prisoners in the United States cost taxpayers about $36,000 per annum. You or I could stay in a fairly nice resort hotel and have three meals a day, and golf, tennis, and pool privileges for 365 days a year for that kind of money.
Solution Company Is Conveying to Problem:	Private management of prisons.

are stepping up our marketing activities in both the domestic and international arenas. During the third quarter we will open a 500-bed expansion in Venus, Texas and finish construction on our 500-bed Florence, Arizona, facility," Grants concluded.

CCA manages prisons and other correctional institutions for governmental agencies. The company is the industry leader in private sector corrections, with 11,639 beds in 24 facilities under contract in seven states, Puerto Rico, Australia, and the United Kingdom. CCA provides a full range of services that include finance, design, construction, renovation, and management of new or existing facilities.

Private enterprise is more efficient than bureaucracies in running prisons—among other services. But many politicians love to hold onto the power of putting friends onto prison boards, and so only 13 states have agreed to let private companies operate their prisons. These politicians are bucking the trend, because their states are running out of money, yet they reject CCA's offer to cut the prision budget by 15 percent per year. How long can they keep up the charade? CCA is a patient company. It now has the financial strength to wait for the states that have not approved prison privatization to climb aboard.

DAVIDSON & ASSOCIATES, INC.

Davidson & Associates is the leading educational software company in one of the most dynamic and rapidly growing industries on the planet and publishes some of the most popular home computer software. Through a series of acquisitions, Davidson owns Chaos Studios, which develops entertainment software for platforms as various as Windows and Sega; and First Byte, developer of a patented software-based text-to-speech technology which gives the company a toe in the telecommunications door.

Janice G. Davidson has carefully built this company, from a series of accidental beginnings. When Apple announced its new personal computer, Davidson, a teacher, sat down and began to learn how to program the computer to meet her students' educational needs. "They had a book on Applesoft and I just followed the directions," says Davidson. The first program that she designed taught speed reading; she named it, appropriately, Speed Reader. That was followed by Word Attack and Mathblaster. Mathblaster, a video arcade-style game in which you solve math equations to shoot aliens out of the sky has been her most successful program, selling more than 1.5 million copies.

Apple Computer learned about Davidson's three programs and offered to list them in the mail order catalog they were initiating. However, the catalog was short-lived, and when Apple decided to discontinue their catalog business and concentrate their efforts on hardware, Davidson looked for a software publisher to work with. She found one in San Diego, and they decided to meet for lunch in San Clemente, which is halfway between Torrance and San Diego. What she didn't know is that the restaurant they chose has two locations, one off the highway just north of San Clemente and one just south of San Clemente. While the publisher was waiting at the southern branch, Davidson and her husband waited at the northern branch.

Davidson considers her husband, Bob Davidson, her "business confidant," who she says has "always encouraged her." While the couple was waiting together for the publisher to arrive, Bob pitched an interesting idea: that Davidson herself publish the software, since she understood education—unlike technical publishers. He also used their current circumstance of waiting for the publisher as evidence that the publisher could be generally irresponsible. Davidson agreed that if she could find a distributor, she would publish her own programs. She

DAVIDSON & ASSOCIATES, INC.

Chief Executive Officer:	Janice G. Davidson
Principal Location:	19840 Pioneer Ave. Torrance, CA 90503
Telephone/Fax:	310-793-0600/310-793-0601
Satellite Locations:	none
Description of Business:	The leading publisher of educational software in the world based on retail-shelf space facings and market-share data. They publish 40 titles, including Mathblaster, which has sold more than 1.5 million copies since its introduction in 1983.
Date Founded:	1982
# Employees Current:	327
# Employees Projected by 6/30/95:	Company withheld
Sales (Annualized) 1994:	$60,468,000
Gross Profit Margin (GPM):	54.4%
SG & A Expense/Sales:	36.4%
% Sales Increase 1991–94:	+365.2%
% Change GPM 1991–94:	-0-
Total Debt/Net Worth:	15.9%
Net Profits Before Taxes:	$11,598,000
Operating Ratio:	19.2%
Net Profits per Employee:	$35,468
Traded On:	NASDAQ/DAVD
Principal Competitors:	The Learning Company, Microsoft, Broderbund Software, Electronic Arts, Sierra On-Line
# Potential Selling Sites:	Domestic: 20 million Foreign: 40 million
Problem Company Is Attempting to Solve:	The need to make the learning process pleasureful to children at an early age in order to engender and make habit-forming the desire to self-teach.
Solution Company Is Conveying to Problem:	Davidson designs, develops, and markets educational software for home and school use targeted at pre-K to 12th-grade age groups.

decided to pitch her software to a distributor called Softsel, now known as Merisel; they bought 100 copies of her software.

By 1986 the company's sales topped $4 million, and Davidson was getting mired in administrative tasks. She found her choice of chief executive nearby: her husband Bob, a lawyer and business school graduate.

In the time-honored tradition of successful consumer products marketers, Davidson competes with itself by offering older products through mass-marketers under the ZugWare and SmartWorks brand names at $12.95 per unit. The top-of-the-line products—Mathblaster, Alge-Blaster, Kid Works 2, Zoo Keeper, Kid CAD, and English Express—carry retail prices three times higher and are sold through conventional software channels. New product development keeps the product line fresh. The company spent $3.5 million on research and development last year. If it does not develop another star product, it has the market capitalization—$300 million—to go out and buy companies that have star products. Do Jan and Bob Davidson have the guts and abilities to remain top dog in the educational technology industry? They have come through some difficult moments together, and they have the admirable ability to somehow make the right decision.

DECISION QUEST

Litigation is a big and growing business. It is catalyzed by an excess of lawyers and their need to put food on the table. There are 750,000 lawyers in the United States; this number increases by 35,000 each year. Although 85 percent of all civil litigation is settled before it gets to court, the costs of trying a case are high. Seeing this trend a decade ago, Donald E. Vinson spotted an opportunity to bring reason into a chaotic market. He would offer mock trials to both parties that would predict the outcome of a trial in advance, and lead to an early settlement. Vinson's idea is catching on.

Litigation is a business. Litigation is a line item in businesses. The structure of both law firms and of client corporations may create counterproductive approaches to litigation. Specifically, corporate managers are fiduciaries who feel most comfortable when they pay their lawyers by the hour. Big defense law firms respond to their clients' accounting requirements by adopting case management systems that allow them to "build a file" that creates a paper trail to justify their bills.

But business defendants can often dispose of lawsuits most cheaply by making low but immediate offers to impecunious plaintiffs who, for entirely subjective reasons, are willing to give an unreasonably large discount to defendants for quick cash. In this circumstance the client's interest and the law firm's interest are diametrically opposed; without months or years of depositions, interrogatories, and pretrial motions, the law firm cannot build a file to justify a large fee—and large fees are necessary to sustain the overhead of large firms. Clients, then, can find themselves engaged in potentially disastrous, all-or-nothing litigation simply because their lawyers are in the litigation business and not the cheap-settlement business. This is chaos. Donald Vinson formed Decision Quest to introduce the notion of settlements for cause.

The professionals at Decision Quest are trained in the behavioral sciences. They are students of jury psychology, persuasion, trial strategy, and courtroom communications. Dr. Donald Vinson, Decision Quest's founder and CEO, introduced the concepts of behavioral research to trial lawyers in the 1970s and is the author of or contributor to 10 books and more than 40 articles on litigation strategy and trial techniques. Decision Quest claims 95 percent accuracy in predicting jury verdicts. It promises that its statistical profiles will weed out "dangerous" jurors and help attorneys tailor their message to the 12 citizens sitting in judgment of their client. But the company's work isn't done when the trial begins.

DECISION QUEST

Chief Executive Officer:	Donald E. Vinson
Principal Location:	2050 W. 190th St. Torrance, CA 90504
Telephone/Fax:	310-618-9600/310-618-1122
Satellite Locations:	Houston, TX; Chicago, IL; New York, NY; Boston, MA
Date Founded:	1991
Description of Business:	Services to litigants: predicting jury trial verdicts and developing trial strategies.
# Employees Current:	45
# Employees Projected by 6/30/95:	50
Sales (Annualized) 1994:	The company is privately-held and therefore not required to make its financial statements public.
Gross Profit Margin (GPM):	not available
Selling Expenses/Sales:	not available
% Sales Increase 1991–94:	not available
% Change GPM 1991–94:	not available
Total Debt/Net Worth:	not available
Net Profits Before Taxes:	not available
Net Profits per Employee:	not available
Principal Competitors:	Litigation Sciences, Inc., Resolute Systems, Inc.
# Potential Selling Sites:	Domestic: 1,000 Foreign: not applicable
Problem Company Is Attempting to Solve:	Surplus lawyers create and sustain litigation and avoid settlement, which cuts into their income.
Solution Company Is Conveying to Problem:	Predicts outcome of jury trials so both sides can be persuaded to settle out of court.

Decision Quest (which is rumored to have advised the prosecution in the O.J. Simpson case) will also provide a "shadow jury," a surrogate panel that watches the trial with hand-held "people meters" to register minute-by-minute reactions. When court is in recess, lawyers can fine-tune strategy based on the group's impressions.

Litigants who hire Decision Quest can select from the following services: trial simulations; drafting of opening statements; witness preparation; trial monitoring with surrogate jurors; post-trial juror interviews; focus groups; juror profiles/jury selection; change of venue studies; preparation for arbitration and mediation; testimony before regulatory agencies; and development and testing of visual exhibits. If clients choose the trial simulation service and see that in all likelihood they will lose the case, they can arrange a settlement and avoid an expensive courtroom battle. If the trial simulation service predicts a likely victory, then some of the other services may be required.

One of Decision Quest's newest services involves the development and testing of visual exhibits. The company has documented that jurors understand and retain more and are more easily persuaded when information is presented visually rather than verbally. Decision Quest has also found that the message of the visuals should be instantaneous and require little explanation. However, some lawyers know that they can produce effects with graphs that are out of proportion to the data. When this occurs, Decision Quest develops competing graphics for its clients. Manipulative? Possibly. But with no end in sight in the litigation business, it makes excellent sense to retain the services of these behavioral scientists. After all, your opponent might sue you and retain Decision Quest simultaneously.

DIGITAL LINK CORP.

The computer industry feeds umbilically on orders of magnitude changes in semiconductor development and networking electronics. Grove's law states that microchip cost-effectiveness rises by the square of the number of transistors crammed onto a single chip. Giden's law states that cost-effectiveness rises by the square of the number of computers connected to networks. Sure PCs are becoming faster and less expensive and networking is forcing managers to reengineer their organizations based on the flow of information. But Silver's law of entrepreneurship states that $V = P \times S \times E$, where V is valuation or wealth, P is the problem that the entrepreneur says she can solve, S is the elegance of her solution, and E is the quality of the entrepreneurial team. To ignore the courage, tenacity, and competitiveness of the entrepreneur is to miss the excitement and dynamism of the greatest show on earth. Case in point:

Vinita Gupta, the founder and CEO of Digital Link Corp., grew up in India, where daughters are married off, where women are not encouraged to do anything bold and unique. But Vinita Gupta's mother was unusual. Undaunted by the traditional cultural roles defined for her daughters, Vinita Gupta's mother encouraged all three daughters to get a good education and instilled in all of them the belief that they were capable of doing anything they wanted to do. Vinita says, "I think that she wanted to prove to everyone that she did not need a son . . . that her daughters were capable of making it."

As an honor math student, Gupta pursued a career in Electrical Engineering. She completed her B.S. in Electronics and Communications Engineering at the University of Roorkee, Roorkee, India, and earned her Master's in Electrical Engineering at the University of California, Los Angeles. Gupta spent the next twelve years working as an Engineering Manager and Design Engineer for two major telecommunications companies. As Design Engineer she developed and patented a new product called the "Solid State Relay." However, Gupta says, "I got edgy. I was not growing professionally. I knew I had to quit. I could not remain in middle management of a major company." The company was not growing and, "I felt that my contributions were not being recognized." However, "I never felt that being an Indian or being a woman held me back. I did not think that anyone was discriminating

DIGITAL LINK CORP.

Chief Executive Officer:	Vinita Gupta
Principal Location:	217 Humboldt Sunnyvale, CA 94089
Telephone/Fax:	408-745-6200/408-745-6250
Satellite Locations:	Germany; United Kingdom
Date Founded:	1985
Description of Business:	Designs, manufactures, and markets data communications products for wide area networks.
# Employees Current:	150
# Employees Projected by 6/30/95:	195
Sales (Annualized) 1994:	$27,817,000
Gross Profit Margin (GPM):	81.9%
SG&A Expenses/Sales:	32.7%
% Sales Increase 1991–94:	+208.9%
% Change GPM 1991–94:	+19.6%
Total Debt/Net Worth:	14.7%
Net Profits Before Taxes:	$4,206,000
Operating Ratio:	15.1%
Net Profits per Employee:	$28,040
Traded On:	NASDAQ/DLNK
Principal Competitors:	Tricord, Parallan, Sun Microsystems, Compaq, Dell, Bay Networks, Inc.
# Potential Selling Sites:	Domestic: 5,000 Foreign: 15,000
Problem Company Is Attempting to Solve:	Large companies with geographically dispersed locations that need a centralized database for such things as inventory management, engineering developments, and electronic financial transactions must have their information transferred quickly.
Solution Company Is Conveying to Problem:	Using T1, T2, and T3 lines, Digital Link transfers computer data up to 3,000 times faster than regular phone lines.

against me. It was that the company was too process-oriented rather than result-oriented. Everyone was worried about covering their behind."

When Vinita Gupta decided to quit her job, she quickly drew up plans to start her own business. With the help of a co-worker, who also quit the company, she incorporated Digital Link in 1985. They both invested their own money, totaling $100,000. Her partner worked on development of new products while she concentrated on marketing and selling. However, after eight months, when the company did not reach the expected volumes that they projected, her partner got nervous and left.

Gupta worked 60-hour weeks for the next eight months. Some payrolls were delayed. Her management skills and her ability to find highly qualified and skilled people to join her company attracted outside venture capital three years later. She managed to bring the company to approximately $4 million in sales. When she was finally able to put together a senior-level management team, the business really began to take off.

Today Digital Link has eight nationwide offices, an office in Germany, and an office in London. Digital Link's sales are growing at more than 50 percent per year and its GPM lept 19.6 percent from 1991 to 1994 (annualized) in a tough climate. Although privately held, Gupta says 1994 sales are approaching $40 million, up from $25 million in 1993.

Digital Link is one of the smallest competitors in the internetworking hardware industry, where publicly held, well-funded manufacturers, including Compaq, Dell, and Bay Networks, Inc., could squash Digital Link like a bug if they chose to. But no corporation can squash an entrepreneur who refuses to let herself be squashed. "It's a challenge to remain upright in this wind tunnel," says Gupta. "But I've come through other challenges with flying colors." Moreover, Gupta has a mother to win for. That is a force bigger than Compaq, Dell, and the others.

DIONEX CORPORATION

J ust how toxic are our waste dumps? Without someone to measure the toxicity, the citizenry can't vote to close them down. That someone is Dionex Corporation. The company produces a line of niche analytical instruments and software that serve three principal needs: ion chromatography, bioseparations, and supercritical fluid separations. In addition to these products the company develops and manufactures columns, detectors, and data analysis systems.

Ion chromatography (IC) is a form of chromatography that separates ionic (charged) molecules, usually found in water-based solutions, and typically identifies them based on their electrical conductivity. The sale of Dionex's IC systems and related columns, suppresors, detectors, automation, and other products accounts for a majority of the company's revenues. Its IC products are used in a wide range of applications, including environmental monitoring, corrosion monitoring evaluation of raw materials, quality control of industrial processes, research and development, and regulation of the chemical composition of food, beverage, and cosmetic products. Major customers include environmental testing laboratories, chemical and petrochemical firms, power-generating facilities, government agencies, and academic institutions.

Bioseparation products are used to analyze biological molecules, such as proteins, carbohydrates, and amino acids. The DX-300 Series, introduced in 1991, as well as the DX-500 and capillary electrophoresis (CE) systems are intended for use by customers in the biological research, biotechnology, and pharmaceutical markets.

The company also manufactures and sells CE systems that utilize an analytical technique that separates molecules based on their charge-to-mass ratios, size, or other characteristics. Dionex's CE systems are used both in the analysis of biological samples as well as for ion analysis. The company's recent R&D has focused on chemistry to improve CE separations through the use of buffers and column technology.

In addition to ion chromatography and bioseparations, the company is also engaged in the emerging market for supercritical fluid separations. (A supercritical fluid is one such as carbon dioxide, that has been put under pressure and heated until it has certain characteristics of both a liquid and a gas.) Its supercritical fluid separation systems are used by a number of industrial, government, and academic institutions worldwide for quality control, product evaluation, and R&D.

DIONEX CORPORATION

Chief Executive Officer:	A. Blaine Bowman
Principal Location:	1228 Titan Way Sunnyvale, CA 94088
Telephone/Fax:	408-737-0700/408-732-2007
Satellite Locations:	Salt Lake City, UT; United Kingdom; Germany; Italy; France; Canada; Belgium; Japan
Date Founded:	1980
Description of Business:	Designs, develops, and manufactures modular systems used in environmental monitoring and in regulating the chemical composition of food, beverages, and cosmetics.
# Employees Current:	633
# Employees Projected by 6/30/95:	Company withheld
Sales (Annualized) 1994:	$108,287,000
Gross Profit Margin (GPM):	68.0%
Selling Expenses/Sales:	36.3%
% Sales Increase 1991–94:	+121.2%
% Change GPM 1991–94:	+0.5%
Total Debt/Net Worth:	23.4%
Net Profits Before Taxes:	$25,560,000
Operating Ratio:	23.6%
Net Profits per Employee:	$40,379
Traded On:	NASDAQ/DNEX
Principal Competitors:	Hewlett-Packard, Floor Corp., Perkin Elmer
# Potential Selling Sites:	Domestic: 10,000 Foreign: 30,000
Problem Company Is Attempting to Solve:	In a world increasingly concerned with food impurity, ozone depletion, acid rain, and the greenhouse effect, we need analytical instruments that test for toxicity.
Solution Company Is Conveying to Problem:	Dionex provides those instruments, and in certain markets it commands a 70 percent share.

Every new market always has two things: a newsletter and a measurement or instrument company. In the emerging market of environmental toxicity measurement, Dionex stepped in and captured the lion's share—70 percent. It has a solid GPM of 68.5 percent, which is not declining under competitive pressure. The company is sitting on $25 million in cash and has virtually no debt. Its management and employees own a tiny 7.7 percent of the company's common stock, which has an overall market capitalization of $270 million.

This small ownership level probably augurs for a conservative business plan. Don't look for a "leap before you look" approach from Dionex; just consistent growth in profitability from measuring defects in our air, land, food, and water.

DNX CORPORATION

The DNX Corporation targeted three areas to focus its business: (1) developing a hemoglobin-based blood substitute; (2) providing pre-clinical and biological testing services to the biotechnology industry; and (3) supporting organ transplantation based on transgenic animal technology. With $6 million provided by venture capital funds and $36 million of manna from the heavenly new-issues market of late 1991, DNX was rich with opportunity. It acquired two affiliated biological testing companies in August 1991 to form Pharmakon (whose revenues are now more than $24 million per annum). But R&D expenses for the blood substitute began to eat into DNX's gross profits from Pharmakon ($4 million) and its available capital. Unable to find a strategic partner willing to share the costs, DNX decided to shut down its blood substitute development program in October 1993.

In November 1992, DNX acquired Hazelton-France (a biological testing lab in Lyon, France, with $15 million in revenues and $1 million in profits) for $10 million in cash and notes. Although expensive, this diversification hedges the company's organ transplantation research by providing it with a stronger foundation.

What makes DNX exciting is the potential behind the large problem that it has identified: organ transplantation, and its elegant solution, genetically altered animal organs. According to The New York Times,[1] the cost of a human kidney is $50,562, a human heart $116,843, and a human liver $186,000, and you can multiply these figures approximately five times to add the surgery costs. Not only are these costs very high, but there are only about 4,000 deaths each year from potential organ donors with 35,000 people on the national waiting list. If DNX can develop commercially viable pig hearts and other organs before it runs out of money—a rather small risk because of its parentage and cash flow from testing services—the company may become one of the most successful health-care delivery companies since Genentech. In August 1994 Baxter International, Inc. entered into a strategic license with DNX and agreed to invest more than $30 million to hasten the development of transplantable pig organs.

---

[1] "Moving to Compensate Families in Human-Organ Market," Peter S. Young, The New York Times, July 8, 1994, p. c1.

DNX CORPORATION

Chief Executive Officer:	Paul J. Schmidt
Principal Location:	303B College Rd. East Princeton, NJ 08540
Telephone/Fax:	609-520-0300/609-520-9864
Satellite Locations:	Lyons, France
Date Founded:	1988
Description of Business:	The leader in xenografts, the transplanting of animal organs into humans.
# Employees Current:	307
# Employees Projected by 6/30/95:	Company withheld
Sales (Annualized) 1994:	$24,659,000
Gross Profit Margin (GPM):	25.1%
Selling Expenses/Sales:	-0-
% Sales Increase 1991–94:	+697.3%
% Change GPM 1991–94:	(20.5%)
Total Debt/Net Worth:	129.3%
Net Profits Before Taxes:	$(18,046,000)
Net Profits per Employee:	not available
Traded On:	NASDAQ/DNXX
Principal Competitors:	Fujisawa-Lyphomed, Vertex Pharmaceutical, Sandoz
# Potential Selling Sites:	Domestic: 35,000 Foreign: 70,000
Problem Company Is Attempting to Solve:	A severe shortage of donor organs, e.g., hearts (30,000 needed in the U.S. annually, 120,000 worldwide), lungs (12,000 and 100,000), kidneys (60,000 and 150,000), and livers (12,000 and 30,000).
Solution Company Is Conveying to Problem:	Organ transplantation has become a successful medical procedure, with most recipients leading normal, useful lives. The company intends to supply this need with animal organs.

The primary obstacle to all forms of organ transplantation is immunological rejection of the transplant by the recipient's immune system. However, as the genetic similarity of the donor and recipient decreases, the complexity and ferocity of the immune system's response to the transplanted organ increase. In human-to-human transplantation, immune rejection can be largely overcome by immunosuppressive drugs. However, in animal-to-human transplantation (xenotransplantation), the immune response is more complex. A pre-existing immune response mediated by antibodies and inflammatory proteins of the complement system may result in the destruction of the transplanted organ within minutes to hours in a process called "hyperacute rejection." Until recently, complement-mediated hyperacute rejection has made the prospects for successful xenotransplantation seem remote. However, DNX is developing technologies that hold great promise in this area. They have

- Developed transgenic mouse prototypes containing multiple human complement-inhibition transgenes.
- Shown that these transgenes are functional, successfully producing the human complement-inhibition factors in critical organs such as the heart.
- Demonstrated the protective capability of this upon xenotransplantation. Hearts from these transgenic mice were perfused with human plasma containing human complement; the activity of human complement was successfully blocked.

In addition, DNX reported the development of transgenic pigs with DNA sequences encoding multiple complement-inhibition factors, similar to those used in the successful prototype transgenic mice.

With the soul kiss from Baxter, DNX has a kitty of more than $40 million to make xenotransplantation a commercial success and save 30,000 lives in the United States and twice that number in foreign countries.

ECOSCIENCE CORP.

EcoScience Corp. has just emerged from its larval stage, after nine years of research and development, and has been selling its product for about one year. It is still an early-stage company racking up huge losses as it continues to develop products, produce them, and implement a marketing strategy. Yet its economic justification is highly demonstrable.

The $20 billion-plus worldwide market for pest and disease control products is dominated by traditional, chemical-based products. EcoScience's product development is targeted at $3.5-$4.0 billion of the total market by introducing products that are at least as effective as the chemical-based ones, at a comparable or lower cost, while reducing or eliminating the use of potentially harmful chemicals. Along with a series of active control agents, the company has developed a set of proprietary core technologies to formulate, stabilize, and deliver biological insecticides and fungicides. Their use of naturally occurring microbes minimizes development problems inherent in gaining EPA approval for genetically engineered and chemical-based products.

EcoScience commercialized its first two products in 1993, the internally developed Bio-Path Cockroach Control Chamber, and Nature Seal, a coating for fruits and vegetables that controls their ripening and extends their shelf life which was developed by the Department of Agriculture. Development continues on other naturally derived products, including bioinsecticides for control of ants, termites, houseflies, and soft-bodied insects (aphids, white flies, etc.), as well as preharvest bioinsecticides for fruit and vegetable crops, and biofungicides for postharvest disease control of some fruits (apples, pears) and citrus fruits. The company has 17 products in development and has filed for EPA registrations since November 1993. It plans to file up to seven additional registrations with the EPA in 1994 for new active ingredients and end-use products.

Market acceptance from the consumers' point of view appears to be a given. Shelf space is another matter. EcoScience will need to be creative in getting its products in front of the consumers to permit them to make a choice. This will require maintaining a high GPM in order to provide flexible discounts and compensate marketing partners. The company's board is heavily loaded with scientists and finance people. It is time to let the marketing folks have sway.

ECOSCIENCE CORP.

Chief Executive Officer:	James A. Wylie, Jr.
Principal Location:	Three Biotech Park Worcester, MA 01605
Telephone/Fax:	508-754-0300/508-754-1134
Satellite Locations:	none
Description of Business:	The discovery, development, and commercialization of natural pest control products for the control of insects and diseases of plants, fruits, and vegetables, as well as naturally derived coatings to preserve food quality and extend the shelf life of fruits and vegetables.
Date Founded:	1982
# Employees Current:	128
# Employees Projected by 6/30/95:	Company withheld
Sales (Annualized) 1994:	$9,691,000
Gross Profit Margin (GPM):	35.3%
Selling Expense/Sales:	62.2%
% Sales Increase 1991–94:	Sales commenced in 1993
% Change GPM 1991–94:	not available
Total Debt/Net Worth:	40.2%
Net Profits Before Taxes:	deficit
Operating Ratio:	deficit
Net Profits per Employee:	deficit
Traded On:	NASDAQ/ECSC
Principal Competitors:	S.C. Johnson & Sons, Miles Labs, Lynwood Laboratories
# Potential Selling Sites:	Domestic: 150,000 Foreign: 300,000
Problem Company Is Attempting to Solve:	Nobody likes roaches, even though, as the joke goes, they only come out at night. But eliminating them and other pests with synthetic pesticides is harming the environment.
Solution Company Is Conveying to Problem:	Developing highly effective natural biopesticides that do the job but do not harm the planet.

EDUCATION ALTERNATIVES, INC.

The potential for the continued success of Education Alternatives is phenomenal. Here's the big picture: Our nation's 15,000 school districts are made up of approximately 80,000 public schools. We spend approximately $236 billion each year to educate more than 40 million children in these public schools. The average cost to educate a single student in 1992–1993 was approximately $5,500.

An astonishing 30 percent of students from low-income families fail to complete high school. In some large, urban areas, the dropout rate of certain minority students exceeds 60 percent. Even those who do complete high school lack the most basic skills and are ill-equipped to fill entry-level jobs. Although the 7.5 percent of gross national product that we spend on education is the second highest percentage spent in the entire world, our students trail the global pack in such important subjects as science and math (test scores of students in 14 comparable, industralized countries exceed the scores of our children). American businesses spend billions of dollars every year on remedial training of its workforce because so many of our young people lack basic skills. In addition, our government spends billions of dollars subsidizing unemployable youth in our welfare system. Many parents desperately want change and a chance for their children to succeed. Corporations need more highly trained personnel.

Over the last few years, some school district officials have been exploring innovative alternatives to inadequate, timeworn concepts in education. One of these alternatives is the private management of public schools. Education Alternatives is the leader in this field.

Education Alternatives is providing its innovative teaching philosophy called the Tesseract Way, which is both cost-effective *and* capable of improving the childrens' education dramatically—the ultimate measures of success. By reducing the cost of noninstructional services, the company reallocates resources in the classroom, resulting in improved academic performance of students without increasing the total cost of educating each student. Teachers guide and encourage children to learn at their own pace.

Education Alternatives has entered into joint ventures with KPMG Peat Marwick and Johnson Controls World Services, Inc. The former provides financial management of school districts, and the latter is subcontracted noninstructional components of the overall task.

EDUCATION ALTERNATIVES, INC.

Chief Executive Officer:	John T. Golle
Principal Location:	7900 Xerxes Ave. South Minneapolis, MN 55431
Telephone/Fax:	612-832-0092/612-832-0191
Satellite Locations:	Baltimore, MD; Hartford, CT; Miami, FL
Date Founded:	1991
Description of Business:	The leader in the private management of schools.
# Employees Current:	133
# Employees Projected by 6/30/95:	133
Sales (Annualized) 1994:	$32,038,000
Gross Profit Margin (GPM):	10.8%
Selling Expenses/Sales:	not available
% Sales Increase 1991–94:	+1,266.2%
% Change GPM 1991–94:	deficit GPM in 1991 and 1992
Total Debt/Net Worth:	8.4%
Net Profits Before Taxes:	$2,524,000
Operating Ratio:	7.9%
Net Profits per Employee:	$18,977
Traded On:	NASDAQ/EAIN
Principal Competitors:	Whittle Communications
# Potential Selling Sites:	Domestic: 15,000 Foreign: not applicable
Problem Company Is Attempting to Solve:	The quality of education throughout the United States is poor and the dropout rate for the nation's 60 million K-12 students is high.
Solution Company Is Conveying to Problem:	The company operates public schools under facilities management contracts. Its basic program is to reduce the costs of noninstructional services and reallocate resources to the classroom.

In 1992 Education Alternatives was awarded a $27 million per annum contract to manage eight Baltimore City elementary schools and one middle school, encompassing 4,800 children. The schools were in need of repair, they were unsafe, and the dropout rate was very high. Within two years, the schools have been renovated, made safe, and students and faculty are becoming computer literate on 1,100 personal computers on lease to the schools.

South Pointe Elementary School in South Miami Beach, Florida was the first public school in the United States to be managed by a for-profit company. Education Alternatives won that contract in July 1990 and opened the school in fall 1991. Today South Pointe is thriving. The school serves 750 students from pre-kindergarten through the sixth grade. Most come from minority families whose financial resources and educational backgrounds are very limited. Education Alternatives has provided continuous staff development at South Pointe since the contract was signed. Associate teachers work side by side with experienced teachers. Students, parents, the business community, and the entire staff are dedicated to achieving an environment that is challenging, nuturing, and personalized.

The Tesseract schools in Eagan, Minnesota and Paradise Valley, Arizona continue to provide the company with an environment that it can use to test new methods and improve on old ones. Attendance is at the maximum with waiting lists growing. Test results are showing dramatic educational gains by nearly all Tesseract students. In April 1994 the Hartford Board of Education called in Education Alternatives. "We need major surgery," Thelma Dickerson, Vice Chairman of the school board, told *The New York Times*.[1] "We're constantly putting on Band-Aids. After so many, they keep erupting and you have a serious problem. We need help." Under the Hartford facilities management contract, Education Alternatives is paid $8,450 per student, a figure that exceeds the national average. The stock market responded by bidding the company's stock price up 10 points, and its P/E ratio to more than 50.0x.

---

[1] William Celis III, "Hopeful Start for Profit-Making Schools," *The New York Times*, October 6, 1993, p. B8.

ENSYS ENVIRONMENTAL PRODUCTS, INC.

Immunoassay technology is a mature science used in health care to detect biological compounds in human blood and urine. It is widely used in tests for pregnancy and drug abuse. Until now, immunoassay technology has not been used in the field of environmental monitoring. Ensys Environmental Products is changing that.

Conventional environmental testing begins with a sample extraction, a step that often takes up to 24 hours. This is followed by compound separation and detection. Instrumentation costs are upwards of $50,000 and typically no more than 30 samples per day can be put through the instruments.

In immunoassay testing, the sophistication is in the reagents and not the instruments, which are lightweight and portable. Ensys has conquered many of the complex problems associated with environmental applications at significant savings. Ensys test methods have demonstrated substantial savings of both time (within minutes vs. several days) and money ($35 per sample vs. $50 to more than $500 per sample) compared to environmental testing laboratories.

Ensys is more than a testing company. It has developed processing technologies to reliably remove contaminants from the media in which they occur. When the processes are combined with test kits, which are proprietary (five basic patents have been applied for), the package is very compelling.

The company is somewhat slow in beating its own drum in the marketplace. Sales are growing, but are just at the $3 million mark. The market size is $3 billion, much of it dominated by commercial laboratories. Ensys's products fit into 40 percent of the market. One of the drivers of revenues is EPA enforcement (demand-pull), another is EPA endorsement (raising the tollgate), and a third is effective marketing (word-of-mouth selling).

Ensys's goals are pioneering the use of immunoassay technology in the environmental testing market, developing proprietary tests, removal processes for 80 percent of all contaminants, obtaining EPA endorsement on all products, and expanding domestic sales and entering foreign markets with strategic partners. Ensys has two enemies. First, it has $17 million in cash on hand and needs to get sales up above break-even to avoid running out of cash. Second, it has large, well-funded competitors—Millipore, Idexx, Ohmicron, and Quantix Systems—breathing down its neck.

ENSYS ENVIRONMENTAL PRODUCTS, INC.

Chief Executive Officer:	Alan H. Staple
Principal Location:	4222 Emperor Blvd. Morrisville, NC 27560
Telephone/Fax:	919-941-5509/919-941-5519
Satellite Locations:	none
Description of Business:	Develops immunoassay-based test kits for environmental testing and monitoring.
Date Founded:	1987
# Employees Current:	65
# Employees Projected by 6/30/95:	Company withheld
Sales 1993:	$2,908,000
Gross Profit Margin (GPM):	52.1%
SG&A Expense/Sales:	131.1%
% Sales Increase 1991–94:	+636.3%
% Change GPM 1991–94:	+403.8%
Total Debt/Net Worth:	6.2%
Net Profits Before Taxes:	$(3,093,000)
Operating Ratio:	deficit
Net Profits per Employee:	deficit
Traded On:	NASDAQ/ENSY
Principal Competitors:	Millipore, Idexx, Ohmicron, Quantix Systems
# Potential Selling Sites:	Domestic: 5,000 Foreign: 15,000
Problem Company Is Attempting to Solve:	The conventional methods for detecting environmental contaminants are expensive, usually must occur off-site, and are time-consuming.
Solution Company Is Conveying to Problem:	The company's test kits are used on-site, automated, user-friendly, and highly effective.

The company has partnered with Hach to enter the German and other markets, including the United States under the Hach brand name. It has partnered with Dragerwerk to sell its test kits and removal processes in Europe. Company management, led by Alan H. Staple, is thinking "associationally" and in terms of developing multiple marketing channels. This is reflected in rapidly rising sales and a rising GPM.

ENVIROTEST SYSTEMS CORP.

Envirotest Systems Corp. came about via the leveraged buyouts of several emissions testing facilities-management companies by a team of primarily minority-oriented entrepreneurs and minority venture funds. The company's leverage of more than $125 million is still on its balance sheet, but interest expenses are easily serviced out of cash flow.

There will be a significant growth in centralized emissions testing programs in the United States. On November 5, 1992, the EPA adopted new regulations under the 1990 amendments that require 83 metropolitan areas, with a total of approximately 59 million vehicles, to implement an "enhanced" emissions testing program using a new, more stringent emissions test. Approximately 42 million of these vehicles are in areas that currently either have decentralized programs or have an emissions testing program. These new regulations also require that an additional 99 areas, with a total of approximately 26 million vehicles, implement a "basic" emissions testing program. Of these 99 areas, 24 currently have no emissions testing program. Centralized testing services such as those offered by Envirotest will capture most of the industry growth resulting from the new regulations. This belief is based on the EPA pronouncement that centralized testing programs are significantly more effective at identifying vehicle-emissions problems than test-and-repair decentralized programs; and no existing decentralized test-and repair program would meet the enhanced testing standards established by the new regulations. Envirotest is therefore in the cat-bird seat with experienced management, advanced software, and systems integration capabilities. The market sees things pretty much the same way, putting a P/E ratio of 59.0x on Envirotest's earnings in mid-1994.

In October 1993, Pennsylvania selected Envirotest to implement and operate its enhanced centralized emissions testing program. The program is scheduled to begin operations in early 1995, and is expected to result in approximately 3.2 million paid tests per year and generate annual revenues of approximately $60 million.

In November 1993, New York selected the company to implement and operate the New York Downstate Region (which includes New York City) enhanced emissions testing program. (The New York program contract is under negotiation.) The Downstate Region is expected to contain approximately 3.7 million of the approximately 5.2 million annual paid tests that will be conducted in New York when the state

ENVIROTEST SYSTEMS CORP.

Chief Executive Officer:	Chester Davenport
Principal Location:	2002 North Forbes Blvd. Tucson, AZ 85745
Telephone/Fax:	602-620-1500/602-620-0981
Satellite Locations:	Bethesda, MD
Description of Business:	The leading provider of centralized vehicle-emissions testing programs for states and municipalities.
Date Founded:	1990
# Employees Current:	1,842
# Employees Projected by 6/30/95:	Company withheld
Sales 1993:	$93,291,000
Gross Profit Margin (GPM):	44.6%
SG&A Expense/Sales:	16.9%
% Sales Increase 1991–93:	+243.0%
% Change GPM 1991–93:	+16.3%
Total Debt/Net Worth:	306.0%
Net Profits Before Taxes:	$10,180,000
Operating Ratio:	10.9%
Net Profits per Employee:	$5,526
Traded On:	NASDAQ/ENVI
Principal Competitors:	Gordon-Darby, Inc., Systems Control, Inc., Allen Group through its MARTA subsidiary
# Potential Selling Sites:	Domestic: 1,000 Foreign: 250
Problem Company Is Attempting to Solve:	A recent EPA study found that the average vehicle emits up to four times the pollutants it was designed to emit and that vehicle emissions produce 50 percent of total ozone air pollution and nearly all of the carbon monoxide air pollution in metropolitan areas.
Solution Company Is Conveying to Problem:	The company's vehicle-emissions testing program is highly effective in reducing noxious and dangerous air pollutants.

selects one or more contractors to implement and operate programs in the three other regions that were bid. The New York Downstate Region, with the exception of Dutchess, Orange, and Putnam counties, will begin operations in early 1996. It is expected to generate annual revenues of approximately $77 million. The other three counties will begin operations in January 1995.

In December 1993, Colorado selected Envirotest to implement and operate its enhanced vehicle inspection program, and contract discussions began in January 1994. The Colorado program is expected to result in approximately 800,000 annual paid tests, generating revenues of approximately $20 million a year.

Also, in December 1993, Connecticut selected Envirotest to implement and operate its new enhanced vehicle inspection program. (Envirotest has operated the current basic centralized program since 1983.) Connecticut's new enhanced program is scheduled to begin testing vehicles in early 1995, at which time the company expects to test approximately 1.2 million vehicles each year and generate revenues of approximately $20 million, or approximately $6.2 million more per year in revenues than it received under the existing contract.

Envirotest's revenues have grown nearly two and one-half times since 1990, and its GPM of 44.6 percent is rising. The ratio of SG&A Expenses/Sales is being held well under 20 percent, and its Operating Ratio is a strong 10.9 percent. Were it not for debt service, the company's Net Profits Before Taxes would be around $30 million and its Operating Ratio approximately 30 percent. These are elegant ratios. States that have hired Envirotest have rehired it: Success is clearly in Envirotest's key of aspiration, arising from the homely realism that if we don't do something about the problem of air pollution it will certainly do something irreparable to us.

FORE SYSTEMS, INC.

Entrepreneurship was defined by the German economist, Joseph A. Schumpeter, in 1912 as a "creative response" to a situation with at least three characteristics:

First, the creative response can practically never be understood ex ante. Second, the creative response shapes the whole course of subsequent events and their "long-run" outcome. Third, the creative response has something to do with the quality of personnel available in the society, with the quality available to a particular field of activity, and with individual decisions, actions, and patterns of behavior. Accordingly, a study of creative response in business becomes coterminous with a study of entrepreneurship.[1] Fore Systems is a company that Schumpeter might have used as an example, had he been alive today.

The market for networking products is cluttered with five substantial companies, three of which are Quantum Companies, that compete tooth and nail for increased market share. Formed in the mid-1980s, they each have about 10 years of solid experience; they know who the top marketing jocks are; they know many of the large customers; and they have spread their webs across the ponds to Europe and Asia. Cabletron, Cisco, 3Com, Bay Networks, Inc., and Newbridge Networks are all fierce competitors.

Yet they left a small door open. And four researchers at Carnegie Mellon University spotted the opening in 1990 and formed Fore Systems, Inc. to capitalize on it. They attracted $5 million in venture capital and by 1992 were shipping their product. Cabletron entered a strategic alliance with the company in 1992 and upgraded it in 1994, to purchase a minimum of $12 million of switch modules. 3Com entered a joint marketing agreement with Fore Systems in 1993.

Revenues at Fore Systems jumped from $5.5 million to $23.5 million from 1993 to 1994. The company isn't the low-end producer either. Its GPM rose from 30.0 percent in 1992 to 55.2 percent in 1994. (Bay Network's is 61.1 percent and Newbridge's is 62.3 percent.)

What is unique about Fore Systems? Its creative response is being the first company to offer asynchronous transfer mode (ATM) local area network (LAN) solutions commercially. ATM is an industry standard for high-speed local-area and wide-area networking. Although many

---

[1] Joseph A. Schumpeter, *The Theory of Economic Development* (Cambridge, Massachusetts: Harvard University Press, 1934).

FORE SYSTEMS, INC.

Chief Executive Officer:	Eric C. Cooper
Principal Location:	174 Thorn Hill Rd. Warrendale, PA 15086
Telephone/Fax:	412-772-6600/412-772-6500
Satellite Locations:	none
Date Founded:	1990
Description of Business:	A leader in the design, development, manufacture, and sale of high-performance networking products based on ATM technology.
# Employees Current:	165
# Employees Projected by 6/30/95:	Company withheld
Sales (Annualized) 1994:	$23,506,000
Gross Profit Margin (GPM):	55.2%
Selling Expenses/Sales:	24.6%
% Sales Increase 1991–94:	+2,253.7%
% Change GPM 1991–94:	+84.0%
Total Debt/Net Worth:	28.7%
Net Profits Before Taxes:	$3,208,000
Operating Ratio:	14.0%
Net Profits per Employee:	$19,442
Traded On:	NASDAQ/FORE
Principal Competitors:	Cabletron, Cisco, Newbridge Networks, Bay Networks, Inc., 3Com
# Potential Selling Sites:	Domestic: 25,000 Foreign: 45,000
Problem Company Is Attempting to Solve:	With more and more PC users entering networking environments, the networks are overloading.
Solution Company Is Conveying to Problem:	Fore Systems products transcend many of the limitations imposed by networking technology.

network equipment suppliers have introduced or announced plans to introduce ATM-based products, and several public carriers have implemented or announced plans to implement ATM services, the ATM market is still emerging and only a limited number of users have installed ATM networks. Substantially, all of Fore System's revenue has been derived from the sale of ATM networking products and related services for LAN- and WAN-access markets (Nippon Telegraph and Telephone Corp. and Tokyo Electron Ltd. represented nearly 30 percent of the company's 1994 revenues), and sales of such products and related services are expected to continue to account for substantially all of the company's revenue in the foreseeable future. Historically, a significant portion of its sales have been attributable to federal government agencies, laboratories, and universities and to users in data-intensive areas of large commercial enterprises that require premium networking capacity and performance. The company's operations are dependent on continued growth and market acceptance of ATM technology as a preferred networking solution for high-performance applications.

In recent years, the power of desktop PCs, workstations, and servers has increased dramatically, and these computers have been linked into LANs to share applications and data. These LANs have in turn been linked into enterprise-wide networks that enable all of the client and server machines in an enterprise to communicate. Further, the greater computational power of PCs and workstations has made possible new, communication-intensive applications, including integrated video, audio, and data. These factors—more users and more powerful network applications—have caused performance degradation in conventional LANs and WANs.

In addition, shared-medium networking technologies such as Ethernet, Token Ring, and Fiber Distributed Date Interface (FDDI) require computers to contend for the total bandwidth of the network. As the number of computers in the network and the volume of network traffic grow, these conventional networking technologies are placed under ever-greater stresses. The performance of an application running over a shared-medium network is unpredictable, because it depends on the amount of competition from other computers contending to use the network.

The task of managing an enterprise network becomes even more difficult and costly when the enterprise network includes links to WANs. WAN technology is separate and distinct from conventional LAN technology and, as a result, LAN information must be processed and transformed prior to its transmission over a WAN. Since existing WAN technologies include many different network protocols, transmission methods, and access technologies, interconnecting LANs across WANs requires costly equipment and complex network management.

Conventional LAN and WAN networking technologies are thus faced with the mounting problems of insufficient bandwidth, administrative burden, and disparate protocols at the gateway to WANs. Fore believes that only ATM offers the combination of scalable bandwidth, simplicity of management, ability to link geographically dispersed LANs into an enterprise-wide backbone, and use of a single protocol across LANs and WANs.

ATM technology transcends many of the limitations imposed by conventional networking technologies. It is the first technology that spans both LANs and WANs, and has been endorsed as a standard by the computer and telecommunications industries. ATM provides a dramatic increase in bandwidth throughout the network, carrying both LAN and WAN traffic faster than conventional network technologies. An ATM-based network is also significantly easier to configure and administer than a comparable conventional network. Network capacity can be increased simply by adding ATM switches and obviating the need for network segmentation and extensive downtime. ATM seamlessly integrates LAN and WAN, facilitating the transmission of data from desktop to backbone wide-area and back to the desktop through a variety of standardized physical interfaces, all of which support a single set of ATM protocols.

ATM technology is integrated easily into customers' existing network environments. It can form the basis of a collaborative work group comprising individual PCs, workstations, and servers equipped with ATM adapter cards. In such a work group, ATM can serve as a complete desktop-to-desktop network solution.

Where were the manufacturers of connectivity hardware products when the ATM opportunity first appeared in 1990? They were busy duking it out with each other for market share, and missed the emerging need. Fore Systems spotted the opportunity and with a relatively small $5 million warchest, it has built a business worth $250 million and growing.

FRONTIER INSURANCE GROUP, INC.

rederick Nietzche wrote, "You must be a chaos to give birth to a rising star." The Chinese have a similar philosophy, expressed in the word "Wei-Ji," which is made up of two characters. The first means danger; the second, opportunity. Fortunes are made in hard times and lost in good times.

Frontier Insurance Group, Inc., lives on the frontier of risk, chaos, and danger. That places it in the opportunistic position to earn larger and larger fortunes. Frontier makes money on its insurance business, which is unusual for insurance companies, many of which rely on investment income for their profits. But Frontier's Combined Ratio in 1993 was 93.3 percent and is marching into the 92 percent range in 1994. It was in the mid-96 percent range in 1992. Thus, the company's insurance business is increasingly profitable.

Its Loss Ratio in 1993 was 65.3 percent, and it has been in that area for several years. This indicates that management understands the risks that it buys. Frontier's Operating Ratio in 1993 was 25.5 percent—better than most companies in high-growth industries—and its net profits per employee were $83,452, roughly equivalent to those of software stars Microsoft and Oracle.

Where does—and will—Frontier's growth come from? Three major areas: (1) Surety bonds—Parts of the United States have to be rebuilt as a result of weather and unrest, and residential construction is booming in the Southwest. The construction industry cannot drive the first nail without surety bonds. (2) Bail bonds—Crime is on the rise, and with it demand for bail bonds. (3) Medical malpractice insurance—Physicians have deep pockets and are easy targets for barratrous lawyers. Frequent litigation can cost a physician his or her coverage. Frontier writes malpractice insurance in two of the most litigious states, New York and Florida.

In fact, medical malpractice represents 45 percent of the company's net premiums. Of that, the New York State piece is the largest, and in 1993, New York State's rates were raised. In 1993, the company also began to write malpractice insurance for physicians who lost their coverage due to peer review problems, drug or alcohol abuse, or excessive claims. Frontier's approach to this class of business involves careful underwriting, intensive risk management, and continuous surveillance. "We want to lose these physicians in about three years as they rehabilitate themselves," says Walter Rhulen, the company's CEO.

FRONTIER INSURANCE GROUP, INC.

Chief Executive Officer:	Walter A. Rhulen
Principal Location:	195 Lake Louise Marie Rd. Rock Hill, NY 12775
Telephone/Fax:	914-796-2100/914-796-1925
Satellite Locations:	Bedford Hills, NY; Los Angeles, CA
Description of Business:	An underwriter and creator of specialty insurance products that service markets that have few competitors and are generally considered unattractive.
Date Founded:	1978
# Employees Current:	363
# Employees Projected by 6/30/95:	Company withheld
Net Premiums Written 1993:	$118,819,000
Combined Ratio (CR):	93.3%
Loss Ratio:	65.3%
% Premiums Increase 1990–93:	164.3%
% Change CR 1990–93:	+3.6%
Total Debt/Net Worth:	181.0%
Net Profits Before Taxes:	$30,293,000
Operating Ratio:	25.5%
Net Profits per Employee:	$83,452
Traded On:	NYSE/FTR
Principal Competitors:	American International Group, Transamerica, Continental, Ranger
# Potential Selling Sites:	Domestic: 500,000 Foreign: not applicable
Problem Company Is Attempting to Solve:	Major insurance companies with a host of portfolio problems and a paucity of talent have shied away from complex and unattractive risks. Someone's got to do the tough jobs.
Solution Company Is Conveying to Problem:	Frontier insures small contractors, physicians whose coverage has been canceled, and construction crane operators. It also writes bail bonds.

"The premiums we charge them while they are our insureds are higher than standard, and we expect this program to contribute to our profitability." Frontier has entered Ohio to begin writing substandard malpractice insurance there. Rather than plunge into a new state with its New York staff, the company hired Michael K. Ng, "who is thoroughly imbued in the alternative risk malpractice business in Ohio," says Rhulen.

The company recently agreed to write malpractice for a book of psychiatrists, previously underwritten by another carrier, with risks located throughout the country. The transfer of this group of physicians to Frontier makes it one of the largest writers of professional liability for psychiatrists in the United States.

"All of this expansion has a threefold purpose: to write more of the profitable and desirable classes of business, to increase the breadth of our underwriting experience, and to better prepare us to be a major player in the managed-care arena, or for that matter, whatever else Clinton's health-care reform has in store for us," says Rhulen.

Frontier is arguably the most exciting insurance company in the country. Its earnings have grown at a 17.1 percent average annual rate since 1989. Bear in mind, Frontier is an insurance company that buys difficult risks, manages them carefully, and earns a profit on its book of insurance business. Its investment income is pure gravy.

GTI CORPORATION

TI is benefiting from the rapid growth in the local area network (LAN) market. Future growth in its networking products is directly related to the growth and direction of the networking industry as a whole. The company produces and sells a broad range of magnetics-based components which enable connectivity. During the last decade, PCs and workstations have brought significant computing resources directly to the user's desktop. Although initially these resources were regarded primarily as personal productivity tools, the benefits of communication among computer users and the ability to share expensive peripherals and other resources, such as printers and storage devices, led to the development of LANs. A LAN typically includes at least the following elements: (1) computers (PCs, workstations, etc.) that are to be linked; (2) adapters, network interface cards, or other mechanisms that physically connect a PC to the LAN; (3) a LAN medium such as copper wire or fiber optic cable; (4) peripherals and other resources to be shared on the LAN; and (5) network server and operating software. GTI's products are used at all connection points between the connected devices and the LAN medium.

The LAN market has grown dramatically in recent years, catalyzed by the availability of low-cost, high-performance PCs and the migration by businesses away from mainframe and minicomputer systems to client/server processing environments. International Development Corporation, the leading gatherer and publisher of computer industry data, has reported the percentage of business PCs attached to a LAN in the United States and other markets in 1992. Its forecasts of business PC connectivity in 1996 show this market has legs (see table). As a result of these trends, IDC estimates 92.4 million PCs being connected to LANs by 1996; 49.2 million PCs were connected to a LAN in 1992.

Percentage of Business PCs Connected to LANs

	Estimated 1992	Forecasted 1996
United States	47%	73%
Western Europe	36%	63%
Rest of World	12%	22%
Worldwide	33%	51%

GTI CORPORATION

Chief Executive Officer:	Gary L. Luick
Principal Location:	9171 Centre Dr. San Diego, CA 92122
Telephone/Fax:	619-578-3111/619-546-0568
Satellite Locations:	Hadley, PA; Hartselle, AL; Abbey Reale, Ireland, Kowloon, Hong Kong; 6 plants in China; Cabuyao, Languano, Philippines
Description of Business:	The leading supplier of magnetics-based components for signal-processing and power-transfer functions in networking products.
Date Founded:	1966
# Employees Current:	6,800
# Employees Projected by 6/30/95:	Company withheld
Sales (Annualized) 1994:	$126,935,000
Gross Profit Margin (GPM):	34.8%
Selling Expenses/Sales:	24.9%
% Sales Increase 1991–94:	+162.9%
% Change GPM 1991–94:	+9.4%
Total Debt/Net Worth:	29.8%
Net Profits Before Taxes:	$16,006,000
Operating Ratio:	12.6%
Net Profits per Employee:	$2,354
Traded On:	NASDAQ/GGTI
Principal Competitors:	Pulse Engineering, Inc., Bel Fuse, Inc.
# Potential Selling Sites:	Domestic: 200 Foreign: 500
Problem Company Is Attempting to Solve:	Constant technological changes in the networking market require filter products and other key components to be continually upgraded.
Solution Company Is Conveying to Problem:	The company has developed a line of magnetics-based components for signal-processing and power-transfer functions in LAN and WAN products.

Several LAN media interface protocols have been adopted as standards, principally Ethernet, Token Ring, and Fiber Distributed Data Interface. They dictate network wiring specifications, transmission speeds, and signaling access methods. While the company's signal-processing and power-transfer products support all major LAN protocols for electronic transmission of data over copper wire, at present the majority of its sales have come from networking products that support Ethernet, specifically 10Base-T cabling systems.

GTI was not formed to develop critical components for the LAN and WAN industries. It was a manufacturer and distributor of electronic components for the first 23 years of its existence, reaching sales of approximately $40 million in those two categories. GTI was relatively unnoticed and certainly undistinguished until Gary L. Luick became President in 1989. Within several months the company had acquired Valor Electronics, Inc., which put it into the manufacture of networking products.

GTI is controlled by Telemetrix PLC, a U.K. investment company that is controlled by a South African electronics manufacturer. GTI operates nine manufacturing plants, of which six are in China. Of the company's 6,800 employees, approximately two-thirds work in the Chinese plants.

GTI is a flexible manufacturer with low labor and overhead costs able to service the needs of its demanding customers—AT&T, Cabletron Systems, Chipcom, Compaq, DEC, Hewlett-Packard, Intel, IBM, Motorola, Sun Microsystems, 3Com, Bay Networks, Inc., and more. The fact that its GPM is rising and its Operating Ratio is a respectable 12.6 percent, is testament to the toughness and skills of GTI's management team.

HARMONY BROOK, INC.

Harmony Brook, Inc., is in the process of laying lots of pipe through which high-quality drinking water will eventually flow. Pipe layers take many years to break into the black, and it appears that Harmony Brook will get there in six.

Supermarket managers love the added income of in-store and affinity marketing schemes. Harmony Brook asks them to yield some floor and wall space to install its dispensing machine, in return for a share in water-dispensing fees. The marketing system is challenging, but the demand for healthful water is pulling more customers to the Harmony Brook solution. That persuades the shopkeeper—thus far Kroger, Wal-Mart, Hy-Vee, and Cub Foods have signed on—and slowly but surely the pipe is being laid.

Bottled water sales represent a relatively small yet significant segment of the massive U.S. retail beverage industry. According to the Beverage Marketing Annual Industry Survey, sales of bottled water in the U.S. market have grown from approximately 1.1 billion gallons in 1984 to 2.2 billion gallons in 1991. This represents a seven-year compounded annual growth rate of 10.4 percent. In 1991 nonsparkling domestic water accounted for 57.7 percent, or approximately $1.5 billion, of the $2.6 billion U.S. bottled water market; it has consistently accounted for more than half of the total U.S. wholesale bottled water market in recent years.

The Harmony Brook Premium Drinking Water System is designed to treat local tap water to make a pure, high-quality product. The water-dispensing system uses four different technologies to treat and purify the water: sediment filters to trap and remove suspended particles and other impurities; activated carbon to remove chlorine and other substances that might affect water odor and taste; reverse osmosis technology that forces the water through a semipermeable membrane to remove most minerals and dissolved solids; and ultraviolet light to kill or neutralize bacteria.

Shopkeepers want to sell the purified water that takes up the least shelf space. That means bottled water, and that is the tollgate Harmony Brook must raise. The company has some built-in persuaders.

Although many of its emerging competitors operate coin-operated dispensing systems, the Harmony Brook system is designed for customer purchase at the retail checkout counter. The Harmony Brook system offers several advantages over coin-operated water-dispensing systems: It can accommodate larger customer volume; it does not need to be

HARMONY BROOK, INC.

Chief Executive Officer:	Michael R. Knox
Principal Location:	1030 Lone Oak Rd. Egan, MN 55121
Telephone/Fax:	612-681-9000/612-688-0616
Satellite Locations:	none
Date Founded:	1989
Description of Business:	Develops, manufactures, markets, and operates equipment that processes ordinary tap water into high-quality drinking water at point of use.
# Employees Current:	50
# Employees Projected by 6/30/95:	60
Sales (Annualized) 1994:	$4,616,000
Gross Profit Margin (GPM):	51.2%
SG&A Expenses/Sales:	28.1%
% Sales Increase 1991–94:	+341.9%
% Change GPM 1991–94:	+34.8%
Total Debt/Net Worth:	12.2%
Net Profits Before Taxes:	$(496,000)
Operating Ratio:	(10.7)%
Net Profits per Employee:	deficit
Traded On:	NASDAQ/HARMBRK
Principal Competitors:	Aqua-Vend, a division of McKesson, Glacier Water Services, Inc.; Evian; local water bottlers
# Potential Selling Sites:	Domestic: 500,000 Foreign: 2,500,000
Problem Company Is Attempting to Solve:	A variety of contaminants are found in water from public water-supply systems that were designed or built during the past 50 years.
Solution Company Is Conveying to Problem:	Offers premium purified drinking water.

opened during working hours to remove coins or to replenish water supplies; and it is designed to prevent spillage and leakage.

Harmony Brook's retail customers typically pay 25 to 49 cents per gallon, excluding the cost of containers, depending on location and retailers' overall pricing strategy. This is significantly lower than the retail price for prefilled bottles, primarily because customers do not have to absorb packaging and freight costs.

Harmony Brook's management team seems to be a cautious group of Midwesterners, willing to wait 10 years to generate the level of sales and profitability that they could have in three if they implemented some multichannel marketing strategies. For example, why not place their dispensing systems in Jiffy Lubes, where people wait with nothing to do for 30 minutes? Jiffy Lube has more "air space" for rent than a cluttered Wal-Mart or Kroger. Sports clubs are another good location; natural foods supermarkets yet another.

Harmony Brook's marketing pieces are technical and mechanical looking. Using Kathy Smith (or another top aerobics instructor) as the product's spokesperson and putting her photo on marketing pieces would remind customers to take their Harmony Brook bottle to the local Wild Oats Natural Food Market for a refill better than anything else. Given another capital injection, perhaps the company will begin to employ some more upbeat marketing strategies.

HAUSER CHEMICAL RESEARCH, INC.

atients with devastating diseases such as cancer and AIDS can benefit from treatments discovered in a leaf or the bark of a tree. However, many valued natural chemical compounds are found in minute concentrations and in the past were often impractical to extract. Hauser Chemical Research's proprietary extraction and purification processes have made these compounds available. Today Hauser is bringing together nature and technology to rapidly become the world leader in specialty products from natural sources.

Hauser's technology is suitable for the large-scale production of high-quality, high-yield, high-concentration natural products, and can often offer them at a lower cost than other producers. The successful production of paclitaxel (Taxol), an unpatented novel anti-tumor agent that has shown a broad spectrum of activity against several types of cancer is a great example.

Taxol received FDA approval at the end of 1992 for use in the treatment of refractory ovarian cancer. At Bristol-Myer Squibb's request, and to meet the increased demand resulting from the earlier-than-anticipated FDA approval, Hauser accelerated its Taxol production in 1993–94. Hauser is the only commercial-scale Good Manufacturing Practices producer of the compound.

Hauser and American Cyanamid entered into a strategic alliance in May 1994 to jointly develop and commercialize Paclitaxel to discover new anti-cancer drugs. Hauser was paid a $1 million signing fee.

There is more to Hauser than Paclitaxel, however. The company has developed the technologies to extract sanguinaria from the bloodroot plant, which grows abundantly in the Southwestern United States. Sanguinaria extract is a completely natural antimicrobial used in toothpaste and oral rinses to fight gingivitis. Hauser produces sanguinaria extract for Colgate's Viadent division.

In 1994, Hauser acquired Ironwood Evergreens, Inc., of Olympia, Washington, (revenues $8.5 million), which makes unique secondary forest products such as decorative greens, boughs, and wreaths sold via catalog. This acquisition is far afield from Hauser's technical strengths, but owning a small forest could be an aid to Hauser's search for other breakthrough cures.

HAUSER CHEMICAL RESEARCH, INC.

Chief Executive Officer:	Dean P. Stull
Principal Location:	5555 Airport Blvd. Boulder, CO 80301
Telephone/Fax:	303-443-4662/303-441-5800
Satellite Locations:	Cottage Grove, OR
Date Founded:	1983
Description of Business:	Produces specialty products—lifesaving and life-enhancing—from natural sources, many of them found in forests.
# Employees Current:	303
# Employees Projected by 6/30/95:	303
Sales 1993:	$60,384,000
Gross Profit Margin (GPM):	39.7%
Selling Expenses/Sales:	10.6%
% Sales Increase 1991–93:	+235.9%
% Change GPM 1991–93:	+50.4%
Total Debt/Net Worth:	4.9%
Net Profits Before Taxes:	$16,140,000
Operating Ratio:	26.6%
Net Profits per Employee:	$40,350
Principal Competitors:	Rhone-Poulenc Rover, NaPro Biotherapetics, Escagenetics, Inc., Givaudan-Roure Corp.
# Potential Selling Sites:	Domestic: 250 Foreign: 500
Problem Company Is Attempting to Solve:	Cancer, AIDS, diabetes . . . the names of our collective Darth Vaders roll off our tongues like the countdown at a million executions. Where and when will the cures be found?
Solution Company Is Conveying to Problem:	Hauser produces Taxol, a highly acclaimed anti-cancer drug, from the bark of the Pacific yew tree, and has licensed it to Bristol Myers-Squibb.

HEALTH MANAGEMENT ASSOCIATES, INC.

When Bill Schoen "retired" to Naples in 1981 at the tender age of 45 after selling his New York brewery, F & M Schaefer Corp., the last thing on his mind was running a group of hospitals.

But a friend asked Schoen to join the board of Health Management, then a small operation only five years old. In two years he was President, then Chairman and CEO.

"I really saw health care as a very, very large business, looking at it from a macro approach," Schoen recounts. "I saw it as a necessary and needed business and one helping mankind, and making a profit in doing so."[1] In 1992, Health Management owned nine hospitals that brought in $38.3 million in revenue. During the next two years, Schoen sold its four urban hospitals, including one in Houston and another in Atlanta, and refocused the company's strategy. "We determined back then that we wanted to set the company in a direction where it would become the dominant provider or the sole provider in certain markets," Schoen explains.

Slowly, Health Management began buying hospitals in small towns and cities: 20,000 to 150,000 in population. Why the small communities? One key could be the paucity of managed-care operations, such as health maintenance organizations (HMOs) and preferred provider organizations (PPOs), that traditionally cut reimbursements to hospitals. Schoen adds another reason. There are three constants in any business, he explains: capital, labor, and marketing. Schoen says he could deal with the money and labor problems in the hospital industry. But he decided that Health Management didn't want to be in urban hospital markets, because they were too marketing intensive. In rural markets, there is frequently one hospital serving several communities.

The downside to the rural health-care market is that many patients do not have health insurance. As a result, Health Management wrote off $30.1 million in 1993. But since some form of universal coverage is expected from health care reform, that will virtually eliminate the company's bad debts.

Schoen has extensive turnaround experience. And what better market to implement these skills than hospitals. When Health Management buys a hospital it quickly moves in its team to slash expenses, remove the top executives, and set up performance goals.

---

[1] "To the Contrary," Chris Roush, *The Tempa Tribune*, October 11, 1992.

HEALTH MANAGEMENT ASSOCIATES, INC.

Chief Executive Officer:	William J. Schoen
Principal Location:	5811 Pelican Bay Blvd. Naples, FL 33963
Telephone/Fax:	813-598-3131/813-597-5794
Satellite Locations:	11 states from Florida to Texas
Description of Business:	The leading operator of nonurban acute-care medical hospitals located in the Southeast and Southwest.
Date Founded:	1977
# Employees Current:	5,500
# Employees Projected by 6/30/95:	Company withheld
Sales (Annualized) 1994:	$368,423,000
Gross Profit Margin (GPM):	24.3%
Selling Expenses/Sales:	not available
% Sales Increase 1991–94:	+150.2%
% Change GPM 1991–94:	+8.0%
Total Debt/Net Worth:	79.4%
Net Profits Before Taxes:	$35,484,000
Operating Ratio:	9.6%
Net Profits per Employee:	$6,452
Traded On:	NASDAQ/HMSY
Principal Competitors:	Principally large, urban hospitals
# Potential Selling Sites:	Domestic: Approx. 1,000 acquisition targets Foreign: not applicable
Problem Company Is Attempting to Solve:	As a general rule, neither the quality of health care nor the providers' experience are good in small rural hospitals.
Solution Company Is Conveying to Problem:	The company acquires and turns around small, underperforming rural hospitals.

Instead of spending money on new computer systems, Health Management buys used equipment, "tweaking" it to get more work for the dollar, Kelly Curry, Chief Financial Officer, told the *Wall Street Journal*. He estimates the company has saved more than $1 million. And analysts say its information system is first-rate. Their efficiency is evident in the time in which Health Management receives payment for a bill: 49 days, compared with the industry average of 75 days. When Health Management considers buying a hospital, the tough question Schoen and his team ask is: Is this a hospital that just doesn't have the demand, or one that physicians would use if it were run better? If the latter, due diligence gets more detailed.

When there is a demand for high-technology equipment in one of its hospitals, Health Management will avoid buying it. Rather, it will subcontract for biweekly visits to an MRI machine owned by a nearby urban hospital.

Thinking creatively, and realizing that it is senior citizens who use the hospital the most, Health Management "plays to that market," extensively. It offers discounts for all senior citizens—not just patients—to eat in hospital cafeterias. The American Association of Retired Persons is the most important lobby in town in management's mind. Health Management has created its own PPO to provide discounts to patients who use its hospitals and selected physicians.

The company's tight-ship philosophy is a sign of things to come. About 1,000 rural hospitals will seek to be acquired in the next 10 years. Health Management will be there with a shovel.

HEALTHDYNE TECHNOLOGIES, INC.

n 1978, Healthdyne Technologies pioneered the development of the first commercially available product for the home monitoring of infants at risk for Sudden Infant Death Syndrome (SIDS). SIDS is the sudden unexpected death of an infant, which remains unexplained after investigation. As the leading cause of death in the United States for infants between one month and one year of age, SIDS is attributed to approximately 7,000 infant deaths. While the causes of SIDS remain unknown, effective monitoring is the most prevalent protocol to reduce and prevent the incidence of death due to SIDS.

Healthdyne Technologies is the leading manufacturer of infant monitors and recording devices. While the company has developed and sells a broad range of monitoring and recording products for the infant market, Healthdyne Technologies' Smart Monitor has attained more than a 60 percent share of this market. The company's most recent unit features an array of technological advantages over competitive devices. Through effective implementation of advanced data storage and telecommunications, the Smart Monitor can record an infant's complete cardiac waveform to change settings via modem, and record five channels of patient waveforms.

Healthdyne Technologies' largest market is respiratory disorders. The company provides a complete product portfolio of oxygen concentrators and medication nebulizers to a group of patients primarily comprising aging adults (who are an increasing proportion of the population) with chronic pulmonary and respiratory conditions. It is estimated that more than 600,000 oxygen delivery systems are currently in use.

The incidence of respiratory disorders is relatively consistent throughout the rest of the world, as is the demographic shift in aging. As the worldwide market continues to grow, constantly refueled by the increasing life expectancy of its aging society, Healthdyne Technologies' share of this market should expand accordingly. Additionally, as managed health-care providers continue to develop strategies for cost containment for this rapidly growing segment of our population, an even greater shift to home care is expected.

The newest market that Healthdyne is entering is *sleep disorders*. While there remain many more patients in need of sleep disorders testing than there are facilities to accommodate them, diagnosis and treatment have expanded significantly in recent years. Diagnosis is usually made through testing at sleep disorders labs, where physicians

HEALTHDYNE TECHNOLOGIES, INC.

Chief Executive Officer:	Craig B. Reynolds
Principal Location:	1255 Kennestone Circle Marietta, GA 30066
Telephone/Fax:	404-499-1212/404-499-0117
Satellite Locations:	Brussels, Belgium
Date Founded:	1978
Description of Business:	Designs, manufactures, and markets technologically advanced medical devices primarily for use in the home.
# Employees Current:	465
# Employees Projected by 6/30/95:	525
Sales (Annualized) 1994:	$72,792,000
Gross Profit Margin (GPM):	41.3%
Selling Expenses/Sales:	24.0%
% Sales Increase 1991–94:	+1,160.0%
% Change GPM 1991–94:	+8.4%
Total Debt/Net Worth:	72.0%
Net Profits Before Taxes:	$9,350,000
Operating Ratio:	12.8%
Net Profits per Employee:	$23,375
Traded On:	NASDAQ/HDTC
Principal Competitors:	Sunrise Medical, Corometrics
# Potential Selling Sites:	Domestic: 250,000 Foreign: 500,000
Problem Company Is Attempting to Solve:	To experience the death of a loved one while sleeping, whether an infant or adult, is a horrible catastrophe.
Solution Company Is Conveying to Problem:	The microprocessor has made it possible to monitor people at sleep and to intervene should they show signs of suddenly expiring.

typically refer patients. There are about 1,500 sleep labs in the United States, far too few for the number of people who need them.

Healthdyne's answer is a full line of cost-effective diagnostic devices designed for hospital and home-based testing. Nightwatch, for example, is a technologically advanced remote sleep recording system, which makes use of telecommunications for the transfer of patient data, allowing patients to be tested for sleep disorders in labs, hospitals, or homes.

Healthdyne's profit margins are impressive. Its GPM has increased by 8.4 percent since 1991 to a robust 41.3 percent. Sales have nearly doubled in the same period, while SG&A Expenses have increased at about the same percentage. Net Profits per Employee are an impressive $23,375. Leverage is too high for a manufacturing company, and limits Healthdyne's flexibility and maneuverability to make strategic acquisitions. Should Sunrise Medical, or another cash-rich competitor, come after Healthdyne in its important market, it could be somewhat vulnerable.

HEART TECHNOLOGY, INC.

The enigmatic U.S. health-care delivery market is an expensive burden on the government and on those persons who pay for their own health insurance. But the flow of capital into research and development labs of start-up health-care companies frequently produces stunning examples of new devices that lower the cost of saving lives. Remove the incentive to invest—i.e., reduce the profitability of pharmaceutical and device producers—and who will pay for R&D? The answer to this question is complex, and hanging in the balance are lives.

In the case of atherosclerotic coronary arteries, one fairly young company, Heart Technology, Inc., has found a remarkable new way to remove plaque. Its new device, the Rotablator, has been designed to treat those classes of complex lesions for which conventional balloon angioplasty has been marginally successful. The FDA approved the Rotablator in the second quarter in 1993 and sales leaped from $21.2 million in 1993 to $50 million (annualized) in 1994. The company had its first profitable quarter in March 1994, and management expects the company to earn about $3 million for the year.

The introduction of traditional balloon angioplasty dramatically affected the way thousands of individuals are treated for coronary artery disease each year. Prior to balloon angioplasty, coronary artery bypass surgery was considered the only therapy, despite its high cost ($40,000–50,000), high risk (six-hour surgery with cardiopulmonary bypass), and lengthy recovery time. Balloon angioplasty provides a less costly, less invasive method of treating atherosclerosis. The technique has become effective for treating short, discrete, noncalcified plaque (type A and B1 lesions) in readily accessible arterial segments. However, it has proven to be less effective for other types of plaque, such as eccentric plaque that is only concentrated on one side of the artery wall, highly calcified plaque, long plaque (10mm in length), and diffuse plaque. These classes of lesions are types B2 and C. Moreover the technique cannot treat plaque when the arterial lumen has become so blocked that only a guide wire can pass through, not the balloon.

Despite this, traditional balloon angioplasty procedures will remain as one of the primary tools available to the cardiologist. In fact, it will most likely remain the technique of choice in roughly two-thirds of the 600,000 percutaneous transluminal coronary angioplasty procedures

HEART TECHNOLOGY, INC.

Chief Executive Officer:	David C. Auth
Principal Location:	17425 NE Union Hill Rd. Redmond, WA 98052
Telephone/Fax:	206-869-6160/206-558-1316
Satellite Locations:	none
Description of Business:	Designs and manufactures new-generation angioplasty devices for the treatment of atherosclerotic coronary arteries.
Date Founded:	1986
# Employees Current:	294
# Employees Projected by 6/30/95:	Company withheld
Sales (Annualized) 1994:	$31,770,000
Gross Profit Margin (GPM):	16,205,000
SG & A Expenses/Sales:	43.8%
% Sales Increase 1991–94:	+514.0%
% Change GPM 1991–94:	+13.5%
Total Debt/Net Worth:	7.0%
Net Profits Before Taxes:	$(1,227,000)
Operating Ratio:	deficit
Net Profits per Employee:	deficit
Traded On:	NASDAQ/HRTT
Principal Competitors:	Vascular Intervention, Interventional Technologies, Spectranetics, Advanced Intervention Systems
# Potential Selling Sites:	Domestic: 300,000 Foreign: 900,000
Problem Company Is Attempting to Solve:	The need for a low-cost and highly efficient alternative to coronary artery bypass surgery.
Solution Company Is Conveying to Problem:	The company produces a "plaque buster" that pulverizes atherosclerotic plaque in persons with coronary artery disease.

performed worldwide each year. This is primarily due to the relatively low cost of the balloon catheters and the high success rate in a majority of the cases.

The Rotablator was designed to treat the remaining one-third of the cases for which balloon angioplasty has shown suboptimal results. The Rotablator utilizes a diamond studded burr rotated at high speed to pulverize atherosclerotic plaque. The system consists of an advancer/catheter, a guide wire, and a control console. The advancer/catheter contains a tiny turbine that drives the flexible shaft with its diamond burr tip. The flexible drive shaft spins within a Teflon sheath that protects the arterial tissue from damage and provides a conduit for saline cooling. With each revolution, the diamond crystals on the catheter tip remove tiny scoops of plaque from the artery. The particulate debris scooped from the plaque is smaller than a red blood cell and is carried through the capillaries and vascular bed with no effect on distal perfusion.

Taking advantage of what is referred to as differential cutting, the Rotablator cuts through the inelastic plaque, while leaving the elastic musculature of the arterial wall unharmed. Since the shaft is rotated at high speeds, all of the longitudinal friction is overcome, thus making the device extremely navigable through the tight turns in the coronary arteries and through the lesions under treatment. It is a "roto-rooter" for diseased hearts.

There are approximately 3,800 interventional cardiologists in the United States, each a target for the company. Heart Technology has created a product with multiple cash flow channels. Primary, of course, is product sales. Second is the catheter attachment, which has to be replaced (purchased) after each procedure. Third is training fees. The company trains about 30 cardiologists per month in the correct use of the device. It is developing and training a sales force to call on these physicians. In the early years of ramping up sales, many companies have a very high Selling Expenses to Sales Ratio—Heart's is 43.8 percent—which eats up the GPM. But as new and improved products are brought forth and the sales department is more experienced, the ratio will decline and Heart Technology could become one of the most profitable medical device companies of all time.

With a market value of $324 million on annualized revenues of $32 million, Heart Technology proves that in Silver's First Law of Entrepreneurship, $V = P \times S \times E$, the size of P (the problem) can generate a very large V (valuation) long before the company produces earnings. If the Rotoblator actually mitigates death from diseased arteries and lowers the cost of heart surgery, then Heart Technology's value will grow into the billions.

HEMOSOL, INC.

Hemosol, Inc., is a biotechnological firm actively developing Hemolink, a human blood substitute derived from human hemoglobin. The company's proprietary and licensed technology involves a cross-linking chemical modification process, originally licensed from Canada's Department of National Defense. The product has completed preclinical animal testing, and the company has recently submitted Investigational New Drug applications in Canada and the United States. Phase I trials are expected to begin by late 1994.

Blood transfusion (donated whole blood) carries with it several difficulties, including the possibility of undetected contaminants; necessity of cross-matching blood types; and limited storage period (no longer than 35 days in Canada, or 42 days in the United States). In incidences of natural disaster, casualties of war, or storage and transportation of organs, the difficulties associated with donated blood transfusion can create significant delays in administration.

Hemolink-Hemoglobin is the active component of the red blood cell that picks up oxygen in the lungs and delivers it throughout the body. When separated from the whole red blood cell, hemoglobin has a tendency to fragment in half (which may be toxic to the kidneys) or lose its oxygen-carrying capacity. To develop a commercially viable oxygen-carrying blood substitute, or hemoglobin-based oxygen carrier (HBOC), Hemosol uses outdated red blood cells and applies two proprietary processes:

- purification of extracted hemoglobin to remove potential contaminants; and
- cross-linking hemoglobin to stabilize and provide oxygen-carrying properties.

The final product possesses very similar properties to blood. A second blood-substitute product (using licensed technology) is also under development by the company, and may have potential for use in a variety of new applications, such as cancer treatment. In March, through acquired technology, Hemosol entered into stem cell research, a complementary field broadening applications for bone marrow transplantation.

The animal studies on Hemolink have been completed, demonstrating a high degree of efficacy. Rats, whose blood was partially replaced by Hemolink, had similar survival data as rats that were given blood instead

HEMOSOL, INC.

Chief Executive Officer:	Alun Davies
Principal Location:	115 Skyway Ave. Etibicoke, CAN M9W 4Z4
Telephone/Fax:	416-798-0700/416-798-0151
Satellite Locations:	none
Description of Business:	Development of an artificial red blood cell substitute.
Date Founded:	1985
# Employees Current:	70
# Employees Projected by 6/30/95:	72
Sales (Annualized) 1994:	The company is in a research and development stage and does not expect to begin selling products for several years.
Gross Profit Margin (GPM):	not available
Selling Expenses/Sales:	not available
% Sales Increase 1991–94:	not available
% Change GPM 1991–94:	not available
Total Debt/Net Worth:	3.2%
Net Profits Before Taxes:	not available
Operating Ratio:	not available
Net Profits per Employee:	not available
Traded On:	TSF/HEM
Principal Competitors:	Conquest Labs, North American Biologicals, Northfield Laboratories, Somatogen, Univax, Biologicals
# Potential Selling Sites:	Domestic: 100,000 Foreign: 1,000,000
Problem Company Is Attempting to Solve:	High risk of transmission of blood-borne infectious diseases, principally hepatitis and AIDS.
Solution Company Is Conveying to Problem:	Purify hemoglobin extracted from red blood cells, then modify it chemically to create an artificial oxygen-carrying hemoglobin.

of Hemolink. In contrast, significantly reduced survival was observed in rats administered with control solutions. Hemolink's oxygen-carrying characteristics were similar to those of intact red blood cells. Hemolink also elicited no serious adverse effects. Hemolink appears to be stable at elevated temperatures for many months.

Hemosol is managed by people with a proven track record. Alun Davies, Chief Executive Officer, was President of Connaught Laboratories, Ltd. from 1978 to 1988, overseeing its growth from $17 million to $200 million in revenues. His Vice President, Medical and Regulatory Affairs, Geoffrey Houlton, held positions of increased responsibility with Glaxo. Anthony A. Magnin, Vice President, Research and Scientific Affairs, worked at Connaught for 17 years where he ran Canada's only large-scale plasma fractionation facility.

This team is too smart to rely solely on Hemolink, and it is positioning Hemosol as a multiproduct company. Several Canadian venture capital funds have $24.2 million invested in the company and the public has $35 million. Hemosol is in a foot race with cash—of which it has about $28 million on hand—and with a handful of other developers of blood substitutes. Several of them, Conquest Labs, Inc., Biopure, and Enzon, do not believe that the impurities can be removed from blood bank hemoglobin, and they are developing transgenic blood from swine and cattle.

Hemosol's strategic plan includes attracting a European strategic partner to make a sizable investment and commercialize Hemolink in Europe.

HOMECARE MANAGEMENT, INC.

After receiving a transplant, organ recipients receive lifelong treatment with immunosuppressant drugs to avert rejection of organs, and adjunctive therapies to counteract the side effects of immunosuppressants. Homecare Management is the largest and most rapidly growing player in the market for medical products used by transplant patients following a transplant—often referred to as "transplantation aftercare."

About 16,000 new transplants are performed each year in the nation's 265 organ transplant centers. In fact, the number of most major organ transplant procedures has been increasing steadily since 1989 (see table below). There are approximately 35,000 people on the waiting lists for organs in this country. At this time, the market for organ transplantation aftercare services is relatively unpenetrated. Homecare Management is the largest player in this market, accounting for only 9 percent of new transplants in fiscal 1993 (up from 4 percent in fiscal 1992). It is receiving referrals from only 26 percent of the 265 organ transplant centers in the United States. Much of the company's future growth will be generated from gaining new patients from existing referral centers and extracting additional new patients from the large pool of transplant centers that do not currently use outside companies to manage their aftercare needs.

Biomedical Business International (BBI), an independent medical consulting and publishing organization, forecasts that the number of transplants performed in the United States will grow at an average annual rate of 9 percent through 1995. BBI attributes this growth to improved surgical, pharmaceutical, and organ preservation technologies. The U.S. market for transplant aftercare products and services is forecast to double from $300 million to $600 million between 1991 and 1995, according to BBI.

Annual Transplants 1989–1992 Transplant Procedure

	Kidney	Heart	Liver	Lung	Heart/ Lung	Pancreas	Total
1989	8,899	1,700	2,164	93	66	401	13,323
1990	9,796	2,085	2,656	202	50	549	15,338
1991	9,943	2,127	2,964	398	52	535	16,001
1992	10,108	2,163	3,025	534	48	552	16,430

HOMECARE MANAGEMENT, INC.

Chief Executive Officer:	Clifford E. Hotte
Principal Location:	80 Air Park Dr. Ronkonkoma, NY 11779
Telephone/Fax:	516-981-0034/516-981-0522
Satellite Locations:	Carrollton, TX; Torrance, CA; Sneads, FL; Pittsburgh, PA
Description of Business:	Provides home care services to patients who have undergone organ transplants.
Date Founded:	1986
# Employees Current:	194
# Employees Projected by 6/30/95:	Company withheld
Sales (Annualized) 1994:	$35,230,000
Gross Profit Margin (GPM):	34.3%
Selling Expenses/Sales:	0.5%
% Sales Increase 1991–94:	+350.7%
% Change GPM 1991–94:	-0-
Total Debt/Net Worth:	31.9%
Net Profits Before Taxes:	$4,767,000
Operating Ratio:	13.5%
Net Profits per Employee:	not available
Traded On:	NASDAQ/HMIS
Principal Competitors:	Quantum Health Resources, CareMark, T2 Medical
# Potential Selling Sites:	Domestic: 16,000 transplants per annum Foreign: not applicable
Problem Company Is Attempting to Solve:	A care provider is needed to tend to transplantation aftercare, particularly in light of the cutbacks by hospitals in these and other peripheral services.
Solution Company Is Conveying to Problem:	Provides post-transplant medical care that includes helping patients deal with complex psychosocial issues associated with their chronic condition.

The number of transplants performed in this country has risen dramatically following the introduction of SandImmune (cyclosporine) by Sandoz in 1986. SandImmune is an immunosuppressant drug that significantly reduces the risk of organ rejection among transplant recipients. The availability of this drug has been responsible for a two- to threefold increase in the number of transplants performed in the United States annually. Cyclosporine, in combination with improved surgical technologies, is also responsible for the increased life expectancy being reported among transplant patients. Cyclosporine accounted for approximately 49 percent of Homecare Management's gross Lifecare revenues in fiscal 1993.

The next treatment advance expected in this field is FK-506, a cyclosporine-like compound under development by Fujisawa-Lyphomed, which is reported to produce less kidney toxicity compared to cyclosporine. A new drug application has been filed in the United States for FK-506 (projected introduction in 1994–1995). Because this product is only a slight advance over cyclosporine, however, FK-506 should not result in a significant increase in the number of transplants performed in this country. However, given the favorable results in clinical studies of FK-506 in liver transplants, FK-506 should increase the dollar value of the transplant aftercare market somewhat, given that this product is likely to be priced at a slight premium to cyclosporine. Homecare Management is well positioned to capitalize on the future availability of FK-506. Senior management has already held a number of prelaunch relationship-building meetings with Fujisawa-Lyphomed's management.

Homecare Management was founded in 1986 by CEO Clifford Hotte as a provider of traditional home care services such as respiratory therapy. In 1989 the company shifted its focus to the organ transplant population with its comprehensive Lifecare program. The company is currently the largest and most rapidly growing national provider of in-home specialized pharmaceutical and support services to organ transplant recipients. It is the only publicly traded pure play in this unique service niche.

Homecare Management also provides traditional home infusion services (e.g., antibiotics, nutrition) to transplant patients and to an established client base of nontransplant patients in the metropolitan New York area. The company serves patients in each of the 48 contiguous states and bills commercial third party insurance carriers, Medicare, and Medicaid directly for its services on behalf of its clients. Private insurers account for about 65 percent of the company's revenues, with the remaining 35 percent coming from Medicare and Medicaid.

Homecare Management's Lifecare model provides the most comprehensive and highest quality pharmaceutical, psychosocial, and economic services to organ transplant patients who enter the aftercare process. Like hemophiliacs, organ transplant patients have a number of needs that go beyond the administration of drugs. For example, patient noncompliance with prescribed drug therapies is the most frequent reason for organ rejection. The company offers a number of services that drastically reduce the occurrence of organ rejection as a result of patient noncompliance.

Through its Lifecare program, Homecare Management provides and delivers all home infusion and orally administered drug therapies taken by organ transplant patients. (In addition to cyclosporine, transplant patients receive on average ten other drug products.) The company's Lifecare program also includes extensive psychosocial counseling to help patients handle the range of problems that emerge as a result of a transplant. The most frequent problems of transplant patients include a lifelong need for medication, constant financial pressures, and adjusting to society after this long-term critical illness. The company sponsors patient support groups headed by social workers and a toll-free information/counseling line. The company also publishes newsletters for patients, families of transplant patients, and transplant professionals. In 1992, Homecare Management was honored by the Organ Transplant Fund "in recognition of its commitment to transplant patients and the willingness of its staff to assist individual patients at a moment's notice." A testimony to the level of loyalty that exists among the company's client base is that there have been no terminations among transplant centers served by the company since its inception. Revenues are growing at about 100 percent per annum, and the company is intensely profitable.

INFORMATION AMERICA, INC.

nformation America, Inc. owns and operates large and informative databases and makes them easily accessible to lenders, lawyers, and others. Its largest and most important database is the *Asset Locator*, which locates and identifies the real property owned by a business or individual in a specific geographic area, finds the real owner, uncovers possible relationships, reports all transactions, and locates stockholders in corporations.

The company's *Executive Affiliation* database profiles more than 30 million business leaders by name, company, title, address, and other affiliations. *Business Finder* contains information on 15 million companies in the United States, 2 million in Canada, and 1.25 million professionals and lists them by address, telephone number, and business categories. *People Finder* provides information on 111 million people, 92 million households, and 61 million telephone numbers. The information includes the person's name, address, telephone number, length of residence, type of residence, median household income, median home value, probability of home ownership, and additional household names. Other databases are more lawyer specific, including *Litigation Prep*, which helps lawyers correctly file complaints, Corporate and Limited Partnership Records, Bankruptcy Records, and UCCs, Liens, and Judgments.

Information America is living proof that large corporations that dominate their industries are blinded to imaginative and profitable niches. Dun & Bradstreet, for example, is the giant of databases, yet it overlooked the niche market for lenders. Mead Data is the major provider of online information services to lawyers, yet it overlooked the legal community's need to know about people and their assets, liabilities, and relationships. Today, 97 of the country's 100 largest law firms are Information America's clients.

Mary Madden found her niche quite by accident. Her launch pad was the insight that in chaos lies opportunity. When Madden visited her friend Burton Goldstein at the Fulton County courthouse one day in 1982, she was amazed at the lack of organization of data and the ensuing chaos surrounding lawyers. She noticed many of the courthouse records were on computer paper. Thus, there had to be a hard copy of the data. Both Goldstein and Madden realized that if they could buy the data on magnetic tape and download the information into a computer, they could create an online service for lawyers that would give them access to

INFORMATION AMERICA, INC.

Chief Executive Officer:	Mary A. Madden
Principal Location:	One Georgia Ctr. Atlanta, GA 30308
Telephone/Fax:	404-892-1800/404-881-0278
Satellite Locations:	none
Date Founded:	1982
Description of Business:	The leading provider of online information and related services designed for the banking and legal industries.
# Employees Current:	193
# Employees Projected by 6/30/95:	195
Sales (Annualized) 1994:	$26,053,000
Gross Profit Margin (GPM):	62.2%
Selling Expenses/Sales:	40.6%
% Sales Increase 1991–94:	+162.2%
% Change GPM 1991–94:	+3.2%
Total Debt/Net Worth:	61.6%
Net Profits Before Taxes:	$(191,000)
Operating Ratio:	deficit
Net Profits per Employee:	deficit
Traded On:	NASDAQ/INFO
Principal Competitors:	Mead Data Central, Dun & Bradstreet, Prentice-Hall, CompuServe
# Potential Selling Sites:	Domestic: 25,000 Foreign: not applicable
Problem Company Is Attempting to Solve:	Madden asked herself the question: What do people in business need to know every day in their business lives that is not presently being provided to them?
Solution Company Is Conveying to Problem:	An inexpensive, easy-to-access service that provides public information to anyone with a personal computer and a modem.

courthouse records. Most of the work had already been done. With Madden's computer experience and Goldstein's legal background, they were able to form Information America.

Sales have grown nearly 200 percent over the last four years. The popularity of the product is evidenced by the company's high (62.2%) and rising GPM: up 3.2 percent from 1991 to 1994. There is considerable price elasticity when selling something to lawyers, as they pass it on to their clients, usually with a markup.

The company stumbled in 1993 because it spent an extreme amount of time attempting to acquire Prentice-Hall Legal and Financial Services from Paramount Communications. With their eye off the ball, Madden and Goldstein saw net profits fall from $1.4 million in 1992 to $139,000 in 1993. The stock market sold "InfoAm," driving its price down to $3 per share. In its 1993 annual report Madden and Goldstein apologized for spending so much time on a failed acquisition attempt and they used the word "focus" many times. One of the keys to building a successful company is to keep your head under the hood while building the motor. What this twosome does best is create and market databases to lawyers and lenders. Good acquisitions will be brought to them as their ability to acquire increases.

As *Quantum Companies* was going to press, Information America's Board of Directors accepted an acquisition offer from West Publishing Corp. at a valuation of $30 million.

INFORMIX CORPORATION

nformix Corporation is one of those perfect companies whose annual reports, 10-K, and 10-Q are a joy to read. Like all software producers, Informix's gross profit margin is high—more than 80 percent—but, what is impressive is that it rises continuously. Its GPM grew from 75 percent in 1991 to 85 percent in the first quarter of 1994. The company's ratio of selling expenses/sales has been holding steady at 40 percent. This is a high ratio, but its software requires smart people to sell it, and these people are paid well. Informix prospects for leads with a telemarketing staff in Lenexa, Kansas.

What are the products that drive Informix's growth and profitability? The most productive products are client server and connectivity software which permit access by PCs to LANs and WANs (local area and wide area networks). Informix's founders recognized the need for connectivity as far back as 1980—a couple of years before IBM created awareness of the PC.

Informix is a *toolmaker*. Its tools enable software designers to develop useful applications. They are designed to be "open," which means they will access data stored on virtually any relational database. Informix's tools have a relatively long product-development life cycle, and are not obsoleted with the rapidity we have become accustomed to in the software market.

The company's customers—end-users, computer original equipment manufacturers (OEMs), value-added resellers (VARs), system integrators, distributors, and dealers—use its relational database management systems (RDBMS) software on over 100 different current models of computers from over 25 open-systems computer manufacturers. The company markets its products directly to end-users through its sales force and indirectly to end-users through OEMs, VARs, distributors, dealers, and system integrators.

Informix is very busy expanding into foreign countries through strategic alliances and by making partial and total acquisitions. There are 610 sales and marketing people in North and South America, 314 in Europe, the Middle East, and Africa, and 90 in South East Asia. Informix's products have been translated into 15 foreign languages, from Czech to Thai.

In May 1993, Informix acquired 15 percent of IntelliCorp, Inc., a developer of visual front-end technology. In November 1993, the company signed an agreement with Frontec AB (formerly IDK Frontec),

INFORMIX CORPORATION

Chief Executive Officer:	Phillip E. White
Principal Location:	4100 Bohannon Dr. Menlo Park, CA 94025
Telephone/Fax:	415-926-6300/415-926-6593
Satellite Locations:	Lenexa, KS
Date Founded:	1980
Description of Business:	Designs, develops, produces, and supports software for client servers and database management.
# Employees Current:	1,718
# Employees Projected by 6/30/95:	Company withheld
Sales (Annualized) 1994:	$371,921,000
Gross Profit Margin (GPM):	84.6%
Selling Expenses/Sales:	41.6%
% Sales Increase 1991–94:	+206.8%
% Change GPM 1991–94:	+12.4%
Total Debt/Net Worth:	54.6%
Net Profits Before Taxes:	$88,677,000
Operating Ratio:	23.8%
Net Profits per Employee:	$51,616
Traded On:	NASDAQ/IFMX
Principal Competitors:	Oracle, Sybase, ASK Group, Gupta Technologies, Powersoft, Uniface, Unify
# Potential Selling Sites:	Domestic: 5,000 Foreign: 15,000
Problem Company Is Attempting to Solve:	Making software easier to use at the applications development level.
Solution Company Is Conveying to Problem:	Relational database management systems (RDBMS) software.

a privately held Swedish corporation, under which Informix acquired 12 percent of Frontec AB's stock for approximately $2.1 million. Both of these investments are aimed at strengthening Informix's relationship with companies developing leading technology that complements the company's own product development strategies. Revenues from foreign sales were 58 percent of total revenues in 1994 (annualized), up nearly 20 percent from 1991. More important, research and development has more than doubled from $16,202,000 in 1991 to $43,619,000 in 1993.

What is this highly connected toolmaker worth? The stock market values Informix at $1 billion—which is a beginning.

INTEGRATED HEALTH SERVICES, INC.

Technological advances, cost containment pressures, and economic incentives combined during the last decade to create an array of alternate site health services, such as outpatient surgery, diagnostic imaging, and infusion therapy/home health services. These concepts have succeeded largely due to the high cost structure of acute-care hospitals, which are typically burdened with such loss leader services as the Emergency Room, high-staffing levels, excess capacity, and a growing indigent caseload. Most of these alternate site efforts focus on the expensive front-end, or traumatic, stage of an illness or injury. Integrated Health Services identified a different niche, the subacute recuperative period, between the hospital's intensive care unit and the home.

The size of the subacute market is difficult to estimate precisely, but perhaps 15 percent of the 1.1 million hospital inpatients on a given day are candidates for care in one of Integrated's facilities. That's a $17 to $20 billion dollar opportunity. The number of patients is growing due to the rising elderly population, our ability to survive previously fatal illnesses or injuries, and the economic mandate to discharge patients from hospitals as soon as clinically practicable. Cancer alone claims almost 1 million new hospital inpatients per year.

Robert Elkins, Integrated's CEO, defines the subacute patient as a very sick patient in need of complex monitoring, but not on the verge of dying. "Integrated's high energy level and rapid growth is one factor that is causing hospitals to close their doors. Subacute care," he says, "overall will save money and close hospitals."

Economic incentive for a health insurer is clear-cut: a $300/day savings for a single 50-day average stay ($15,000 total) could mean the difference between profit and loss for the insurer on a 250-employee group. Although Integrated's validity is owing to cost-savings, the company is committed to quality clinical services. All of its facilities have applied for Joint Commission of Accreditation of Healthcare Organizations (JCAHO) accreditation; more than half of its facilities have received commendations (the highest award), compared to a 6 percent national average. Moreover, the company has compiled two years of outcome data, verified by a third-party insurer, which demonstrate its patients recover as fast or faster than would be predicted in a hospital setting.

INTEGRATED HEALTH SERVICES, INC.

Chief Executive Officer:	Robert Elkins
Principal Location:	10065 Red Run Blvd. Owings Mills, MD 21117
Telephone/Fax:	410-998-8400/410-998-8700
Satellite Locations:	The company operates 148 facilities in 27 states.
Date Founded:	1986
Description of Business:	One of the nation's leading providers of subacute health-care services.
# Employees Current:	13,500
# Employees Projected by 6/30/95:	19,000
Sales 1993:	$356,928,000
Gross Profit Margin (GPM):	26.8%
SG&A Expenses/Sales:	5.8%
% Sales Increase 1991–93:	+248.5%
% Change GPM 1991–93:	-0-
Total Debt/Net Worth:	32.0%
Net Profit Before Taxes:	$33,263,000
Operating Ratio:	9.3%
Net Profits per Employee:	$2,464
Traded On:	NYSE/ITG
Principal Competitors:	National Rehab Centers, Continental, Rehab Clinics, NME, Caremark
# Potential Selling Sites:	Domestic: 1,000 Foreign: not applicable
Problem Company Is Attempting to Solve:	Medically complex patients who do not need the high-level care of acute-care hospitals should be moved to less expensive facilities, particularly in this age of managed care.
Solution Company Is Conveying to Problem:	To buy/lease and operate geriatric facilities and upgrade them to provide levels of care equal to those at acute-care hospitals, but at prices 30 to 60% less.

Robert Elkins started Integrated in 1986 when he saw the need for alternative facilities for medically complex patients in need of the high level of care provided in acute-care hospitals. In addition, he also noted that third-party payors and government reimbursement programs generally do not provide adequate reimbursement for patients in an acute-care hospital. Integrated serves patients in a low-cost setting. Integrated establishes Medical Specialty Units (MSUs) at its geriatric care facilities; these subacute specialty units provide levels and quality of care similar to those provided by an acute-care hospital but at lower costs.

Integrated is adding specialties in the MSUs, including inhalator, wound management respirator, and psychiatric therapy. It is beginning to capitate its prices, i.e., charge insurers a fixed amount per day to remain a first-choice provider with HMOs. Perhaps concerned about the effect on Integrated of changes in the prices providers can charge insurers, the stock market places an unrealistically low P/E ratio on Integrated, which is not reflective of its rapid growth rate and solid earnings.

INTERNATIONAL HIGH TECH MARKETING INC.

Maria Elena Ibanez, founder and CEO of International High Tech Marketing, Inc. (IHTM), is a combative entrepreneur. "When someone tells me that a certain market is difficult to penetrate," she says, "that's the one I want to go after. Because there will be very little competition."

Ibanez was founder of International Micro Systems (IMS) which she began in 1979 and sold in 1988. It distributed PCs and computer-related equipment in Latin America. After two years of being a beach bum, Ibanez launched IHTM, going after customers in Africa, the Middle East, Russia, and Eastern Europe.

Developing countries contain vast markets of young people who see computer literacy as their road to job security and career success. Conveying PCs and related equipment to this eager but disparate market is a challenge: from language barriers to currency, credit, and collection issues. It is not the kind of business that would naturally and easily attract credit. Lenders to IHTM have to make "character" loans, and Ibanez, some might say, is a real character. However, IHTM does not sell direct, but rather goes through more than 25,000 distributors in over 40 countries, continually adding new names to its list.

Ibanez was suspended from school at the age of 15 for objecting to repetitive praying to the Virgin. As punishment, her father made Ibanez take a computer course offered by Boris Computers. Ibanez loved it and became the only person in Barranquilla, Columbia (population 1 million) who had completed the course and knew how to program in Assembly. Ibanez continued going to school, but after school she would program accounting packages in Spanish for Boris Computers.

At 16 she began selling the software she had developed for a high price and saved a lot of money so she could come to the United States to go to college. She did not speak any English, but enrolled in Florida International University, where she majored in Computer Science. She graduated in 1978 with high honors and a degree in Computer Science and went to work for the school's computer lab as a troubleshooter, where she had spent most of her time while she was a student. "I was a nerd. I was always in the Computer Lab whether I had work or not. I loved it, so I put a lot of time into learning everything about computers." It did not take her long to realize that she was not going to get anywhere working for the University. "My boss was making nothing and he had been there for 20 years."

INTERNATIONAL HIGH TECH MARKETING INC.

Chief Executive Officer:	Maria Elena Ibanez
Principal Location:	12285 SW 129th Ct. Miami, FL 33186
Telephone/Fax:	305-254-8731/305-254-8736
Satellite Locations:	none
Date Founded:	1990
Description of Business:	International distributor of personal computers and computer-related products to developing countries.
# Employees Current:	27
# Employees Projected by 6/30/95:	38
Sales (Annualized) 1994:	$15,000,000
Gross Profit Margin (GPM):	The company is privately-held and not required to disclose its financial statements.
Selling Expenses/Sales:	not available
% Sales Increase 1991–94:	not available
% Change GPM 1991–94:	not available
Total Debt/Net Worth:	not available
Net Profits Before Taxes:	not available
Operating Ratio:	not available
Net Profits per Employee:	not available
Principal Competitors:	Compaq, Apple, IBM, AST, Dell, Gateway, Packard Bell
# Potential Selling Sites:	Domestic: not applicable Foreign: 100 million
Problem Company Is Attempting to Solve:	Most developing countries use computer systems that are archaic and lack the knowledge of how computers can benefit business.
Solution Company Is Conveying to Problem:	Produce seminars in developing countries showing business owners new computer systems and explaining how these systems can make them more money.

With the development of personal computers came a cheaper and more powerful machine. The cost of a PC was a fraction of the cost of the big computer systems that they had in Columbia. Realizing this, Ibanez says, "I saw an opportunity to become a distributor of personal computers to Columbia. I knew the Columbian market." She proceeded to find a small manufacturer and became their distributor. "I began to call all of the people I had done programs for in Columbia and right away I was selling computers." Having no business experience at all, Ibanez had quite a bit to learn. "I knew about accounting and I knew a little bit about exporting from my father, but I did not know anything about marketing, sales, or finance."

Ibanez proceeded to consume book after book, learning as much as she could about marketing and sales. "If you can read you can learn," says Ibanez. Before she made the switch to hardware, Ibanez was producing accounting software in Spanish. She pulled in $60,000 in the first month. But soon after sales began to decrease, so she spent her money advertising in a major computer magazine, following the advice of one of the books she had read. Unfortunately, she did not realize until after most of her money was gone that there were no copyright laws in Latin America and that people were buying and selling pirated copies of her software. This did not stop Ibanez. She scraped together whatever money she had left, spent two days calling every computer manufacturer, and ended up with a distributorship for five computer companies.

Ibanez now had the product but no clients, and so she traveled to Latin America, stopping at all major cities and cold-calling from every hotel room. "I ended up stealing the yellow pages from every hotel room I stayed in. It was the best source book I could get my hands on. I began to call companies with the biggest ad that I thought would be interested in my services." She ended up coming back home with $100,000 in orders and was able to get back on her feet in three months. That was the beginning of IMS, a company that was ranked 55 of the top 500 fastest-growing companies in the United States in 1987. In 1988, with sales at about $10 million, Ibanez sold IMS to a larger computer company when they made her an offer she could not refuse. "They offered me more money than I could make in 10 years."

Ibanez's goal is to take IHTM to sales of $150 million by the year 2000.

INVISION SYSTEMS CORPORATION

Think for a moment of the many novel things and events that can be enhanced or improved by making a phone call and seeing something and/or someone at the receiving end. You might say, "accessing a book from a library in Russia," or "watching a distinguished surgeon at work," or you might say, "calling my sales managers all over the United States to monthly teleconferences." Well, you're about to experience it. The visual communications market has three subsets: Group Video Systems—large, roll-about, or dedicated systems typically designed for conference room use; Desktop Video Systems—PCs that have been integrated with video conferencing capabilities; and Personal Video Systems—standalone video phones (e.g., the Dick Tracy watch) for use by businesspeople as well as consumers. InVision Systems is an important player in the Desktop Video Systems market. The company was formed in 1990 by James G. Geddes Jr., the Chief Executive Officer, and several top-flight systems engineers from Wiltel Communications, Inc., in Tulsa. Venture capital was provided by Bill Melton, the co-founder of Verifone, the telecommunications success. Geddes met MCSB, a Malaysian systems integrator at a trade show in 1993, and following a brief courtship, MCSB entered into a strategic alliance with the company, involving South East Asian marketing rights, and invested second-stage venture capital.

The most compelling reasons for organizations to purchase group visual communications products are: to achieve savings on travel costs and to be able to study blueprints, drawings, plots, and data files with remote offices. For desktop video conferencing, users add a third driver: to support file/data sharing and message annotation; you write on my screen, I write on yours.

Some of InVision System's customers are commodities traders and brokerage firms—they have to get the price right; engineers who want to pull together their colleagues in offices around the world to jointly design and develop a product or project on the whiteboard on everyone's PC; and physicians, in order to consult with colleagues 1,000 miles away during an operation by using a remote endoscopic camera.

The market size for Desktop Video Systems is driven by the installed base of PCs plus the percentage of PC users who want or need video—as well as price. The number of PCs in use worldwide is expected to grow from 125 million units in 1994 to 225 million in 1997, and prices are

INVISION SYSTEMS CORPORATION

Chief Executive Officer:	James G. Geddes Jr.
Principal Location:	8500 Leesburg Pike Vienna, VA 22182
Telephone/Fax:	703-506-0094/703-506-0098
Satellite Locations:	Tulsa, OK
Date Founded:	1990
Description of Business:	The company develops, markets, and supports the software that brings full-motion video to a PC screen if the PC is attached to a network.
# Employees Current:	17
# Employees Projected by 6/30/95:	45
Sales (Annualized) 1994:	$3 million
Gross Profit Margin (GPM):	The company is privately-held and therefore not required to make public its financial statements.
Selling Expense/Sales:	not available
% Sales Increase 1991–94:	not available
% Change GPM 1991–94:	not available
Total Debt/Net Worth:	not available
Net Profits Before Taxes 1994:	not available
Net Profits per Employee:	not available
Principal Competitors:	PictureTel, Vtel, Compression Labs, Workstation Technologies
# Potential Selling Sites:	Domestic: 15 million Foreign: 30 million
Problem Company Is Attempting to Solve:	The desire and need for business people separated by great distances to have face-to-face meetings and resolve issues together *without* incurring airplane and travel costs as well as the opportunity costs of traveling to meetings.
Solution Company Is Conveying to Problem:	Online, real-time, full-color video communication through desktop PCs linked via networks.

coming down. InVision sells its software and camera for approximately $1,500 per installation. A price break under $1,000 would undoubtedly bring in more customers.

InVision was the first company to develop the software that brings video to the PC screen. The color is realistic, the timing is instantaneous (although there are still a few jerkies), and the ease of use is friendly. More important, perhaps, is that with the InVision System unit, the customer does not have to be operating over digital dial-up lines such as Integrated Services Digital Network (ISDN), but can operate on any network so long as the PC is hooked up to a local area network (LAN) or a wide area network (WAN). This proprietary feature gives the company an estimated nine-month lead on its competitors.

InVision Systems sees the LAN/WAN market as its territory. With one-half of the world's 60 million PCs tied to a LAN or WAN, and both numbers growing, chances are when these users want to communicate visually, they will select InVision.

JUST FOR FEET, INC.

Harold Ruttenberg is old enough to remember that record stores in the 1950s provided their customers with listening rooms where they could try out the record before buying it. Perhaps believing they invented the concept of try-before-you-buy, some computer software companies have recently adopted a form of selling that they call "shareware," in which the customer can use the software and pay for it if he or she likes it. Ruttenberg may not know about shareware or the heightened spirit of cooperation between customers and vendors catalyzed by the intensely competitive 1990s; but he has certainly brought back the listening room. The variation is that Ruttenberg uses it to sell athletic shoes, and his concept works so well that the typical young male customer buys multiple pairs at Just For Feet. This translates into sales per square feet per year of $512.

The company operates 20,000 sq. ft. athletic shoe stores in which it strives to create an exciting and high-energy shopping experience through the use of bright colors, upbeat music, an enclosed "half-court" basketball court for use by customers, a multiscreen video bank, a snack bar featuring Chicago-style hot dogs and hamburgers, and appearances by well-known sports celebrities, including national spokespersons for the company's leading vendors. Each Just For Feet superstore features 16 separate branded "concept shops," displaying the brand's product line and typically built and periodically updated by the vendors to tie into their national advertising campaigns. All of the stores benefit from the upscale appearance of the branded fixturing. The company also sponsors creative promotional events such as "Midnight Madness" sales and family frequent buyer programs.

Because of the large selection of footwear carried and to further differentiate its superstores from other retailers, Just For Feet devotes substantial time and resources to training and testing its employees in footwear technology, the performance attributes of the company's merchandise, and common foot problems. It staffs its stores with a high ratio of sales associates to customers. More unusual: Customers can try out the shoes on the store's half-court basketball court, while TV screens show slam dunk contests.

Just For Feet guarantees that it will match any competitor's advertised price. Its family frequent buyer program gives participating customers the thirteenth pair of shoes free. In addition, the company seeks to enhance its reputation for value-oriented pricing by offering a

JUST FOR FEET, INC.

Chief Executive Officer:	Harold Ruttenberg
Principal Location:	3000 Riverchase Galleria Birmingham, AL 35244
Telephone/Fax:	205-987-3450/205-987-9878
Satellite Locations:	Atlanta, GA, Nashville, TN; San Antonio, TX; Las Vegas, NV; Kansas City, MO
Date Founded:	1977
Description of Business:	Operates superstores that specialize in brand name athletic and outdoor footwear.
# Employees Current:	344
# Employees Projected by 6/30/95:	Company withheld
Sales (Annualized) 1994:	$19,355,000
Gross Profit Margin (GPM):	41.7%
SG&A Expenses/Sales:	7.4%
% Sales Increase 1991–94:	+228.6%
% Change GPM 1991–94:	+31.5%
Total Debt/Net Worth:	30.3%
Net Profits Before Taxes:	$1,247,000
Operating Ratio:	6.4%
Net Profits per Employee:	$3,635
Traded On:	NASDAQ/FEET
Principal Competitors:	The Athlete's Foot, Foot Locker, Sports Authority, Niketown
# Potential Selling Sites:	Domestic: 40 million Foreign: 80 million
Problem Company Is Attempting to Solve:	To make shopping for athletic shoes a learning and entertaining experience.
Solution Company Is Conveying to Problem:	Customers leave a Just For Feet store having shot some hoops, had some fun, and created a larger than typical cash register ring-up.

limited selection of close-out merchandise at prices generally ranging from 30 percent to 60 percent below manufacturer's suggested retail prices and displayed at the front of each store called the "Combat Zone."

An interesting development in the athletic footwear industry is that Nike, a major manufacturer, is vertically integrating forward and opening retail outlets called "Niketown," in competition with their customers, such as Just For Feet. Niketowns are multistory, downtown mini-department stores that offer brand name clothing, half-court basketball courts, and a plethora of Nike's philosophical bumper stickerisms about using athletic shoes for finding one's true path through life's jungles. For the moment, Niketowns are occupying expensive retail real estate while Just For Feet is in suburban mall space. But the two concepts will clash somewhere, someday. Just For Feet is making shopping an aerobic and fun experience. This chain will be copied, but it has the financial backers to run the "D."

LANDSTAR SYSTEMS, INC.

There is a correlation between the growing popularity of baseball and the intensification of the entrepreneurial revolution. Baseball is the sport of entrepreneurs. Real estate developers tend to buy football teams, with their more rigid, militaristic rules. Entrepreneurs buy baseball teams. Attendance at baseball games is increasing. The expansion team Colorado Rockies drew 4.6 million people in its first year and was going to beat that in 1994.

In baseball, unlike sports played against the clock, the game is not over until one team gets ahead of the other team after nine innings are played. The fields are irregular. The positions offer variety to the players as well. Scoring is called "coming home." A player helps another player by "sacrificing." There are "utility" infielders and "relief" pitchers, and other helpful, cooperative names.

Entrepreneurship is a dynamic force: Man's (and woman's) need to make a commercial statement that defines who they are. The need to build a monument to one's brief life on earth: "Joe Jones was here for 75 years and he accomplished the following things . . . ."

That brings us to a most unusual trucking company, Landstar Systems, Inc., that recognizes the entrepreneurial need in truck drivers and optimizes it. Rather than have its trucks driven by employee-drivers, Landstar puts its truck drivers in businesses of their own. Then they contract to drive their trucks for Landstar.

High employee turnover rates are very costly to trucking companies. Landstar's turnover rate is an industry-low 64 percent. One out of three Landstar independent contractors stay with the company for more than one year.

Landstar's four owner-operator companies—Ranger Transportation, Inc. (Ranger); Independent Freightway, Inc. (Inway); Gemini Transportation Services, Inc. (Gemini); and Ligon Nationwide, Inc. (Ligon)—together generated 83.3 percent of Landstar's 1993 revenue. Each of the four has independent market recognition as an individual transportation services company. Together they utilize approximately 4,900 independent contractors supplying more than 6,480 tractors and a network of 750 independent commission sales agents who perform most of the marketing functions. There are also more than 30 company sales locations. That's more than 5,600 people running their own small businesses and selling their time and skills to Landstar and presumably others.

LANDSTAR SYSTEMS, INC.

Chief Executive Officer:	Jeffrey C. Crowe
Principal Location:	1000 Bridgeport Ave. Shelton, CT 06484
Telephone/Fax:	203-925-2900/203-925-2916
Satellite Locations:	30 locations throughout the country
Date Founded:	1991
Description of Business:	Operates five long-haul trucking companies, four of which manage and create opportunities for their drivers, who are entrepreneurs; the drivers in the fifth are company employees.
# Employees and IC's Current:	7,800
# Employees Projected by 6/30/95:	9,000
Sales (Annualized) 1994:	$869,600,000
Gross Profit Margin (GPM):	21.1%
Selling Expenses/Sales:	8.6%
% Sales Increase 1991–94:	+191.7%
% Change GPM 1991–94:	+11.0%
Total Debt/Net Worth:	171.7%
Net Profits Before Taxes:	$30,000,000
Operating Ratio:	34.5%
Net Profits per Employee and IC's:	$3,846
Traded On:	NASDAQ/LSTR
Principal Competitors:	KLLM, Swift Transportation, J. L. Hunt, Consolidated
# Potential Selling Sites:	Domestic: 15,000 Foreign: not applicable
Problem Company Is Attempting to Solve:	The desire of people to own their own businesses no matter how small, and to create something in their own image.
Solution Company Is Conveying to Problem:	The company creates independent business opportunities for thousands of truck drivers and assists them in creating personal wealth.

In addition, Landstar is online with its customers to locate their shipments in seconds and to receive their orders as well. The company communicates with its drivers via both a satellite-based communications system and pagers. This obviates the need for drivers to get out of their trucks and telephone the company for information on new loads.

This seems good for the drivers. But does it benefit Landstar's stockholders? Yes. Landstar's return on stockholders' equity in 1993 was 23.3 percent. Its Net Profits Before Taxes have grown from $1.3 million in 1989 to $30.0 million (annualized) in 1994. The average annual growth rate of Landstar's profits over the last five years exceeds 50 percent per year. Revenues are growing at about 10 percent per annum.

Landstar's growth has been fueled by leverage. Debt-to-worth is 171.7 percent, but with growth in demand for long-haul, full-load trucking, Landstar will work its debt down. Then it will be poised to make five or six acquisitions of languishing trucking companies, convert their drivers to entrepreneurs, sell them company-owned rigs to streamline the balance sheet, and grow to several billion dollars in revenues by the year 2000.

If I told you the earnings growth rate, GPM improvements, and return on stockholders' equity for a company named "Landstar," but didn't tell you it was in trucking, what P/E ratio would you put on its earnings? 40.0x maybe? The stock market gives it a 21.0x in mid-1994.

LIFE RESUSCITATION TECHNOLOGIES, INC.

Life Resuscitation bases its technologies on independent scientific studies on the potential of hypothermia and certain drugs and other chemical compounds to inhibit damage to an oxygen-deprived brain or other organs. The company believes that, if successfully developed, its technologies may overcome many obstacles that have led to irreversible brain damage in, or death of, victims of cardiac arrest and other catastrophic illnesses or injuries. Life Resuscitation is developing two portable devices designed to be used by providers of emergency medical care, such as ambulance drivers and paramedics, to help prevent damage to the brain and neurological tissue.

The company's patented prototype Brain Resuscitation Device is a briefcase-sized cerebral heart-lung bypass pump designed to infuse chilled oxygen-impregnated fluid laden with drugs and other chemical compounds that the company believes will not only reduce the temperature of, and supply oxygen to, the brain but will also deliver substances believed to counteract the chemical reactions that disrupt DNA, cripple enzymes, sabotage molecular gates, and weaken and damage cell membranes of the brain.

Its patented prototype Brain Cooling Device is a helmetlike device designed to envelop the head of a patient with an expansion chamber into which carbon dioxide is injected to form dry ice, which the company believes will rapidly reduce the temperature of the brain. As proposed, the device also will include a neck-supporting back plate that will lend additional cooling to the back of the patient's head and neck.

While the heart, kidneys, liver, and other vital organs generally can survive considerably longer than the brain, such organs are also damaged by oxygen deprivation. In addition to the Brain Cooling Device and the Brain Resuscitation Device, the company intends to develop other organ resuscitation or preservation technologies that may extend organ preservation for purposes of transplant or otherwise for anywhere from a few hours to a day or possibly even several days.

Human resuscitation technology is in its earliest stages of development. Life Resuscitation intends to capitalize on its proprietary technologies by developing the Brain Cooling Device, the Brain Resuscitation Device, and its other proposed devices into commercially viable products and to market these products, either directly or through joint ventures or licensing arrangements, to hospitals, physicians, senior citizen facilities, and other providers of emergency medical care.

LIFE RESUSCITATION TECHNOLOGIES, INC.

Chief Executive Officer:	Dr. Robert Goldman
Principal Location:	2434 N. Greenview Ave. Chicago, IL 60614
Telephone/Fax:	312-528-1000/312-929-5733
Satellite Locations:	none
Date Founded:	1993
Description of Business:	Researches and develops organ resuscitation and preservation technologies to significantly reduce brain and other organ damage stemming from oxygen deprivation.
# Employees Current:	7
# Employees Projected by 6/30/95:	15
Sales (Annualized) 1994:	not available
Gross Profit Margin (GPM):	The company is privately-held and is not required to publish its financial statements.
Selling Expenses/Sales:	not available
% Sales Increase 1991–94:	not available
% Change GPM 1991–94:	not available
Total Debt/Net Worth:	not available
Net Profits Before Taxes:	not available
Net Profits per Employee:	not available
Principal Competitors:	none
# Potential Selling Sites:	Domestic: 20,000 Foreign: 100,000
Problem Company Is Attempting to Solve:	CPR fails to revive victims 95 percent of the time.
Solution Company Is Conveying to Problem:	Life Resuscitation Technologies has developed more effective ways to prevent death or brain damage within the first six and a half minutes of cardiac arrest.

MEDICENTER, INC.

We address the issue of cost control," says Jim Lee, co-founder and Executive Vice President of MediCenter. "Unlike HMOs, we are not interested in reducing the quality or amount of health care we provide." MediCenter offers the company doctor option to the employees of large corporations with whom it contracts.

When MediCenter contracts with a corporation, it carefully documents all of the savings. Financial information is traced by computer; MediCenter furnishes a monthly comparative report detailing expenses versus the cost of using outside community services. "We believe cost savings result from elimination of markups on laboratory, X-ray, and pharmacy services, and from increasing economies of scale. Accounting, inventory management, and other functions from all MediCenter facilities are handled by a central MediCenter computer system," says Lee.

MediCenter slashes health-care costs in the first instance by centralizing overhead functions such as billing, collection of receivables, inventory management, purchasing, productivity reporting, and medical records. Doug McElvey, Director of Human Resources at South Wire Corp., a MediCenter client, says, "MediCenter saves us several hundred thousand dollars a year in primary health-care costs." The company recruits and hires all medical personnel, just as any facilities-management contractor, and puts them on its payroll. MediCenter is rewarded for delivering health care at less than the amount of its contract with the hiring corporation. Consequently, its physicians have a negative incentive to order unnecessary tests or prescribe unnecessary services and procedures.

The company-owned medical center operates like its public counterparts. Services include routine family medical care, X-ray, laboratory, and pharmacy. Physicians refer patients to specialists when necessary, and follow patients during hospitalization. The medical staff is on-call 24 hours a day, seven days a week, and operating hours of the medical center can be tailored to meet the needs of the company and the employees. In addition, physicals, wellness programs, and special health projects are included to increase employee participation. Medicare assignment is also included for retirees of the sponsoring company.

MediCenter's long-term plans include adding additional services to meet industry and employee needs. These services are as follows:

- Infusion therapy
- Expanded outpatient surgical procedures

MEDICENTER, INC.

Chief Executive Officer:	Cheryn Lee
Principal Location:	13 NW 44th St. Lawton, OK 73505
Telephone/Fax:	405-357-3686/405-357-5622
Satellite Locations:	Savannah, GA; Carollton, GA; Solon, OH; Fondule, WI; Luke, MD; Boogalousa, LA
Description of Business:	Offers facilities management of health-care operations to large employers.
Date Founded:	1984
# Employees Current:	110
# Employees Projected by 6/30/95:	150
Revenues 1994:	$13,000,000
Gross Profit Margin (GPM):	The company is privately-held and is not required to publish its financial statements.
Selling Expenses/Sales:	not available
% Sales Increase 1991–94	not available
% Change GPM 1991–94:	not available
Total Debt/Net Worth:	not available
Net Profits Before Taxes:	not available
Net Profits per Employee:	not available
Principal Competitors:	Columbia Health Systems, Homecare Management, Quorum Health Group, Vivra
# Potential Selling Sites:	Domestic: 10,000 Foreign: not applicable
Problem Company Is Attempting to Solve:	As anyone knows who hasn't lived on Mars for the last five years, health-care costs in the United States are one-seventh of the Gross National Product and rising at more than 20 percent per year.
Solution Company Is Conveying to Problem:	MediCenter offers the "company doctor" solution—providers are on its payroll and the company contracts with corporations who offer MediCenter as an option.

- Psychological services
- Physical therapy
- Stress evaluation services

Other medical specialties, such as optical care, may be included as needs and economics dictate.

Quality of care is the major focus of the MediCenter program. MediCenter is able to attract highly qualified physicians and pharmacists for several reasons, including: (1) physicians can focus exclusively on patient care, since MediCenter handles administrative tasks and pays for malpractice insurance and other operating costs, and (2) MediCenter clinics are top-quality operating facilities, featuring the latest laboratory and X-ray equipment.

"We find very qualified physicians who just want to practice medicine and not be hassled by paperwork, HMOs, PPOs, and filling in insurance forms," says Lee. The patient's ailments are not disclosed to his or her employer. Could MediCenter be the beginning of a return to simpler times in the health-care industry? "It's a start," responds Lee. "Cheryn and I believe that after 10 years we've got the formula down pretty good and we're ready to roll it out."

MEDICUS SYSTEMS CORP.

Health-care information services are a large and largely untapped market. Ironically, the health-care industry is the most information-intensive industry and perhaps the greatest laggard in terms of utilizing information management technology. With the transition to managed or capitated health care, the investment in information technology for the past several years has been focused on, and will be increasingly in the future, further streamlining transaction processing, tools, and systems that assist providers in better managing the cost of delivering quality care. Health-care providers, as well as payors and perhaps consumers, will need to track both the effectiveness and the efficiency of care provided on an absolute and comparative basis in order to measure the outcome.

Hospital information systems are 10 years behind virtually all other industries. Primarily focused on processing financial and administrative data, they have no standards of care, or protocols, against which to measure quality. Few use cost accounting, and as a result, do not know what their costs are for a given patient experience. Compounding the problem, hospitals have made substantial investments in closed, proprietary systems, often dedicated to mainframes, which operate as isolated information centers. This has resulted in huge inefficiencies, bad business judgments, and inflated expenses. With capital budgets now under severe pressure and the future of health-care insurance uncertain, providers have been slow to move to the newest frontiers of information management.

However, payors, employers, and the federal and state governments are all demanding that providers assume fiscal accountability for the delivery of care. This is manifested in a dramatic shift from fee-for-service (essentially cost-plus) to managed-care and capitated payment, whereby providers must compete by providing value-quality outcomes at the lowest possible cost—*and* to accept the economic risk of underperforming. This dynamic is a major wave that will occur regardless of the shape of health-care reform.

In short, there has evolved in the hospital market a critical need for timely access to integrated clinical, administrative, and financial information in order to understand costs and better manage the business of providing medicine. Providers must be able to reliably identify, select, and document the most efficient and effective method of care. This need is driving a philosophic about-face in managing health-care information

MEDICUS SYSTEMS CORP.

Chief Executive Officer:	Richard C. Jelinek
Principal Location:	One Rotary Center Evanston, IL 60201
Telephone/Fax:	708-570-7500/708-570-7622
Satellite Locations:	Alameda, CA; San Diego, CA; Cincinnati, OH; Clayton, MO
Description of Business:	Develops, markets, and supports information management systems used by physicians, nurses, and administrators in the health-care industry.
Date Founded:	1969
# Employees Current:	292
# Employees Projected by 6/30/95:	379
Sales (Annualized) 1994:	$36,214,000
Gross Profit Margin (GPM):	44.3%
Selling Expenses/Sales:	23.0%
% Sales Increase 1991–94:	+108.8%
% Change GPM 1990–94:	+1.4%
Total Debt/Net Worth:	32.7%
Net Profits Before Taxes:	$6,616,000
Operating Ratio:	18.3%
Net Profits per Employee:	$22,658
Traded On:	NASDAQ/MECS
Principal Competitors:	Clinicom, Cerner, HBO & Company
# Potential Selling Sites:	Domestic: 22,000 Foreign: 10,000
Problem Company Is Attempting to Solve:	In complexity there is opportunity. The health-care delivery business has gone into information overload and is seeking solutions to manage the data.
Solution Company Is Conveying to Problem:	The company markets to hospitals a line of software products to improve clinical data management, staff productivity management, and financial data management.

and a requisite shift from mainframe-based, closed-administration, and financial systems to open-architecture networks that are designed to manage the process more productively.

Today, there are no dominant players with strong positions offering information management services to health-care providers to manage their costs. But meet Medicus Systems, which has developed three primary products for this market:

Medicus' Clinical Data Systems, which allows medical records personnel and other health-care professionals to classify, analyze, and manage clinical data, monitor the quality of patient care and outcomes, and ensure optimal reimbursement to the provider. Through an automated expert system, each patient admission is appropriately identified on the basis of industry-standard codes.

Patient Focused Systems consist of *Medicus Clinical and Financial Case Manager* and *Medicus' Resources Management Systems Case Manager*, which allows health-care providers to develop and use care protocols to manage and evaluate the effectiveness of patient care from a clinical perspective. This product is being co-developed with Henry Ford Health System in Detroit. *Medicus' Resources Management Systems* measures and monitors continuing levels of staff productivity, clinical acuity, and related staffing requirements by assessing nursing resource needs, as well as the financial impact of individual high-cost cases.

Decision Support Systems gives health-care professionals access to integrated clinical, financial, cost accounting, and other information from internal and external data sources. User-friendly modeling allows management to make informed operational and strategic decisions. The budgeting and accounting packages are the result of the acquisition, in May 1992, of Innovate Software Solutions, Inc.

Medicus Systems Corp. is in the right place at the right time with a line of software products that merge clinical data systems and financial systems. Selling solutions to hospital administrators and to their boards frequently stacked with doctors is not an enviable proposition. Moreover the company waits a long time for payment: 93 days in 1994 versus 91 in 1991 and 102 in 1992. But, perhaps it's worth the wait. GPM is 44.3 percent and rising. The company's Operating Ratio is 18.3 percent. The stock market awards Medicus a cautious P/E ratio of 18.0x.

MEDRAD, INC.

Health insurance underwriters are people of passionate taciturnity—people with whom you do not joke. In a 1994 speech, Hillary Rodham Clinton accused these people of "bankrupting" the U.S. health-care system. She bearded the lion, then left the podium for the Senate to come up with cost reductions.

The insurers got the message. They have been writing smaller checks to providers for about two years. The providers, in turn, are writing smaller checks to pharmaceutical, device, and service companies. Equipment must perform better and last longer in the health-care delivery market. Mrs. Clinton's jaw-boning has had a lasting effect.

Enter Medrad, Inc. Medrad has been around since 1969 but didn't gain a sense of purpose until Tom Witmer began calling the shots in 1982. Witmer joined Medrad following a stint as CEO of Union Carbide Imaging Systems, Inc. He spun off a Medrad division to Eli Lilly in 1985 and settled down to making imaging enhancement products to help physicians make better diagnoses.

The company makes vascular injection systems (28 percent of its 1994 sales) that are used in angiography and CT scanning to control the flow rate, volume, and pressure of a contrast media injection; syringes (42 percent of 1994 sales), used in angiography to deliver and control the injection of contrast media through the vascular system; and magnetic resonance products (12 percent of 1994 sales) used in magnetic resonance imaging systems to enhance the image.

Medrad dominates the U.S. market but is a small factor abroad. Witmer says, "Our challenge is to grow more in international markets. There is a lot of opportunity for Medrad outside the United States. We own high market shares, generally 70 to 75 percent, in the United States, but often less shares in selected countries outside the United States. The international market represented approximately 22 percent of our sales this past year and has the potential to grow to as much as 40 or 50 percent of our sales."

The company has also announced its intention to grow through acquisitions. With a strong balance sheet, including $11.6 million in cash and only $1.8 million in debt, Medrad is well-positioned financially if an opportunity arises. While there is always risk involved—particularly since the company has never made an acquisition—management is deeply experienced in production and marketing and could easily fit an acquired company into its operating modality.

MEDRAD, INC.

Chief Executive Officer:	Thomas H. Witmer
Principal Location:	271 Kappa Dr. Pittsburgh, PA 15238
Telephone/Fax:	412-967-9700/412-967-9735
Satellite Locations:	Maastricht, the Netherlands; Wurzborg, Germany
Description of Business:	A leading developer, manufacturer, and marketer of equipment and disposable products that enhance the clarity of medical images of the human body.
Date Founded:	1969
# Employees Current:	736
# Employees Projected by 6/30/95:	Company withheld
Revenues 1994:	$74,238,000
Gross Profit Margin (GPM):	51.0%
Selling Expenses/Sales:	29.5%
% Sales Increase 1991–94	+129.1%
% Change GPM 1991–94:	+4.3%
Total Debt/Net Worth:	29.3%
Net Profits Before Taxes:	$9,503,000
Operating Ratio:	12.8%
Net Profits per Employee:	$12,912
Traded On:	NASDAQ/MEDR
Principal Competitors:	Liebel-Flarsheim, E-Z Em, Medical Advances
# Potential Selling Sites:	Domestic: 5,000 Foreign: 12,500
Problem Company Is Attempting to Solve:	Need for enhancement products to make medical imaging equipment operate longer and enable physicians to make superior diagnoses.
Solution Company Is Conveying to Problem:	Makes products that fit into medical imaging devices like blades into razors and give superior images to the physicians.

MEGAHERTZ HOLDING CORP.

Beginning in 1986 with a 1,200bps modem for the IBM PC convertible laptop, Megahertz has since introduced over 100 modem products for use with laptop and notebook computers. The company is the dominant factor in the business of extending the utility of the portable computer to provide the capabilities of an office on the road.

Until 1993 Megahertz offered two basic product types: internal Data/FAX modems designed to fit the proprietary specifications of portable computers from leading manufacturers such as Apple, Compaq, Toshiba, and Zenith; and pocket-sized external modems designed to connect to the serial port of personal computers. Because each notebook computer required a unique modem design, Megahertz's internal modem line was compatible with only a portion of the total mobile computer market. Lack of economies of scale prevented the company from expanding its product offering to include modems for less popular machines, leaving much of the mobile computing market unavailable to them.

However, in 1989 the Personal Computer Memory Card International Association (PCMCIA) began work to establish a standard for peripheral devices, including modems, to be used in mobile computers. And in 1992 they released the specification for credit card-size internal modem cards, which defines physical dimensions, as well as the interface necessary for "plug and play" capability. The PCMCIA standard is being adopted widely by portable computer manufacturers and peripheral device vendors. In December 1992, Megahertz was among the first to begin volume shipments of PCMCIA modems.

The emergence of the PCMCIA standard allows Megahertz to manufacture modems to be used in an increasing number of computers, including notebook, sub-notebook, palmtop, and pen-based computers, as well as personal digital assistants (PDA), and even desktop computers—substantially expanding the potential market for the company's products. Its greatest opportunity and challenge lie in exploiting this market by continuing to differentiate its product through the integration of emerging technologies with innovative product design. A second challenge is to capture greater market share abroad. A mere $4 million of product was sold internationally last year.

Now, Megahertz is in the enviable position of being unable to keep up with demand. Producing branded and OEM products, it enters foreign

MEGAHERTZ HOLDING CORP.

Chief Executive Officer:	Spencer F. Kirk
Principal Location:	4505 South Wasatch Blvd. Salt Lake City, UT 84124
Telephone/Fax:	801-320-7000/801-273-6770
Satellite Locations:	none
Description of Business:	A leading manufacturer of high-performance data/fax modems for mobile computing.
Date Founded:	1986
# Employees Current:	480
# Employees Projected by 6/30/95:	450
Sales (Annualized) 1994:	$91,178,000
Gross Profit Margin (GPM):	47.7%
Selling Expenses/Sales:	13.8%
% Sales Increase 1991–94:	+890.2%
% Change GPM 1991–94:	+49.8%
Total Debt/Net Worth:	11.2%
Net Profits Before Taxes:	$14,389,000
Operating Ratio:	15.8%
Net Profits per Employee:	$29,977
Traded On:	NASDAQ/MEQZ
Principal Competitors:	Logicode, Axonix, Hayes, Motorola
# Potential Selling Sites:	Domestic: 15 million Foreign: 30 million
Problem Company Is Attempting to Solve:	You're on a travel assignment, hopping from meeting to meeting, and you need to fax data back to headquarters, review your incoming faxes, E-mail, and snail mail. How can this be done?
Solution Company Is Conveying to Problem:	A fax/modem that plugs into the back of your laptop computer. You can buy one made by Megahertz at most office supply and computer stores.

markets via strategic alliances, as it did with Tokyo-based Integram for Japan. To maintain market dominance, Megahertz lowered prices on some key products, yet management revenues doubled in 1994 to more than $90 million. With portable computer shipments projected to reach 16.1 million units in 1997, from 7.3 million units in 1993, and modem penetration to increase from 26 percent in 1993 to 60 percent in 1997, Megahertz is addressing an elegantly expanding market opportunity.

Megahertz lacks a stock market following. Its stock price languishes below $6 per share, notwithstanding a GPM increase of nearly 20 percent since 1991, which suggest price elasticity for PCMCIA plug-in products; revenue growth of more than 100 percent per annum in each of the last four years; a tiny Selling Expense/Sales ratio of 13.8 percent; a miniscule leverage ratio of 11.2 percent; and an Operating Ratio of 15.8 percent. If these numbers don't suggest a P/E ratio in the 25.0x atmosphere, then I haven't read my Graham & Dodd correctly. Yet, Megahertz's P/E ratio languishes at 10.0x.

One picayune issue: the cover of Megahertz's Annual Report states the company's name as "Corporation"; the back page of the Annual Report states it as "Inc."; and the 10-K states it as "Holding Corporation." This lack of attention to detail is off-putting but not enough to lower the company's P/E ratio in 10.0x.

As *Quantum Companies* was going to press, Megahertz accepted an acquisition offer from U.S. Robotics.

MITEK SURGICAL PRODUCTS, INC.

One would normally be concerned by the existence of three seasoned venture capitalists on the board of directors of a publicly-held company whose sales are growing at more than 50 percent per annum, Operating Ratio is nearly 30 percent, GPM is 77.5 percent and rising in each of the last four years, and Net Profits per Employee is a stratospheric $76,857. But there they are, with one of them serving as Chairman of the Board. One would have assumed they would have taken their capital gains years ago and began scanning the horizon for the next winner.

Thus, it was with caution that I reviewed Mitek Surgical Products, Inc., a company with outstanding numbers and a good story. The story is about an anchor. The company's anchor makes it easier for surgeons to reattach torn ligaments and tendons to bones in shoulders, knees, ankles, and other parts of the body. Use of the tiny implants has increased surgeons' success rates and speeded up patients' recoveries, helping athletes and the rest of us get back to work faster. Mitek has a 65 percent market share and more than 2,000 hospitals have surgeons who have been trained in the use of the company's anchors. Mitek's anchors are ubiquitous in soft tissue reattachment surgeries.

Mitek developed its anchor products to address the need for more effective soft tissue reattachment devices. Its anchors are based on a patented system involving components made of nitinol, a super-elastic nickel-titanium alloy that has performance characteristics superior to those of stainless steel and plastic, the most common materials used in contemporary orthopedic fixation devices. The unique structural properties of the nitinol components allow them to retain their original shape and strength after extreme deformation by the physical pressures caused during anchor insertion into a hard substance like bone. Because of their small size and ease of use, Mitek's anchors are increasingly used in arthroscopic and less invasive smaller incision procedures.

Mitek's anchors are bimetallic implants, inserted below the surface of the bone, which use attached sutures to hold soft tissue against bone during the healing period. Over time, the sutures degrade and are metabolized by the body, while the bone grows over and around the anchor. Each Mitek anchor consists of one or more nitinol wire arcs attached to a titanium alloy body. A hole is provided in the body for suture attachment.

MITEK SURGICAL PRODUCTS, INC.

Chief Executive Officer:	Kenneth W. Anstey
Principal Location:	57 Providence Hwy. Norwood, MA 02062
Telephone/Fax:	617-551-8500/617-551-8517
Satellite Locations:	Cincinnati, OH; Carlsbad, CA
Date Founded:	1986
Description of Business:	The leading supplier of minimally invasive proprietary surgical implants that facilitate the reattachment of damaged tendons, ligaments, and other soft tissue to the bone.
# Employees Current:	108
# Employees Projected by 6/30/95:	130
Sales (Annualized) 1994:	$22,303,000
Gross Profit Margin (GPM):	77.5%
SG&A Expenses/Sales:	45.2%
% Sales Increase 1991–94:	+266.0%
% Change GPM 1991–94:	+5.4%
Total Debt/Net Worth:	7.7%
Net Profits Before Taxes:	$6,456,000
Operating Ratio:	28.9%
Net Profits per Employee:	$76,857
Traded On:	NASDAQ/MYTK
Principal Competitors:	American Cyanamid, Bristol-Myers Squibb, Arthrex, Biomet, AME, Innovasive
# Potential Selling Sites:	Domestic: 3,500 Foreign: 7,500
Problem Company Is Attempting to Solve:	Historically, in performing surgery, a surgeon has had to make a relatively large incision in the body to gain direct physical and visual access for the removal, repair, or simple inspection of internal tissue.
Solution Company Is Conveying to Problem:	Mitek is a leader in developing and manufacturing minimally invasive surgical implants.

The company has been introducing new products, at higher GPMs, to supplement its highly successful tissue-to-bone anchors. The new anchors include Anterior Cruciate Ligament and Rotator Cuff. On the drawing board is a urology anchor, one where Mitek's anchor is used in bladder neck suspension procedures for the treatment of female urinary stress incontinence. Anchors for use in oral/maxillofacial surgery are pending, subject to FDA review.

Since the competition is back at the starting gate, the company lifted prices 6 percent in January 1994, or $120 per anchor, and sales continued their pell-mell growth. A heavy SG&A Expenses/Sales ratio of 45.2 percent indicates that Mitek is building a sales force. Thirteen new salespersons were added in the first quarter of 1994.

This machine is getting oiled, and credit goes to a fairly new CEO, Kenneth W. Anstey, 47, who has run an Ostomy and Surgical Products division for Bristol-Myers Squibb, has served as President for Edward Weck, a surgical products maker, and as Vice President of Baxter International, Inc. Anstey is an excellent jockey, the horse is a thoroughbred, and the three breeders—well they come out for every race.

MOLTEN METAL TECHNOLOGY

Christopher J. Nagel, 36, came upon the idea of breaking down harmful wastes in molten metal while he was a researcher at U.S. Steel. The technology is an extension of attempts to cut steel production costs by dissolving used tires. Nagel left the giant steel maker to pursue a chemical engineering degree at MIT, and it is there in 1989 that he approached John Preston, MIT's Director of Licensing, to discuss ways of commercializing the process. Preston obtained MIT's permission to help Nagel form a company to exploit the technology; in return MIT received equity in the company.

Preston introduced Nagel to William N. Haney III, who was 26 years old at the time. Haney had launched his first company, Fuel Tech, Inc., which makes air pollution control systems, while a freshman at Harvard University. In 1989, two years after selling Fuel Tech, he started Energy Bio Systems Corp. to develop a biotechnology process for removing the sulfur from fossil fuels. The company went public in March 1993, making Haney's 27.1 percent share worth approximately $25.6 million. Haney became instrumental in raising $135 million for Molten Metal, including two public offerings that raised $104 million. In mid-1994 Molten's market value was $392 million—Haney's share was worth about $100 million.

Molten Metal holds 18 U.S. and foreign patents and it has filed 19 more; they merge chemical engineering with metallurgy. Nagel discovered that most chemicals break down into their constituent elements at 3,200° F, which then dissolve in the liquid metal. The bath is hotter than volcanic lava. The intermediate result is that the ingredients—motor oil, paint thinner, plastic containers—are reduced to harmless materials, such as carbon and hydrogen. When special reactants are added, these elements can be recovered as new commercial products—metals and alloys such as chromium, cobalt, and nickel; valuable gases, such as carbon monoxide and hydrogen; and specialty inorganics, such as abrasives and calcium chloride. These can be recycled back into the manufacturing process. What of the unusable lava? The company is thinking about casting it into useful forms such as telephone poles.

Molten Metal claims that its plants cost half as much to build as comparable incinerators with the same capacity (50,000 tons of waste a year), and cost a third as much to operate. And the technology may have a valuable ally in the regulatory system, which is forcing U.S. industry to meet rigid cleanup requirements. With such systems, American

MOLTEN METAL TECHNOLOGY

Chief Executive Officer:	William N. Haney III
Principal Location:	51 Sawyer Rd. Waltham, MA 02154
Telephone/Fax:	617-487-9700/617-487-7870
Satellite Locations:	none
Date Founded:	1989
Description of Business:	A waste-disposal system, using a bath of molten metal, that destroys hazardous materials yet recovers the dissolved materials. Basic elements in the form of gases, metals, and other inorganics can be used by industry.
# Employees Current:	179
# Employees Projected by 6/30/95:	230
Sales (Annualized) 1994:	$7,596,000
Gross Profit Margin (GPM):	53.2%
Selling Expenses/Sales:	36.3%
% Sales Increase 1991–94:	+387.6%
% Change GPM 1991–94:	+33.3%
Total Debt/Net Worth:	7.6%
Net Profits Before Taxes:	$(14,769,000)
Operating Ratio:	deficit
Net Profits per Employee:	deficit
Traded On:	NASDAQ/MLTN
Principal Competitors:	Providers of hazardous waste treatment services
# Potential Selling Sites:	Domestic: 2,500 Foreign: 500
Problem Company Is Attempting to Solve:	Each year more than 200 million tons of hazardous waste are generated in the U.S. Under environmental laws, the companies that generate the waste are responsible for disposing of it.
Solution Company Is Conveying to Problem:	The combination of intense heat and the catalytic effect of molten metal transforms toxic and nontoxic materials into harmless basic materials.

companies may be able to reclassify their waste products as "process intermediates." That could help them to evade costly regulations and long-term legal liability.

Molten Metal built a $10 million facility, in Fall River, Massachusetts, in 1991 to demonstrate its Catalytic Extraction Process (CEP) to visiting corporations. Shortly thereafter, it began selling CEP plants, and Fluor Daniel Environmental Services advanced $5.2 million to the company to obtain the rights to build CEP plants. Early customers include Hoechst Celanese Corp., Clean Harbors Environmental Services, Inc., and Rollins Environmental Service, Inc., the largest U.S. commercial hazardous waste incineration company. In Oak Ridge, Tennessee, Westinghouse and Molten Metal are jointly working to clean up low-level and mixed radioactive waste. A University of Tennessee study has estimated that the cost of removing all the waste generated by decades of nuclear weapons production nationwide could total $300 billion over the next three decades.

What about Nagel's degree? He obtained his doctorate in 1991, while managing the science and technology aspect at the company. Nagel's shares are worth more than $20 million.

Molten Metal's market value is approaching one-fifth that of U.S. Steel's. At its current rate of growth, Molten Metal will be a more valuable company than the company where Nagel conceived the idea. Such is the "creative destruction" that Joseph A. Schumpeter called "entrepreneurship."[1]

---

[1] Joseph A. Schumpeter, *The Theory of Economic Development*, Cambridge, Mass.: Harvard University Press, 1934. (First published in German in 1912.)

MOTHERS WORK, INC.

Rebecca Matthias launched Mothers Work in 1982. She defines the company's market as the upscale maternity apparel market, with a target customer of 25 years or older. The U.S. Bureau of Census reports that during the 1980s births to mothers aged 25 or older rose from 50 percent of all births in 1980 to 61 percent at the end of the 1980s. The census further indicates that fertility levels have risen since the late 1980s and are expected to remain constant through at least the year 2000. Mothers Work believes that the combination of the fertility rate and the trend toward older mothers will favor continued strength in its customer segment.

The company currently owns 142 stores, after acquiring 22 Page Boy stores in January 1994. Revenues are growing at more than 75 percent per year. Mothers Work's GPM increased 3.6 percent from 1991 to 1994 and 14.3 percent from 1993 to 1994. This is due to slower growth in factory overhead as manufacturing output grows.

Real-time retailing is the company's term for monitoring consumer fashion demand with computerized point-of-sale and merchandising systems, and satisfying it with fast-turn, in-house design and manufacturing. Matthias believes that real-time retailing provides certain competitive advantages, including reduced fashion risk, since the company can schedule production two weeks before it is needed to service daily items and allows a broad assortment in small retail space. The company's systems and manufacturing capabilities permit it to be more responsive to consumer demand by reserving an estimated 40 percent of its purchasing budget for testing new styles and responding to new fashion ideas that appear in the designer or ready-to-wear markets during the season. Real-time retailing also assists the company in maximizing its in-store inventory turns and sales per square foot, improving its gross margins, and reducing its cost of goods sold.

Looking back over the past 12 years, Matthias modestly says that luck had a lot to do with her success. "The timing was right," she contends. "The business took off at a time when a lot of women were moving into key business positions. And there were so many women who believed in what I was doing because my products made a difference in their lives."

RoseAnn Rosentha, Senior Vice President of the Pennsylvania Industrial Development Corp. (PIDC), and a member of the Mothers Work board of directors, was one of Matthias' early supporters. While

MOTHERS WORK, INC.

Chief Executive Officer:	Rebecca Matthias
Principal Location:	1309 Noble St. Philadelphia, PA 19123
Telephone/Fax:	215-625-9259/215-440-9845
Satellite Location:	none
Date Founded:	1982
Description of Business:	The leading specialty retailer of upscale maternity clothes.
# Employees Current:	954
# Employees Projected by 6/30/95:	1,500
Sales (Annualized) 1994:	$43,301,000
Gross Profit Margin (GPM):	57.6%
SG&A Expenses/Sales:	51.5%
% Sales Increase 1991–94:	+301.1%
% Change GPM 1991 94:	+3.6%
Total Debt/Net Worth:	53.0%
Net Profits Before Taxes:	$2,796,000
Operating Ratio:	6.5%
Net Profits per Employee:	$8,738
Traded On:	NASDAQ/MWRK
Principal Competitors:	Maternity apparel chains, catalog retailers, department stores
# Potential Selling Sites:	Domestic: 3,500,000 Foreign: 15,000,000
Problem Company Is Attempting to Solve:	Pregnant working women need attractive, classic apparel to wear to work.
Solution Company Is Conveying to Problem:	A chain of well-stocked maternity apparel stores in high-traffic metropolitan areas caters to this growing need.

Matthias often fantasized about selling her company during trying times, Rosenthal and other investors never doubted that she had the strength, intelligence, and business savvy to launch a successful business. Although the two women didn't actually meet until 1986, Rosenthal bought clothing from Mothers Work when she was pregnant with her first child in 1982. From that point on, she followed the company's progress closely. When Matthias approached the PIDC for funding in 1986, Rosenthal was largely responsible for helping her secure her loan. "By the time we invested, she already had a profit track record and was ready to roll out her company-owned stores," Rosenthal explains. "The concept was proven. It was just a question of gaining market share."

NATIONAL HEALTH CORP.

Recognizing that the self-employed and small-business owners are the healthiest segment of the population, Paul Wood Jr., a Texas insurance salesman, developed the concept of association-based group health insurance. His company, National Health Insurance Co., managed by G. Scott Smith, a former auditor, has a 1,200-person captive sales force whose job it is to gather in large numbers of policyholders, who join a related association. The health insurance is deemed "group" by the state insurance commissioners and therefore bears lower rates than individual health insurance. The health insurance policy offers fairly narrow coverage, has high deductibles, and is geared to paying catastrophic claims.

Association-based health insurance plans encourage policyholders to shop carefully for health care because wastefulness causes them to lose the privileges of club membership. The Law of Reciprocity that governs all commerce brings down the costs of health care because the buyers are more careful with their money.

Here's how it works. I buy health insurance for myself and for my employees and everyone's family, and all of us join a "buying club." The insurance costs my company about $115 per month per employee, and the club membership costs another $20 per month per employee. National Health has banded together about 80,000 people like my employees and me, and it uses this leverage to obtain significant discounts on a wide variety of products and services—beyond health insurance.

These discounts include $100 off the price of eyeglasses from Lenscrafters, a 20 percent discount on athletic shoes from Foot Locker, 50 percent off Alamo rental car rates, and much more. There are significant discounts on pharmaceuticals as well, refunded by check in about 30 days.

Let's look at an example of the benefits of association membership. My company has five employees; we take four airline trips per month, and we buy food, pharmaceuticals, and other products. A typical trip costs about $1,200 in airfare, $150 for the hotel room, and $100 for the rental car. The savings on one of these trips is $144 on the airfare, $72 on the hotel room, and $50 on the rental car, or $266 total. The monthly savings for four trips is $1,064. My cost for health insurance plus the association membership is $675 per month. So I actually *make* money on my health insurance; about $400 per month.

NATIONAL HEALTH CORP.

Chief Executive Officer:	Paul Wood Jr.
Principal Location:	1901 North State Hwy. 360 Grand Prairie, TX 75070
Telephone/Fax:	817-640-1900/817-640-3477
Satellite Locations:	None
Date Founded:	1978
Description of Business:	A fully integrated health insurance company that offers its policyholders noninsurance-related benefits through an affiliated association.
# Employees:	320
# Employees Projected by 6/30/95:	Company withheld
Premiums 1993:	$180,000,000
Operating Ratio (OR):	93.0%
Loss Ratio:	60.0%
% Sales Increase 1991–93:	+40.2%
% Change Optg. Ratio 1991–93:	-0-
Total Debt/Net Worth:	733.0%
Net Profits Before Taxes:	$12,000,000
NPBT/Premiums:	6.7%
Net Profits per Employee:	$39,735
Principal Competitors:	John Alden, Capitol American, American Service Life, PPL Life
# Potential Selling Sites:	Domestic: 10 million Foreign: 100 million
Problem Company Is Attempting to Solve:	Lack of economic benefits to compensate for loss of income arising from catastrophic illness.
Solution Company Is Conveying to Problem:	Offers affordable health insurance to the self-employed and small-business owners, with an emphasis on catastrophic illness.

Health-care coverage varies, depending on employees' age, the size of their family, their children's ages, and their health. Checkups are not covered at all. Injuries resulting from accidents are covered from the first dollar up to reasonable limits. Elective surgery has a $2,500 deductible in most cases. Dental coverage is excellent. One of our employees needs braces; her condition is pre-existing. I can pay $23.75 per month, and the insurance company will pay $1,350 to the dentist in two installments 13 months apart. This leaves $1,000 for the employee to pay, or considerably less if she chooses a dentist who belongs to the insurance company's Preferred Provider Organization. She can earn the few hundred dollars by putting in some overtime.

How likely is she or my other employees to file needless claims and risk losing their discounts? Not very. How likely is she or my other employees to search out the lowest-cost health providers? Very.

It is the noninsurance benefits offered by the association—the cost savings and discounts—that persuade my employees and me to renew our National Health policy every year and to watch our health-care costs closely. If the myriad associations that provide services to small-business owners began to offer association-based health insurance to their members, the cost of health insurance nationwide would begin to drop sharply, pulled by the features of club membership. The government, then, would have only the unemployed to provide coverage for, which it could accomplish inexpensively by taking a page from the association-based health insurers' book.

NetFRAME SYSTEMS, INC.

Opportunities for entrepreneurial companies do not always arise because large needs suddenly develop; but most assuredly, that is the primary causative factor. They also develop when large, powerful, dominant corporations refuse to cannibalize their sales forces in order to develop products that are sold through marketing channels that do not require feet on the street. Wang Laboratories, Inc. had one of the best mid-size computers in the market throughout the late 1970s and into the early 1980s, and one of the most highly skilled sales forces on the planet. But how do you get that salesperson to sell a $1,200 PC when her commissions exceed that amount on a single installation? That was the crossroads that Wang came to in 1985, and it chose the wrong road.

Now IBM and Digital Equipment Corp. (DEC) are at that intersection. DEC is repressing superior RISC and UNIX technologies in order to protect its VAX/VMS installed base. Its service fees were $1.5 billion for the quarter ending March 31, 1994, or about 45 percent of DEC's total revenues. It lost $183,000 for the quarter, six times its previous year's loss. Service fee income for the quarter was down 11 percent from the comparable period a year earlier; not a very good sign.

Multiterminal computer users are doing their math. They see $1,000,000 going out to DEC to service their mainframe, which frequently breaks down, as old machinery will. And they compare that with the $300,000 total cost of a brand new client/server computer, which can link all of a company's PCs into local area networks (LANs).

Most client/server networks run on industry-standard software known as UNIX, for which DEC and, for that matter, IBM, are not providers. Snatching the client/server opportunity from DEC and IBM are a handful of rapidly emerging entrepreneurial companies, perhaps the best of which is NetFRAME Systems, Inc. The company designs, develops, manufactures, markets, and supports superservers that provide network file and application server functions. NetFRAME's engineers developed its proprietary MultiProcessor Server Architecture, which is optimized for network computing, i.e., it combines the high-performance features of mainframe computing with the cost advantages of PCs and workstations.

The PC server business is expected to climb from $4.7 billion in 1993 to $7.4 billion in 1996, according to International Data Corp. Moreover,

NetFRAME SYSTEMS, INC.

Chief Executive Officer:	Enzo Torresi
Principal Location:	1545 Barber Lane Milipitas, CA 95035
Telephone/Fax:	408-944-0600/408-434-4100
Satellite Locations:	Cologne, Germany; Milan, Italy; Paris, France; Tokyo, Japan; Toronto, Canada
Date Founded:	1987
Description of Business:	Designs, develops, manufactures, markets, and supports superservers for linking PCs in local area networks.
# Employees Current:	232
# Employees Projected by 6/30/95:	Company withheld
Sales (Annualized) 1994:	$73,832,000
Gross Profit Margin (GPM):	54.4%
Selling Expenses/Sales:	28.1%
% Sales Increase 1991–94:	+346.1%
% Change GPM 1991–94:	+12.2%
Total Debt/Net Worth:	21.3%
Net Profits Before Taxes:	$7,843,000
Operating Ratio:	10.6%
Net Profits per Employee:	$33,806
Traded On:	NASDAQ/NETF
Principal Competitors:	Compaq, Dell, Sun Microsystems, Hewlett-Packard, Tricors, Parallan
# Potential Selling Sites:	Domestic: 5,000 Foreign: 15,000
Problem Company Is Attempting to Solve:	Corporations and organizations want to move complex network management issues off of mainframes and on to superservers.
Solution Company Is Conveying to Problem:	NetFRAME provides the superserver architecture and the LAN system to enhance the move to network environments.

servers carry GPMs of 30 percent or more. NetFRAME's GPM is 54.4 percent in 1994, up from 46.9 percent in 1991.

Strategic alliances were *de riquire* in the launch of NetFRAME, as befits a company founded by computer industry retreads, whose first ventures did not provide them with the personal satisfaction they had sought. Enzo Torresi, the CEO of NetFRAME, was previously a co-founder of Businessland, one of many failed computer retail chains. His co-founder at NetFRAME is Carlton G. Amdahl, who founded Trilogy Ltd., a large-scale integrated semiconductor and system manufacturer that fared about the same. NetFRAME's Vice President of Operations, Marty Di Pietro, was with Scientific Micro Systems, which also filed for protection.

Notwithstanding, Kleiner, Perkins, Caulfield & Byers, the most highly regarded venture capital fund in Silicon Valley, two other venture capital funds—MK Global Ventures and Bessemer Venture Partners—plus one corporate venture player—Olivetti Holding N.V.—chipped in close to $30 million to launch NetFRAME. NetFRAME granted Olivetti an exclusive distribution license for Europe which ran through 1993. Olivetti accounted for about one-third of its sales during the lift-off years. Businessland became an important value-added reseller (VAR) customer, accounting for as much as 100 percent of NetFRAME's sales in 1989.

NetFRAME broadened its thrust and began selling UNIX-based superservers in mid-1993, which made it directly competitive with the full gamut of server producers—Compaq Computer Corp., Sun Microsystems, Inc., Dell Computer Corp., Parallan Computer, Inc., Tricord Systems, Inc., Hewlett-Packard, and the aforementioned DEC and IBM. Some of NetFRAME's competitors also make PCs and workstations, which gives them the ability to bundle their server with a couple dozen deep-discounted PCs. But cut-throat competition is not new to Messrs. Torresi, Amdahl, et al. They may be driven by a higher and less visible power than beating a competitor—the power of overcoming a previous loser.

NEUROGEN CORP.

Estimates by the National Institutes for Mental Health (NIMH) suggest that anxiety is the most common mental illness in the United States, affecting almost 25 million people. The American Psychiatric Association defines anxiety as an irrational sense of dread or fear; the symptoms can be so severe that patients are almost totally disabled. Current treatment with anxiety-reducing drugs, or anxiolytics, serves to alleviate some of the symptoms but causes numerous side effects, including drowsiness, impairment of motor skills, memory loss, and addiction. The largest class of anxiolytics, benzodiazepines, can cause coma or death when consumed with alcohol.

Despite the shortcomings of anxiolytics, studies by various market sources indicate that the market for such drugs is approximately $3 billion worldwide and $1.4 billion in the United States. Neurogen believes that the development of improved anxiolytic drugs that achieve the therapeutic efficacy of existing compounds, but eliminate or reduce the side effects, would represent a major medical advance in the treatment of anxiety disorders—and provide a significant opportunity for expansion of the anxiolytic market.

In March 1994, Pfizer, the company's collaborative partner, filed an IND for NGD 91–1, Neurogen's leading drug candidate, which appears to be a nonsedating, nonaddicting anxiolytic in nonhuman models. Through its research of the gamma-aminobutric acid (GABA) receptor, Neurogen has been able to create a new class of anxiolytic compounds that exhibit greater therapeutic efficacy and an improved side-effect profile compared with currently marketed anxiolytic drugs. The company is also developing several alternative anxiolytic drug candidates that may have therapeutic properties similar to or better than NGD 91–1. While evaluation in the laboratory is needed to more thoroughly characterize all its drug candidates and assess their therapeutic actions, the company believes these compounds may represent significant advances in the treatment of anxiety disorders.

Neurogen was founded to capitalize on advances in neuroscience and molecular biology—specifically those involving the mechanisms and clinical utility of drugs that affect the central nervous system—by building a multidisciplinary research and development organization around a core of scientists from the academic community who have contributed significantly to many of these advances. Neurogen believes this strategy has enabled it to develop compounds and evaluate their

NEUROGEN CORP.

Chief Executive Officer:	Harry H. Penner Jr.
Principal Location:	35 NE Industrial Rd. Branford, CT 06405
Telephone/Fax:	203-488-8201/203-483-8651
Satellite Locations:	none
Date Founded:	1987
Description of Business:	Seeks to capitalize on advances in neuroscience and molecular biology in order to develop new pharmaceutical treatments for brain disorders.
# Employees Current:	72
# Employees Projected by 6/30/95:	100+
Revenues (Annualized) 1994:	$5,095,000
Gross Profit Margin (GPM):	Neurogen is not expected to ship product for several years; its revenues are from research contracts and interest income.
Selling Expenses/Sales:	not available
% Sales Increase 1991–94:	not available
% Change GPM 1991–94:	not available
Total Debt/Net Worth:	9.3%
Net Profits Before Taxes:	deficit
Operating Ratio:	deficit
Net Profits per Employee:	deficit
Traded On:	NASDAQ/NRGN
Principal Competitor:	Cambridge Neurosciences, Eli Lilly, Merck & Co., Glaxo
# Potential Selling Sites:	Domestic: 40 million Foreign: 120 million
Problem Company Is Attempting to Solve:	There are no effective treatments for anxiety, depression, psychosis, sleep disorders, or neurodegenerative disorders such as Parkinson's and Alzheimer's diseases.
Solution Company Is Conveying to Problem:	Neurogen conducts R&D in these areas and has made its greatest strides in developing a promising anxiety-reducing candidate.

therapeutic efficacy more quickly and efficiently than traditional approaches permit. The company's business plan is to focus on the discovery and development of drug candidates and continue to develop strategic alliances in order to draw on the resources of other collaborators.

Neurogen's expertise is in molecular biology, medicinal chemistry, pharmacology, electrophysiology, and behavioral science; the company's approach to drug development combines medicinal chemistry with an advanced understanding of the biological systems affected by certain mental disorders. Neurogen's drug development approach has allowed its chemists to synthesize a new group of therapeutic compounds that it believes will have greater receptor specificity and will, consequently, produce fewer side effects than currently marketed drugs. Complementing its medicinal chemistry efforts, the company's molecular biology staff has cloned the individual subtypes of cell receptors that are thought to play essential roles in the action of certain mental disorders. Cloning receptor subtypes has helped the company develop therapeutic compounds with greater specificity.

To enhance its drug discovery methodology, Neurogen is developing a combinatorial chemistry program, an emerging field in the pharmaceutical industry. The program combines the use of established databases of molecules with robotic, high-volume, biological screening procedures to create large libraries of potentially hundreds of thousands of distinct compounds with identifiable and appropriate properties. It will utilize Neurogen's proprietary assays to identify compounds that are highly selective to specified neuron receptor subtypes.

Neurogen was conceived and founded by David Blech, who has an excellent record in the field of biotech start-ups, primarily as a lift-off expert rather than as a manager. The company has achieved two private placements, a strategic alliance financing, and an IPO, and it is sitting on about $10 million in cash plus $25 million in contingent funding from Pfizer. It needs to begin earning royalties on NGD 91-1 before it uses up its cash.

NEWBRIDGE NETWORKS CORP.

Throughout the world, corporate information networks represent one of the fastest-growing business sectors in the telecommunications industry. Newbridge has become a leader in this business with its ability to design, manufacture, market, and support digital networks for private and public operators worldwide. Its high-performance *MainStreet* line of networking products has become synonymous with high quality, flexibility, and value for money. *MainStreet* products are standards-based and provide very reliable multiprotocol connectivity for voice, data, image, and video.

Newbridge Networks was founded by Terry Matthews, who with Mike Cowpland, CEO of Quantum Company, Corel Corporation, co-founded Mitel Corp., a telecommunications success story. Newbridge's sales are growing at 50 percent per year with a rising GPM, presently holding at 62.3 percent. Its Operating Ratio is 27.4 percent and its Net Profits per Employee are $41,476. With this kind of track record, the stock market underrewards Newbridge with a P/E ratio of 21.0x in mid-1994.

The company is a formidable money-making machine. GPM grew by almost 5 percent since 1991, and its inventory is turning every two months, a significant indicator of operational efficiency. Sales to telephone companies exceed sales to private customers and account for about 60 percent of revenues: Newbridge currently supplies over 100 telephone companies around the world with advanced digital networking products which deliver extremely reliable and flexible communications. Its customers include Copenhagen Telephone Co., Chilean Telephone Co., MCI Communications Corp., Moscow Local Telephone Network, Shenzhen Telecommunications, NYNEX, Southwestern Bell, and the FNA (a consortium of major telephone companies offering communications services to financial institutions worldwide).

Newbridge's management continues to differentiate its product offerings. The *4602 MainStreet* Intelligent NetworkStation manages Frame Relay and Asynchronous Transfer Mode (ATM), as well as traditional circuit-switched paths. To keep up with the demand for comprehensive, sophisticated management of very large networks, the latest generic of the *4602 MainStreet* network manager is being developed with the power to manage many thousands of nodes in a single network.

NEWBRIDGE NETWORKS CORP.

Chief Executive Officer:	Terrence H. Matthews
Principal Location:	600 March Rd. Kanata, Ontario, CAN K2K 2E6
Telephone/Fax:	613-591-3600/613-591-3680
Satellite Locations:	San Jose, CA; Moscow, Mexico City, Rio de Janeiro, London, Paris, Auckland, Hong Kong
Date Founded:	1986
Description of Business:	Develops, produces, markets, and supports a line of integrated digital networking equipment enabling companies and organizations to expand and manage world link communications networks.
# Employees Current:	1,462
# Employees Projected by 6/30/95:	Company withheld
Revenues (Annualized) 1994:	$221,450,000
Gross Profit Margin (GPM):	62.3%
Selling Expenses/Sales:	20.6%
% Sales Increase 1991–94:	+206.3%
% Change GPM 1991–94:	+4.4%
Total Debt/Net Worth:	34.0%
Net Profits Before Taxes:	$60,638,000
Operating Ratio:	27.4%
Net Profits per Employee:	$41,476
Traded On:	NASDAQ/NNCXF
Principal Competitors:	Ascom/Timeplex, Network Equipment Technologies, General DataComm Industries, StrataCom
# Potential Selling Sites:	Domestic: 25,000 Foreign: 75,000
Problem Company Is Attempting to Solve:	To remain competitive, companies are increasingly required to manage information on a worldwide basis.
Solution Company Is Conveying to Problem:	Newbridge supplies the equipment necessary for worldwide communications networks.

The company has formed several strategic partnerships for the joint development and marketing of router and ATM products. With its partners, Advanced Computer Communications of Cupertino, California, and MPR Teltech of Vancouver, British Columbia, Newbridge is significantly advancing the features, functions, and availability of new *MainStreet* networking products.

The market for networking equipment will grow much larger because, to paraphrase Elias Canetti in *Crowds and Power*, all kinds of crowds experience the need to get bigger.

NEXTEL COMMUNICATIONS, INC.

Nextel Communications, Inc., has spent $4 billion, mostly in its common stock, to acquire, through 125 transactions, local radio dispatch companies and rename them Specialized Mobile Radio (SMR) companies. Nextel is number three in wireless communication in most major markets, serving about 176 million proportionate population equivalents (pops). It is in 45 of the nation's 50 largest markets and occupies 10 to 12 MHz of the available 800-MHz SMR spectrum. Using Motorola Integrated Radio System (MIRS) technology, this provides double the capacity of analog cellular and about two-thirds of the capacity of Time Division Multiple Access (TDMA) digital cellular. In a word: inexpensive transmission costs. SMR is a digital net; it will charge Workstation Technologies, Inc., and InVision Systems, Inc., two digital video conferencing companies, a whole lot less to transmit movies and live classrooms on a wireless basis than will the long-distance telephone carriers.

To pay for its "railroad" of the next century, Nextel has established strategic partnerships with four global telecommunications technology leaders: Motorola and Northern Telecom will assist with radio frequency design and manufacturing as well as switching; Motorola and Matsushita will aid in handset design and manufacturing and other required electronic technologies; Nippon Telephone & Telegraph (NTT) will work with the company in network design and management; and MCI will provide marketing muscle. The equity infusion by Comcast and NTT, the implementation and demonstration of MIRS technology, and the rapid acquisitions of DisCom American Mobile Systems (AMS), Questar Telecom, Inc. (QTI), American MobileComm, Inc. (AMI), PowerFone, and Motorola's common service area SMR operations have contributed heavily to increased realization of the company's aggressive plans.

Up until now Nextel has been a quiet consolidator of radio dispatch companies—the press-and-speak radios that have dispatched taxis and construction crews for decades. Seven years ago Morgan E. O'Brien, Nextel's founder, was a D.C. lawyer who represented clients at the FCC and got to know its arcane laws very thoroughly. O'Brien discovered a discrepancy in the FCC regulations: Cellular phone systems were soaring in market value while radio dispatch companies were languishing, yet both used the radio-wave spectrum. They even used the same bandwidth, 800 MHz. The FCC had created artificial barriers between

NEXTEL COMMUNICATIONS, INC.

Chief Executive Officer:	Brian D. McAuley
Principal Location:	201 Route 17 North Rutherford, NJ 07070
Telephone/Fax:	201-438-1400/201-438-5540
Satellite Locations:	California, Ohio, Pennsylvania, Connecticut, Delaware, Illinois, Indiana, Maine, Maryland, New York, Texas, Utah, Vermont, Virginia, Washington, D.C.
Date Founded:	1987
Description of Business:	Provides wireless communications services utilizing SMR frequencies licensed by the FCC.
# Employees Current:	769
# Employees Projected by 6/30/95:	Company withheld
Sales (Annualized) 1994:	$76,613,000
Gross Profit Margin (GPM):	54.6%
SG&A Expenses/Sales:	58.0%
% Sales Increase 1991–94:	+142.1%
% Change Optg. Ratio 1991–94:	(14.6)%
Total Debt/Net Worth	95.6%
Net Profits Before Taxes:	$(105,522,000)
Operating Ratio:	deficit
Net Profits per Employee:	deficit
Traded On:	NASDAQ/CALL
Principal Competitors:	McCaw Cellular, AT&T, MCI Communications, Sprint
# Potential Selling Sites:	Domestic: 30 million Foreign: not applicable
Problem Company Is Attempting to Solve:	As the world market is being knitted together by PCs and network connectivity software and switches, transmission costs need to be contained.
Solution Company Is Conveying to Problem:	Nextel is building the lowest-cost digital cellular network to compete with AT&T/McCaw, Qualcomm, and more expensive analog networks such as the telephone.

the two. But why hadn't entrepreneurs bought up cheap dispatch airspace and built a competitive network?

O'Brien persuaded his law firm to fund a start-up, which he would run. He bid $3 million to buy two systems in Bakersfield and Fresno, California. O'Brien had no financing, but he knew the FCC would take about eight months to review the sale—enough time to raise the money. O'Brien then hired Brian D. McAuley, who had been CFO of a telecommunications company, as president of his new company.

Today Nextel is an operational, nationwide cellular company. MCI Communications is its primary long-distance carrier and provider of long-distance connections for Nextel's transmitters and switches. A merger of Nextel and MCI (which owns a minority interest in Nextel) may be in the cards someday, particularly if Nextel develops systems to bypass MCI.

ON ASSIGNMENT, INC.

On Assignment, Inc., through its first operating division, Lab Support, is a leading nationwide provider of temporary scientific professionals to laboratories in the biotechnology, environmental, chemical, pharmaceutical, food and beverage, and petrochemical industries. As of December 31, 1993, the company served 28 metropolitan areas through a network of 35 branch offices. In January 1994, the company established its second operating division, Finance Support, with the acquisition of 1st Choice Personnel, Inc., of Walnut Creek, California. 1st Choice is expected to form the core of the new division, which will specialize in assignment professionals for the banking, lending, credit, and mortgage industries.

On Assignment was founded in December 1985, as a California corporation under the name Lab Support, Inc.; it changed its name in November 1991 to Temporary Professional Support, Inc. The company reincorporated in Delaware as On Assignment, Inc. on September 15, 1992.

The company's strategy is to serve industries' needs for quality assignments of temporary professionals. In contrast to the mass-market approach used for temporary office/clerical and light industrial personnel, the company believes effective assignments of temporary professionals require significant knowledge of the client's industry and the ability to assess the client's specific needs as well and the temporary professionals' qualifications. To accomplish this, the company developed the Account Manager System. Here's how it works:

All Account Managers have scientific degrees, at least two years of nonacademic laboratory experience, and two to ten years of total work experience. They are responsible for the entire assignment process, including recruiting and assessing the qualifications of employees, maintaining client contacts, inspecting labs, identifying specific job requirements, assigning employees, and following up with both clients and employees. The company is continuously engaged in recruiting and training new Account Managers to increase coverage of existing markets, extend into new geographic markets, and replace open Account Manager positions.

Temporary personnel assigned to clients are employees of On Assignment. Clients provide on-the-job supervisors for temporary personnel, overseeing performance, and approving hours worked, while Account Managers are responsible for many of the activities typically

ON ASSIGNMENT, INC.

Chief Executive Officer:	H. Tom Dueltor
Principal Location:	26651 W. Agoura Rd. Calabasas, CA 91302
Telephone/Fax:	818-878-7900/818-878-7930
Satellite Locations:	35 offices throughout the United States
Date Founded:	1985
Description of Business:	A leading provider of temporary scientific professionals to laboratories in the biotechnology, environmental, and pharmaceutical industries.
# Employees Current:	115
# Employees Projected by 6/30/95:	130
Sales (Annualized) 1994:	$39,514,000
Gross Profit Margin (GPM):	30.4%
Selling Expenses/Sales:	21.0%
% Sales Increase 1991–94:	+149.0%
% Change GPM 1991–94:	-0-
Total Debt/Net Worth:	12.1%
Net Profits Before Taxes:	$4,187,000
Operating Ratio:	10.6%
Net Profits per Employee:	$44,074
Traded On:	NASDAQ/ASGN
Principal Competitors:	ManPower, Kelly Services, Olsten, AIDA Services
# Potential Selling Sites:	Domestic: 2,500 Foreign: 7,500
Problem Company Is Attempting to Solve:	To manage cash flow more efficiently, companies hire temporary personnel in the valleys, and if they return to the peaks, they convert them to full-time employees.
Solution Company Is Conveying to Problem:	The company is the leader in the rent-a-chemist field.

handled by the client's personnel department. If a temporary employee is converted to a regular employee by the client during the first six months of an assignment, the client typically pays On Assignment a fee. These fees account for approximately 1 percent of On Assignment's total revenues.

CEO H. Tom Buelter spent six years at Kelly Services Inc., the temp agency, rising through the ranks to become Chief Operating Officer of Kelly's Home-Care division. That was exactly the kind of steady, predictable record that the venture capital investors were looking for when it hired Buelter to run On Assignment, Inc., in 1989.

Founded by a couple of chemists, the company started out providing scientists on a temporary basis to companies that needed skilled staff for short-term projects. The concept worked fine when it was first put into practice. The problem was that On Assignment kept expanding into new areas, such as consulting and recruiting. Costs soared, and so did losses. In 1989, the red ink amounted to $1.5 million on sales of just $7 million. Buelter quickly got On Assignment back on track, and closed down the consulting and recruiting businesses. Then he went to work finding new customers for the temp business. He didn't have to look far. By 1990, many companies that had downsized jumped at the chance to hire temps to perform some of the functions of their laid-off staff. That same year, On Assignment turned profitable again. It earned 10.6 percent on annualized revenues of $39.5 million in 1994, and a lofty $44,074 Net Profits per Employee. This business is going to grow like a rocket if mandatory company-paid health insurance is approved by Congress.

ORBITAL SCIENCES CORP.

The three greatest inventions of the last 30 years, and the ones that have spawned such a large number of applications by entrepreneurial companies, are the discoveries of DNA, the semiconductor, and the satellite. The federal government, owner of many tollgate businesses, identified satellites as a business it would like to monopolize. The public, for the most part, stood back and let that happen. But in 1986, when the Challenger exploded, the government placed a moratorium on commercial launches from its space shuttles. This opened the door for entrepreneurs.

David Thompson founded Orbital Sciences Corp. in 1982 to offer commercial satellite communications services. Talk about space junkies, Thompson sent monkeys into space in homemade rockets while still in high school (two returned safely, one died). He did not contemplate getting into the launch rocket business, but when the government abdicated, he set Orbital's engineers to work on designing a low-cost rocket called Pegasus that would launch small satellites into low orbit from high-flying jets. The company's business plan calls for 26 low-orbit satellites to receive and transmit data using the Orbcomm hand-held, wireless communications device. It's strategic partner in developing Orbcomm is Teleglobe, a Montreal telecommunications device developer.

Orbital's satellites weigh as little as 50 pounds and cost as little as $1 million to build. The low capital costs mean less expensive data transmission to the user—about 25 cents from Singapore to New York for a dozen words.

Following its first launch in 1990, Orbital has put five more satellites into orbit at about 500 miles above the Earth. In June 1994 Orbital announced the acquisition of Fairchild Space & Defense Corp. for $93 million from Matra-Hachette, which will double Orbital's employee base and increase revenues to $310 million.

But since this segment of the market could become *overcrowded* with competitors, Thompson is moving his company into new markets. One new service, known as Eyeglass, offers high-resolution satellite imagery for mapping and natural resources management. Another, Seastar, uses satellites to detect changes in oceans. To add to its cachet of skilled engineers, Fairchild will bring $160 million to Orbital's revenues, mainly from space and information technology products. Overcrowding in the communications satellite market! The thought seems ridiculous that

ORBITAL SCIENCES CORP.

Chief Executive Officer:	David W. Thompson
Principal Location:	21700 Atlantic Blvd. Dulles, VA 20166
Telephone/Fax:	703-406-5506/703-406-3509
Satellite Locations:	Chandler, AZ; Pomona, CA; Boulder, CO; Chantilly, VA; Huntsville, AL
Date Founded:	1982
Description of Business:	Launches small satellites into low orbits around the Earth to transmit inexpensive data messages.
# Employees Current:	2,000
# Employees Projected by 6/30/95:	4,000
Sales 1993:	$187,311,000
Gross Profit Margin (GPM):	19.9%
Selling Expenses/Sales:	9.6%
% Sales Increase 1991–94:	+138.8%
% Change GPM 1991–94:	+28.4%
Total Debt/Net Worth:	89.1%
Net Profits Before Taxes:	$7,497,000
Operating Ratio:	4.0%
Net Profits per Employee:	$6,676
Traded On:	NASDAQ/ORBI
Principal Competitors:	Motorola, American Mobile Satellite, Loral, Qualcomm, TRW, Teledesic
# Potential Selling Sites:	Domestic: 5,000 Foreign: 15,000
Problem Company Is Attempting to Solve:	Inexpensive wireless data transmission and communication, as well as mapping and high-resolution satellite imagery services.
Solution Company Is Conveying to Problem:	The private ownership and operation of a large quantity of orbiting satellites.

there is a superfluity of providers of low-cost wireless long-distance data transfer and telecommunications. That's good for consumers of voice, data, and video communications and a realization of Marshall McLuhan's forecast of a "Global Village" back in 1964:[1]

"At the moment of Sputnik the planet becomes a global theater in which there are no spectators but only actors."

McLuhan visually united the satellite and xerography for us:[2]

". . . Sputnik created a new environment for the planet. For the first time the natural world was completely enclosed in a man-made container."

Of the new inhabitant of the Global Village, McLuhan had this to say:[3]

". . . electronic man shares much of the outlook of preliterate man, because he lives in a world of simultaneous information, which is to say, a world of resonance in which all data influence other data."

How McLuhan would have enjoyed the birth of Orbital Sciences Corp. and the sale of its services to movers of information. Will video teleconferencing companies rent space on Orbital Sciences' satellites? "If the price is right," says Chris Miner of Workstation Technologies, another Quantum Company. Most Quantum Companies are actors in the global theater and Orbital Sciences is a stage builder.

It was at Fairchild Semiconductor in 1960 that Andrew Grove was introduced to Gordon Moore and Robert Noyce, who would hatch the idea of forming Intel, one of the first semiconductor manufacturers. The ever-widening circles of entrepreneurship are elegant to observe.

---

[1] Marshall McLuhan, *The Man and His Message*, George Sanderson and Frank MacDonald, Fulcrum, Inc., Golden, CO, 1989, p. 71.
[2] Ibid., p. 72.
[3] Ibid., p. 72.

ORTHOGENE, INC.

D r. Robert F. Shaw is one of the most prolific entrepreneurs in the health-care field. He holds more than 45 issued U.S. patents and more than 40 patents pending, as well as foreign counterparts. One of his companies pioneered the field of intravenous pumps for the automated administration of parenteral fluids, and another pioneered in-vivo oximetry, two fields that have become major health-care industries. He has established companies in the fields of critical care, artificial blood, and hemostatic and endoscopic surgery.

Now Dr. Shaw and his team of world-class scientists and clinical leaders in the orthopedic field—including Ernst B. Hunziker, Clement B. Sledge, and Joseph A. Bruckwalter IV—have collaborated to develop and perfect a pharmaceutical to counteract the effects of osteoarthritis, the "wear and tear" arthritis that we have come to accept as a normal accompaniment of aging.

Osteoarthritis is caused by the thinning and loss of articular cartilage, the tissue that covers bones where they articulate with adjacent bones to form joints. Articular cartilage, unlike other tissues in the body, does not regenerate when it is damaged or worn away. When cartilage is lost on a joint surface, an osteoarthritic lesion develops, causing pain and eventually joint destruction. Loss of articular cartilage can be markedly accelerated by overuse of joints or physical injuries such as fractures, torn ligaments, and torn menisci; individuals' particular anatomy can also make them more susceptible.

Typically, osteoarthritis patients suffer many years of pain and progressive limitation of their activities. These symptoms are little relieved and in no way reversed or slowed by the billions of dollars spent on nonsteroidal, anti-inflammatory, aspirin-like drugs manufactured by almost every major pharmaceutical company. Over half a million patients each year undergo surgery for osteoarthritis of their knees, hips, and shoulders, and comparable numbers undergo surgery for osteoarthritis of the spine. This is major and painful surgery, requiring a week or more of hospitalization, six weeks or more of convalescence, and six months or more of rehabilitation. The artificial joints themselves each costs several thousand dollars; their manufacture and sale is a $2 billion industry. The total cost of an individual's surgery and hospitalization ranges from $20,000 to $40,000. The direct cost to the nation of over half a million joint replacement surgeries each year totals many billions of dollars.

ORTHOGENE, INC.

Chief Executive Officer:	Robert F. Shaw
Principal Location:	2330 Marinship Way Sausalito, CA 94965-2853
Telephone/Fax:	415-331-7800/415-331-2505
Satellite Locations:	None
Date Founded:	1986
Description of Business:	Offers genetically engineered solutions to problems associated with osteoarthritis and other bone, joint, and cartilage diseases.
# Employees Current:	5
# Employees Projected by 6/30/95:	20
Sales (Annualized) 1994:	None
Gross Profit Margin (GPM):	The company is privately-held and therefore not required to make its financial statements public.
Selling Expenses/Sales:	not available
% Sales Increase 1991–94:	not available
% Change GPM 1991–94:	not available
Total Debt/Net Worth:	not available
Net Profits Before Taxes:	not available
Net Profits per Employee:	not available
Principal Competitors:	Zimmer division of Bristol-Myers Squibb, Danek, Smith & Nephew, Biomet
# Potential Selling Sites:	Domestic: 200 million Foreign: 2 billion
Problem Company Is Attempting to Solve:	The dearth of effective treatments for osteoarthritis, which affects a large percentage of the population.
Solution Company Is Conveying to Problem:	Developed a new drug that induces regeneration of articular cartilage.

Dr. Shaw's team has filed patents on a new topical drug called Chondrogeneron, which is capable of producing regeneration of articular cartilage, resurfacing damaged joints in three to six weeks.

The drug has been demonstrated to induce the regeneration of articular cartilage in rabbits and pigs when applied locally. Decades of study involving a wide variety of bone and cartilage experiments have demonstrated that results in these two species are directly translatable to humans. Chondrogeneron can be topically applied to the osteoarthritic lesions of patients on an outpatient basis in an arthroscopic procedure requiring less than an hour.

Until now, Chondrogeneron has been manufactured under university laboratory conditions suitable for these experimental animal studies. However, with a forecasted yearly demand for millions of doses of several-milliliter vials of Chondrogeneron, the manufacturing process suitable for such large quantities should be optimized for large-scale production in an FDA-approved facility. Dr. Shaw expects the FDA approval process to take no more than a year, and says Orthogene should be treating humans experimentally by mid to late 1996.

Dr. Shaw's previous companies have addressed market needs in the hundreds of millions of dollars. Orthogene represents the largest medical problem that he has ever attempted to tackle—in the billions of dollars. "It's one of the biggest problems in health care today," says Dr. Shaw, as he rubs the spot of his own knee surgery.

PARAMETRIC TECHNOLOGY CORP.

Obscene profits! $88 million pre-tax on annualized sales of $204 million. Parametric's Operating Ratio is 43.3 percent; its GPM is 93.2 percent. The company's cash on hand at April 1994 was $169 million, roughly equal to net worth. If it doesn't make an acquisition soon or begin making strategic investments in newer technologies, Parametric will be considered much too conservative to be included in "best" lists. The stock market seems somewhat frustrated with this profits powerhouse, giving it a 23.0x P/E ratio net worth, a low ranking based on the following earnings growth rates:

	Net Profits Before Taxes $(000s)	Percentage Change
1994	$88,380	+29.1%
1993	68,470	106.1
1992	33,222	109.3
1991	15,886	-
Three-Year Average		+81.5%

What is Parametric Technology's value added that affords it this level of profit growth? Parametric's software improves the productivity of manufacturers in quantum leaps, enabling manufacturers to get their products to market at least twice as fast as before.

With Parametric's Pro/ENGINEER software, companies are driving down the cost of product development. Its team approach enables designers to consider "downstream" requirements early on, lowering final production costs. Federal-Mogul's CB Ball Bearings division integrates design-through-manufacturing with Parametric's Pro/ENGINEER software. "By ensuring accurate numerical control tool set-ups and tool paths, Pro/ENGINEER is cutting costs in every application," says Product Designer Laura Wakeford.

Pro/ENGINEER also minimizes expensive rework by displaying designs as highly accurate, realistic images. At Electro-Wire, "Pro/Engineer has all but eliminated expensive tooling errors," notes Al Vanderstuyf, Director of Engineering. "It has proven absolutely critical in managing the cost side of our business."

Manufacturers are also reducing costly prototyping by analyzing and validating designs right on the computer. "Our average number of

PARAMETRIC TECHNOLOGY CORP.

Chief Executive Officer:	Steven C. Walske
Principal Location:	128 Technology Dr. Waltham, MA 02154
Telephone/Fax:	617-398-5000/617-398-6000
Satellite Locations:	43 sales offices throughout the U.S.
Date Founded:	1986
Description of Business:	Develops, markets, and supports a family of fully integrated software products that automate the mechanical design through the manufacturing process.
# Employees Current:	900
# Employees Projected by 6/30/95:	Company withheld
Sales (Annualized) 1994:	$204,071,000
Gross Profit Margin (GPM):	93.2%
Selling Expenses/Sales:	39.6%
% Sales Increase 1991–94:	+456.4%
% Change GPM 1991–94:	-0-
Total Debt/Net Worth:	21.2%
Net Profits Before Taxes:	$88,380,000
Operating Ratio:	43.3%
Net Profits per Employee:	$98,200
Traded On:	NASDAQ/PMTC
Principal Competitors:	IBM, Computervision, EDS, Intergraph Corp., Structural Dynamics Research Corp.
# Potential Selling Sites:	Domestic: 1,000 Foreign: 5,000
Problem Company Is Attempting to Solve:	Competitive demands on manufacturers to bring high-quality products to market more rapidly and at lower costs.
Solution Company Is Conveying to Problem:	Parametric Technology is a leader in fully associative solid modeling for desktop PCs and workstations.

prototypes has dropped 30 percent, which translates into big savings," says George Henry, Precor's Vice President of Engineering.

By operating in a heterogeneous computing environment, Pro/ENGINEER further enhances cost-effectiveness. "We run Pro/ENGINEER on different platforms," reports John Celli, Director of Spacecraft Engineering at Space Systems/Loral. "With Pro/ENGINEER, we're clearly maximizing our existing hardware investment."

Pro/ENGINEER's ability to link with other software is key to both cost containment and team engineering. "With Pro/ENGINEER, we can transfer design data to related software used by other departments, which is absolutely critical to the success of our concurrent engineering environment," says Mike Kennedy, Technical Staff Senior Member at Texas Instruments.

With Pro/ENGINEER, users are able to optimize the quality of a product design. They can instantly change its shape, expand its features, and adjust its dimensions with just one keystroke—gaining time to create many more iterations.

At Medtronic Inc., Pro/ENGINEER users are turning out 40 designs for complex medical devices in the time it took to do just four with their previous systems. "Pro/ENGINEER's greatest benefit is its creative freedom," explains Principal Engineer Gus Caicedo of Archive Corporation, a tape drive manufacturer. "Anyone can be a Michelangelo of design without devoting a lifetime to the project."

Pro/ENGINEER designers are also free to evaluate each new iteration, asking "what if" questions to achieve design optimization. Restricted by its former system, engineers at Eastman Kodak's Polymer Processing division spent 80 percent of their time creating designs and only 20 percent optimizing them. "With Pro/ENGINEER, that ratio has been reversed," says Enterprise Director Darryl Miller, "allowing us to meet our mandate for developing the highest-quality component products."

With these kinds of testimonials, Parametric still spends about 40 percent of its revenues on sales and marketing costs, unusually high for a productivity-improving, high-tech software manufacturer. But its product requires hands-on sales and support by intelligent people, and this ratio is in decline as word-of-mouth kicks in.

PARCPLACE SYSTEMS, INC.

I t is a truth universally acknowledged that established organizations, entrenched in their ways, will die, fall back, or split up.

In the 1970s, Xerox Corp. created the Palo Alto Research Center, better known as Xerox PARC. The center's director, Bert Sutherland, attracted many bright people to Xerox PARC to generate innovations for the company, resulting in products such as "windows," the "mouse," the personal copier (pioneered by Canon), very large-scale integrated circuit design, Ethernet, and the notebook computer. However, Xerox's senior management chose not to attempt to commercialize any of these new products; as a result, their developers left with their innovations and have become the happier and the wealthier for it.

Adele Goldberg was one of the pioneers of object-oriented technology, another Xerox PARC innovation. Goldberg left with her ideas in 1988 and started PARCPlace Systems, acknowledging her company's origins. After raising $12 million in venture capital, she began to develop software.

Before PARCPlace, software programming techniques were fundamentally unchanged for four decades. Programming methods by and large still resemble feudal craftsmanship, with each program handcrafted from scratch. When a program needs modification, it is necessary to call in the craftsman who wrote it.

Object-oriented technology is poised to transform the software industry and create a factory approach to application development. The crafts guild is giving way to the power tools industry, leading to more rapid applications development and lower maintenance costs. Object-oriented technology permits software developers to evolve from programming individual lines of code to assembling reusable, specific-function software components called objects. PARCPlace is at the frontier of re-engineering organizations based on the flow of information and work. The company may someday be spoken of in the same manner that we describe Charles Lindberg's flights as ushering in air mail.

Object-oriented technology represents a new approach to developing software applications. The basic concept of object-oriented technology is to construct software in terms of objects, independent modules that can be modified independently, reused in new applications, and reused and extended to create new objects. Thus, object-oriented technology can offer substantial productivity gains by enabling programmers to reuse

PARCPLACE SYSTEMS, INC.

Chief Executive Officer:	William P. Lyons
Principal Location:	999 East Arques Ave. Sunnyvale, CA 94086
Telephone/Fax:	408-481-9090/408-481-0214
Satellite Locations:	Sales offices in Colorado, Georgia, Illinois, Massachusetts, Michigan, New York, Oregon, Texas, U.K., Germany
Date Founded:	1988
Description of Business:	Designs, develops, markets, and supports object-oriented programming tools, a technology that represents a paradigm shift in software development.
# Employees Current:	177
# Employees Projected by 6/30/95:	Company withheld
Sales (Annualized) 1994:	$26,631,000
Gross Profit Margin (GPM):	73.0%
Selling Expenses/Sales:	39.6%
% Sales Increase 1991–94:	+492.6%
% Change GPM 1991–94:	+5.3%
Total Debt/Net Worth:	25.7%
Net Profits Before Taxes:	$2,141,000
Operating Ratio:	8.0%
Net Profits per Employee:	$12,096
Traded On:	NASDAQ/PARQ
Principal Competitors:	Borland, Gupta, Knowledgeware, Microsoft, Powersoft, Uniface
# Potential Selling Sites:	Domestic: 5,000 Foreign: 15,000
Problem Company Is Attempting to Solve:	To remain competitive, many companies need to create new ways of organizing their internal decision-making processes, management structures, and methods of exchanging information.
Solution Company Is Conveying to Problem:	Lets programmers represent business models in software in a way that corresponds to real-world business relationships.

more of their application code in developing new applications or adding new functionality to existing applications.

This technology allows programmers to represent business models in software applications in a way that more closely corresponds to real-world business relationships. The goal is to eliminate the requirement of translating a business problem into lines of software code and instead allow modeling of the business problem with software objects that directly represent the business model. Object-oriented programming allows prototyping of partial systems, which can then be extended and modified incrementally, thereby eliminating the need to define the entire scope of the business model at the onset of the development project. This enables organizations to start the development process earlier, build and refine the business model as the system is being developed, and modify the system dynamically in response to evolving business requirements. In addition to providing for direct modeling of business processes, the distribution of functionality among objects and the ability of objects to communicate with each other makes object-oriented technology ideally suited for the client/server environment.

PARCPlace purchased $3 million worth of software from Solborne in September 1992, resulting in a book loss. William P. Lyons came aboard as CEO in the same year. He had been CEO of Ashton-Tate Corp., a desktop database company, where he dealt with chaos and rapid growth. Lyons got a firm hand on the rudder, and for its fiscal year ended March 31, 1994, PARCPlace earned $2.1 million on revenues of $26.6 million. The stock market has fallen in love with PARCPlace, anointing it with a P/E ratio of 56.0x in mid-1994.

PHENIX BIOCOMPOSITES, INC.

Consumer demand, cacophonous environmentalists, and incessant regulation are driving building materials manufacturers to produce products from post-consumer waste and to recycle their own scraps. One such effort sprung full-born from the physics department at Mankato State University after scientists there heard about a Minnesota sixth-grader, Molly DeGezelle, who experimented with old newspapers, Elmer's Glue, and her mother's blender for a science fair project. The result was a sturdy, nailable "Mollyboard." The process has been refined into "a whole new technology," by Phenix Biocomposites, says Rod Skillman, the company's CEO. "We feel like it's akin to the invention of plastics, only this time with positive global impact for our mountains of waste paper." The new material—called Environ—can replace wood or stone in a variety of building, furniture, and decorative applications. It has the appearance of polished granite, yet can be fastened, sawed, milled, routed, drilled, and worked with traditional woodworking tools; glued together with standard wood glues and standard construction adhesives; and glued and joined together with traditional woods, unlike other solid-surface, hydrocarbon-based, plastic materials, or real stone.

The material has been tested in-house and by Twin City Testing Labs under standards associated with hardboard and particleboard. It currently meets all specified conditions for interior applications and most requirements for protected exterior application.

In addition to Environ, Phenix Biocomposites is creating a new class of materials for use in high-humidity environments in countertop applications; in biomass-oriented strand products and synthetic-oriented strand products in structural applications; in custom inlays; and in extrusions for use in millwork.

Phenix Biocomposites is one of a handful of eco products companies that are attempting to capture market share from the Weyerhauesers and Boise Cascades of the world. The company received a $1 million award from the Alternative Agricultural Research and Commercialization Center to bring Environ to market. It is in the process of building its own sales and distribution network. Soon we'll be going to "Environland" for Environ building materials, rather than to conventional lumberyards.

PHENIX BIOCOMPOSITES, INC.

Chief Executive Officer:	Rodney D. Skillman
Principal Location:	1511 Gault St. St. Peter, MN 56082
Telephone/Fax:	507-931-9787/507-931-5573
Satellite Locations:	Mankato State University
Date Founded:	1992
Description of Business:	Produces a composite building material that looks like granite, and acts like wood, but is made from used newspaper and soybeans.
# Employees Current:	35
# Employees Projected by 6/30/95:	70
Sales (Annualized) 1994:	The company is a start-up and has only modest sales to date. It does not make its financial information public.
Gross Profit Margin (GPM):	not available
Selling Expenses/Sales:	not available
% Sales Increase 1991–94:	not available
% Change GPM 1991–94:	not available
Total Debt/Net Worth:	not available
Net Profits Before Taxes:	not available
Operating Ratio:	not available
Net Profits per Employee:	not available
Principal Competitors:	AbTco, Fiber Stone Quarries, Schoolcraft, CoverAge, Fypon
# Potential Selling Sites:	Domestic: 15 million Foreign: 15 million
Problem Company Is Attempting to Solve:	One of our planet's universal problems is the overuse of our natural resources: Rain forests are being depleted at an alarming rate; e.g., the planet loses forests equal in size to the state of Wisconsin every year.
Solution Company Is Conveying to Problem:	Phenix Biocomposites has developed a new artificial material that can replace wood or stone in a variety of building, furniture, and decorative applications.

PLEASANT COMPANY

D oll companies are generally run by men, who produce female dolls according to *their* image of what dolls should look like. When they create a doll for girls, it is, like Barbie, a highly sexual creation that encourages the little girls who adore it to think of their sexuality long before they reach puberty. (Barbie was actually invented by a woman but was acquired by the male-dominated Mattel.) "This takes away an important part of their childhood," Pleasant Rowland says. Her dolls go directly against this trend. They are not sexual objects but rather instruments of learning and adventure as well as playthings.

Pleasant Company has developed a line of six dolls, representing six different American ethnic groups. All the dolls, and their accessories, are designed to educate.

There are six or so short books to accompany each doll. In the first of the black doll's books, *Meet Addy*, young readers find her living in slavery. An advisory panel consisting mainly of black women, including psychologists, educators, and entertainer Melba Moore, concluded that slavery was a crucial part of Addy's story.

The other dolls include a pioneer girl, Kirsten; a World War II patriot, Molly; and the cosmopolitan, turn-of-the-century Samantha, the collection's most popular character. Each doll has her own wardrobe, and there are coordinated clothes to fit young owners.

A German company manufactures the dolls. Vendors in the Far East, Sweden, Spain, Russia, and the United States make the period accessories. The clothes come from China, and the furniture is from Taiwan. Trunks that holds the dolls' clothing are made in the United States.

Each doll is priced at $200; accessories include a doll's table and chairs for $75 and a trunk for $175. At those prices, it is no surprise that parents account for 75 percent of sales and adult collectors account for about 7 percent. The company's catalogs are mailed to 19 million homes.

Although the dolls and their trappings are the line's most eye-catching offerings, Rowland considers the books the heart of the collection because they enable girls to get to know the characters and develop a continuing relationship with them. The books—$5.95 for paperbacks and $12.95 for hardcovers, with boxed sets of six available at a slight discount—are the only part of the line available in stores, mainly book chains. (The books are also available through the catalogs.)

PLEASANT COMPANY

Chief Executive Officer:	Pleasant T. Rowland
Principal Location:	8400 Fairway Place Middleton, WI 53562-2554
Telephone/Fax:	608-836-4848/608-836-0761
Satellite Locations:	none
Date Founded:	1986
Description of Business:	Produces books, dolls, and accessories that educate young girls about growing up in different periods of American history.
# Employees Current:	365
# Employees Projected by 6/30/95:	Company withheld
Sales (Annualized) 1994:	$90,000,000
Gross Profit Margin (GPM):	The company is privately-held and does not release its financial statements to the public.
Selling Expenses/Sales:	not available
% Sales Increase 1991–94:	not available
% Change GPM 1991–94:	not available
Total Debt/Net Worth:	not available
Net Profits Before Taxes:	not available
Operating Ratio:	not available
Net Profits per Employee:	not available
Principal Competitors:	Mattel, Fisher Bros., Marx, Lewis Maloof
# Potential Selling Sites:	Domestic: 20 million Foreign: 20 million
Problem Company Is Attempting to Solve:	Toys that are educational and represent positive values are virtually nonexistent.
Solution Company Is Conveying to Problem:	Pleasant Company brings American history to life through its books and doll collections.

Pleasant Company class-markets rather than mass-markets its dolls. It has done no licensing. It spends no money on advertising. "We are in for the long pull," says Rowland. "If we wanted to lower our prices and sell through the chains, our sales would go to $200 million and everyone would copy us."

Now Pleasant Company is watching its competitors try to figure it out.

THE PROGRESSIVE CORP.

The more confusion and the less reliable information in a marketplace, the more money service providers can charge and the higher their profits. This is especially true in the marketplace for legal services, where laypeople are provided with zero information by the courts and, unless they have a good deal of time and intelligence, must resort to hiring lawyers. The more complex the area, and the more dire the consequences, the greater the fees that lawyers can charge and be paid.

Another example is auto insurance. Who among us knows the claims-paying record of our underwriter, or whether we have paid the lowest possible rate? Not many of us.

Progressive Corp.'s CEO, Peter B. Lewis, is a man who "reveres honesty." At Progressive, he says, "We adhere to high ethical standards, report completely, encourage disclosing bad news, and welcome disagreement." It is not surprising, then, that Progressive became the first auto insurer to offer consumers comparable, competitive quotes for their specific situation from the companies with the largest market share in their state; perhaps it is not surprising, either, that some standard carriers charge more to low-risk drivers than Progressive charges its high-risk drivers. Progressive's online information service is currently available to consumers in several states, and the company plans to take it nationwide.

Progressive is a low-cost, high-profit insurance underwriter. It makes a profit on its insurance business, a rarity in the insurance industry. Its Combined Ratio was 94.9 percent in 1994 (annualized), and the company has a Loss Ratio of 56.4 percent, which means that it pays out a little more than 50 cents on the dollar. That speaks for a superb underwriting department: trained personnel who know which risks to buy and which not to buy.

"Six years ago, Progressive was enjoying what was our greatest year until then," Lewis recalls. Then the company was "shocked into action" when California voters passed Proposition 103, "threatening auto insurance as we know it. It opened our eyes to auto insurance consumers' anger and mistrust and our vulnerability to capricious legislation and regulation," says Lewis. "Consumer dissatisfaction with auto insurance appeared to put Progressive's existence in danger; we knew we had to do something. We pulled back in California, but the situation required much more positive action.

THE PROGRESSIVE CORP.

Chief Executive Officer:	Peter B. Lewis
Principal Location:	6300 Wilson Mills Rd. Mayfield Village, OH 44143
Telephone/Fax:	216-461-5000/216-446-7936
Satellite Locations:	Tampa, FL
Date Founded:	1965
Description of Business:	Underwrites nonstandard property and casualty insurance for people canceled and rejected by other insurers.
# Employees Current:	6,101
# Employees Projected by 6/30/95:	Company withheld
Net Premiums (Annualized) 1994:	$1,955,600
Combined Ratio:	94.9%
Loss Ratio:	56.4%
% Premiums Increase 1991–94:	+147.6%
% Change Combined Ratio:	−8.4%
Total Debt/Net Worth:	302.0%
Net Profits Before Taxes:	$364,800,000
Operating Ratio:	18.7%
Net Profits per Employee:	$59,793
Traded On:	NYSE/PGR
Principal Competitors:	Allstate, State Farm, Farmers, Penn Central
# Potential Selling Sites:	Domestic: 5,000,000 Foreign: not applicable
Problem Company Is Attempting to Solve:	Conventional insurers are quick to cancel policyholders following an accident, suspended license, or bankruptcy. Where do these individuals go for auto insurance?
Solution Company Is Conveying to Problem:	Progressive underwrites these higher-risk drivers.

"About the same time, we learned that Allstate had passed us in total U.S. volume on our specialty of nonstandard auto insurance, making it our most threatening competitor. After 25 years of observing Progressive's success, Allstate and other competitors, like the Penn Central companies, recognized that our high expense ratios and wide profit margins gave them a perfect opportunity to take market share from us by mimicking our programs, operating at lower cost, and accepting slimmer profit margins. We saw that Allstate, with its distribution and data advantages, could overwhelm us unless we acted quickly and decisively." Lewis was compelled to act like an inside raider and tighten the company's cost structure.

"Auto owners and operators regard Progressive in direct proportion to how our service, quality, and cost compare to their options," Lewis says. "In five years of intensive study of U.S. auto owners and operators, we are learning their needs and attitudes. We have concluded that Progressive has an opportunity to continue to grow profitably if we work within our highly regulated, highly competitive, very staid industry, figuring out how to lower consumers' costs and improve their experience sufficiently to turn their anger with auto insurance to delight."

Turning anger to delight. What a remarkable business challenge. And to do that through the company's 30,000 independent agents is an uphill battle of extraordinary proportions. Any of the competitors in the $115.3 billion marketplace could have used the available information to win consumers' confidence; only Progressive, one of the smallest players, one with a mere 1.5 percent market share, chose to do it. Its profit margins did not suffer—they improved. In 1991, net income before taxes was $32.9 million, or 2.5 percent, on revenues of $1.3 billion. A mere two years later, net income before taxes had grown to $373.1 million, or 18.7 percent on revenues of $1.8 billion.

This remarkable company's stock trades on the New York Stock Exchange at an unprogressive P/E ratio of 12.0x. Management should delist and move to NASDAQ, where growth stocks flourish and innovation is rewarded.

QUALCOMM, INC.

Qualcomm, Inc. may become to telecommunications what Microsoft has become to personal computers. In 1995 it plans to introduce Code Division Multiple Access (CDMA), a technology that will bring the capabilities of the personal computer to the cellular telephone. If it succeeds, and if wireless communications can compete with fiber optics in the quality and price arenas, then Qualcomm could be licensing CDMA to all the telephone carriers in the same way that nearly all PC manufacturers pay licensing fees to Microsoft for its ubiquitous DOS operating system.

Here's some background: Cellular systems operate in a total spectrum space of 50 megahertz (millions of cycles per second), in two frequency bands near the 800-megahertz level. The U.S. cellular telephone industry is a duopoly (i.e., the FCC awards only two licenses to provide cellular service in any given cellular market), and these cellular carriers compete intensely on cost of service, system performance, transmission quality, and other bases. In certain large markets where carriers have reached system capacity on their existing analog-based systems, they are transitioning to digital systems. The cellular industry association approved a competitive digital system in 1989 known as TDMA, for Time Division Multiple Access. TDMA's signal processing technique is incompatible with the company's CDMA; thus, if one competitor in a market adopts TDMA, it is unlikely to license CDMA. However, CDMA has 10 to 15 times the capacity of TDMA.

Qualcomm has licensed AT&T, Motorola, and Northern Telecom to manufacture network equipment. It has licensed Oki, Alps, and Nokia to develop subscriber equipment that utilizes the company's CDMA technology. But AT&T, L. M. Ericsson, Hughes Network Systems, Motorola, Northern Telecom, and Oki have invested heavily in TDMA as well and are developing TDMA equipment. McCaw Cellular Communications and Southwestern Bell, two cellular carriers, have installed TDMA equipment in some of their markets. CDMA's advantage is that it uses the entire 12.5 megahertz of the cellular bandwidth, whereas TDMA and analog systems use a frequency in one cell out of seven.

Cellular companies are paralyzed with fear of backing the wrong system. To make matters worse, Steinbrecher Corp. of Burlington, Massachusetts, has announced that it is able to put an entire cellular base station—now requiring some 1,000 square feet and costing $1.5 million—in a briefcase-size box that costs $100,000. Moreover, the box,

QUALCOMM, INC.

Chief Executive Officer:	Irwin M. Jacobs
Principal Location:	6455 Lusk Blvd. San Diego, CA 92121
Telephone/Fax:	619-658-4820/619-658-2501
Satellite Locations:	none
Description of Business:	Qualcomm is a leader in digital wireless technologies. It operates the OmmTRACS system, a satellite-based, two-way mobile communications and tracking system.
Date Founded:	1985
# Employees Current:	900
# Employees Projected by 6/30/95:	Company withheld
Sales (Annualized) 1994:	$192,363,000
Gross Profit Margin (GPM):	62.9%
Selling Expenses/Sales:	9.6%
% Sales Increase 1991–94	+213.9%
% Change GPM 1990–94:	−5.2%
Total Debt/Net Worth:	27.9%
Net Profits Before Taxes:	$21,328,000
Operating Ratio:	11.1%
Net Profits per Employee:	$23,698
Traded On:	NASDAQ/QCOM
Principal Competitors:	Motorola, American Mobile Satellite Corp., Rockwell, Nextel, Mitsubishi
# Potential Selling Sites:	Domestic: 25,000 Foreign: 75,000
Problem Company Is Attempting to Solve:	How to deliver high-quality voice, data, and video service anytime, anywhere.
Solution Company Is Conveying to Problem:	Qualcomm plans to offer cellular telephone carriers CDMA that digitally expands one channel to more than 30, then reassembles it at the receiving end.

known as the MiniCell, is superior to the existing cellular base station; it is more capacious and more easily programmable, and it can accommodate stores of different models of cellular handsets.

US West, PacTel Cellular, and Bell Atlantic Mobile Systems have all announced agreements to purchase CDMA cellular equipment for deployment in their markets. These systems will use Qualcomm's CDMA technology in equipment to be manufactured by the company and its licensees, Motorola and Northern Telecom. Qualcomm recently signed a letter of intent for a multiyear agreement with US West, under which Qualcomm will provide the company with a minimum of 36,000 CDMA dual-mode digital cellular phones.

PacTel announced plans to offer CDMA digital cellular service in its Los Angeles market beginning in early 1995, with future installations planned in its San Diego, Atlanta, and Sacramento markets. PacTel's multiphased CDMA infrastructure installation in Los Angeles is scheduled to begin later this year, enabling the system to be fully tested and widely deployed prior to the start of commercial service. Network equipment will be supplied by Motorola Nortel, a joint venture of Motorola and Northern Telecom. PacTel also announced an agreement to purchase more than 30,000 dual-mode CDMA portable cellular telephones from Oki.

Bell Atlantic announced plans for initial deployment of CDMA in its Connecticut and Rhode Island markets in 1994, with future installations planned in its other existing markets in the Mid-Atlantic.

Of the telecommunications companies competing for market share in the wireless world, these are the wild ones. They have gone back as far as it is possible to go toward primitivism. The stock market loves companies that do not fear hand-to-hand combat on the frontier of cyberspace. It gives Qualcomm a P/E ratio of 50.0x.

QUANTUM HEALTH RESOURCES, INC.

Quantum Health Resources, Inc. (QHRI) was founded in June 1988 to provide therapies and related support services to patients affected with certain chronic disorders. The company's original focus was hemophilia, a bleeding disorder that occurs in some 20,000 people in the United States. Now the company has developed a program called Chronicare for all the chronic diseases it treats. The program focuses on the unique needs of patients with rare chronic disorders that require costly, long-term, recurring therapy. The company not only delivers therapy to these patients but assists them and their families in coping with the psychosocial issues related to their disease and in receiving reimbursement for the care. QHRI also provides the more traditional home infusion therapies, such as antibiotic and parenteral and enteral nutrition. It currently delivers its services through 23 branches and 16 satellites throughout the United States, having expanded through a combination of internal growth and acquisitions.

The treatment of hemophilia accounted for 60.2 percent of QHRI's total revenue in 1993. Hemophilia is an inherited, chronic bleeding disorder caused by the lack or improper functioning of a key blood plasma protein that enables blood to clot. Treatment involves the use of intravenous infusions of anti-hemophilic Factor VIII products, which have, until recently, been available only in a form derived from blood plasma. More recently, biotechnology-derived recombinant forms of Factor VIII have become available.

QHRI is the second-largest provider of products and services to the hemophiliac population behind Caremark and currently has about 15 percent of the total market, which is estimated at some $800 million. This market is growing to some degree because of the ongoing conversion to higher-priced recombinant therapy.

Other chronic diseases QHRI treats using its Chronicare model include:

Alpha$_1$-Antitrypsin Deficiency—This inherited disease is related to a deficiency in the alpha$_1$-protinase inhibitor, which results in damage to the lungs and progressive emphysema. QHRI estimates that about 6,000 people have this disorder and are in need of therapy. According to the company, about 1,800 patients are currently being treated with Prolastin, a purified form of the inhibitor derived from human plasma. This product is approved for treating patients who have overt signs of emphysema; while it has not been definitively proven that the compound

QUANTUM HEALTH RESOURCES, INC.

Chief Executive Officer:	Douglas H. Stickney
Principal Location:	790 The City Dr. South Orange, CA 92668
Telephone/Fax:	714-750-1610/714-750-3235
Satellite Locations:	39 satellite offices throughout the U.S.
Date Founded:	1988
Description of Business:	Provides therapy and support services to patients affected by chronic disorders requiring lifelong therapy.
# Employees Current:	589
# Employees Projected by 6/30/95:	Company withheld
Sales 1993:	$201,729,000
Gross Profit Margin (GPM):	26.9%
Selling Expenses/Sales:	not available
% Sales Increase 1991–93:	+105.8%
% Change GPM 1991–93:	+3.1%
Total Debt/Net Worth:	124.0%
Net Profits Before Taxes:	$27,877,300
Operating Ratio:	13.8%
Net Profits per Employee:	$47,330
Traded On:	NASDAQ/QHRI
Principal Competitors:	Caremark, Homecare Management, Vivra
# Potential Selling Sites:	Domestic: 15,000 Foreign: 30,000
Problem Company Is Attempting to Solve:	Providing long-term care to patients with chronic illnesses can be among the most expensive forms of health care.
Solution Company Is Conveying to Problem:	For the five niches—five rare chronic illnesses—the company has selected, it delivers long-term care on a capitated basis.

slows the progression of emphysema, the medical community generally believes that weekly infusions of the compound, at home, do have merit. Of the patients currently being treated, QHRI believes that it has about a 25 percent market share.

Primary Immunodeficiency Diseases (PIDs)—These include a variety of chronic disorders, all of which are related to the inability of the immune system to produce sufficient quantities of immunoglobulin to protect against infection. About 7,000 people are thought to suffer from these diseases. Treatment involves replacement therapy with immune globulin prepared from human plasma. Monthly intravenous administration of immune globulin in the patient's home has become the standard therapy.

Gaucher Disease—This is a chronic disorder resulting from an enzyme deficiency and the accumulation of fats in the spleen, liver, and bone marrow. Between 2,000 and 3,000 people are believed to suffer from this disease. A modified form of the deficient enzyme is available under the brand name Ceredase, a product approved by the FDA and administered intravenously.

The managers at QHRI want to stay one step ahead of managed-care companies and their plans to capitate patients—using a flat per-member, per-month (instead of fee-for-service) fee. QHRI is planning to convert to capitation as well, by arranging for the payers—HMOs and PPOs—to charge their enrollees $150 per month and carving out 70 to 80 cents per member for QHRI. A one-million-member HMO would pay QHRI about $9 million per year, notwithstanding the number of hemophiliacs in the HMO. A risky plan, but a necessary one.

Gatekeeper companies, even specialty ones such as QHRI, have the implicit responsibility to take leadership roles in their markets and not to be continually reactive. QHRI could do worse than create its own PPO for its market and become proactive ahead of the managed-care companies. Its P/E ratio would move up from a laconic 15.0x.

QUORUM HEALTH GROUP, INC.

here are several venture capital funds in the United States whose track records in selecting and monitoring early-stage companies are so outstanding and whose dealings with investors—private, institutional, or public—are so notably fair that to ignore the portfolio companies they bring to market is to miss outstanding investment opportunities. One such venture fund, known for its Silicon Valley picks, is Kleiner, Perkins, Caulfield & Byers. Another, known for its Eastern investments in medical and computer-related deals, is Welsh, Carson, Anderson & Stowe (WCAS). Quorum Health Group, Inc. is a WCAS deal, and that is reason enough to pay serious attention to it.

Quorum was formed in 1990 to buy or manage acute-care hospitals of 100 to 400 beds in markets of 100,000 to 400,000 people. WCAS was approached by knowledgeable hospital managers in 1989 and was persuaded that there were opportunities in the health-care delivery market to catch some falling hospitals, turn them around, and send them skyward once again. WCAS decided to dig for gold in this deep vein. It loaned and invested approximately $73 million, for which it received 21.7 million shares of stock between 1989 and 1993, at an average price of $3.36 per share.

The company bet on the right jockeys. James E. Dalton Jr., Quorum's CEO, and his team bought 11 hospitals and entered into contracts to manage 260 hospitals, producing net profits before taxes of $38,542,000 on revenues of $442,257,000 for the fiscal year ended June 30, 1993. That is an amazing achievement in three years. One of Quorum's biggest bites was its $340 million cash purchase of Charter Medical's 10 acute-care hospitals in August 1993. Charter was founded in 1969 by William A. Fickling Jr., who leveraged everything he could find to buy hospitals. Charter's fall from grace 25 years later is testament to the treatise that leverage is a bountiful mother who sometimes eats her offspring.

WCAS approached underwriters in late 1992 and asked them to join it in loaning $300 million to Quorum to keep its acquisition machine rolling. It sold the underwriters Quorum stock at $6 per share. The underwriters would earn a fee on Quorum's IPO in May 1994, but they took a significant risk as well: a $112.5 million risk. Then in September 1993, WCAS bought $42.9 million of Quorum's stock at $7.50 per share, a price *above* what the underwriters paid. Mind you, WCAS controlled Quorum and could have set the price per share anywhere they wanted. They are not "LIFO" (last-in-first-out) investors, and their record of

QUORUM HEALTH GROUP, INC.

Chief Executive Officer:	James E. Dalton Jr.
Principal Location:	155 Franklin Rd. Brentwood, TN 37027
Telephone/Fax:	615-320-7979/615-340-5853
Satellite Locations:	11 owned and 260 managed hospitals
Date Founded:	1990
Description of Business:	Owns and manages acute-care hospitals in 44 states; is growing by acquiring inefficiently managed 100- to 400-bed hospitals in medium-size markets.
# Employees Current:	8,500
# Employees Projected by 6/30/95:	Company withheld
Sales Annualized 1994:	$644,306,000
Gross Profit Margin (GPM):	61.5%
Operating Expenses/Sales:	8.7%
% Sales Increase 1991–94:	+634.1%
% Change GPM 1991–94:	+59.7%
Total Debt/Net Worth:	276.8%
Net Profits Before Taxes:	$50,589,000
Operating Ratio:	7.9%
Net Profits per Employee:	$5,952
Traded On:	NASDAQ/QHGI
Principal Competitors:	Healthcare Management Associates, Humana, National Medical Enterprises, among numerous hospitals
# Potential Selling Sites:	Domestic: 2,500 Foreign: not applicable
Problem Company Is Attempting to Solve:	There are more than 5,000 hospitals in the U.S.—the most inefficiently run hospitals will go out of business or be acquired in the next five to ten years.
Solution Company Is Conveying to Problem:	Quorum manages acute-care hospitals *profitably*. It will acquire or manage many of the poorly run hospitals.

sticking with their investments and treating every group fairly is significant in an era in which some venture capitalists have been criticized for personal greed and atavistic behavior.

Quorum is not an easy business to operate and to grow. Hospital managers must deal with physicians, and that is frequently more punishment than anyone deserves. They must also deal with HMOs and PPOs who are dictating price to them. This is not how hospital managers are used to being treated. Managers used to pay whatever price the providers put on their services; thinking wasn't a requirement. Now it is. Are there enough thinking hospital managers to keep hospitals afloat in this age of downsizing? Probably not. Hence the need for Quorum.

The *1993 Almanac of Hospital Financial & Operating Indicators* reports that there is a widening gap between the best- and worst-performing hospitals and that the major challenge in the U.S. hospital industry is to achieve further cost reductions without sacrificing quality. Hospital managers are afraid; they are sitting on cash and either not paying bills or paying them more slowly in order to get the attention of their vendors—pharmaceutical, device, and service companies—to cut costs. According to the report, the average Operating Ratio of the 2,000 U.S. hospitals in the study was 2.9 percent. It is 8.7 percent for Quorum. The best-performing hospitals in the country had an average Operating Ratio of 6.2 percent, while the worst-performing hospitals were at 1.6 percent. Quorum's ratio is above the best. The hospital industry's debt-to-worth ratio is running at 106.8 percent, indicating an unwilling-ness to borrow money for capital improvements. Quorum's debt-to-worth ratio at March 31, 1994, was an aggressive 276.8 percent. Indeed, the average age of hospital plants has increased 10 percent, to 8.2 years. The plant is getting older, the equipment is aging, and the operating ratios—cash flows—are shrinking.

It took guts to start Quorum, but if you review its year-to-year financial results since 1990, you will see that its profit margins and its cash flow are improving. As it grows and puts more hospitals under management contracts, the company will be able to duke it out with the HMOs, PPOs, and health insurers, which should reflect positively on Quorum's future profitability.

RES-CARE, INC.

A number of problems indigenous to American society are elegantly addressed by Res-Care, including downsizing of the health-care industry, privatization of state agencies, and homelessness among the mentally retarded and developmentally disabled (MR/DD).

An estimated 3 percent of the U.S. population has at some point in their lives some form of mental retardation or developmental disability. Approximately 1.6 percent, or just over half of these individuals, require some form of lifelong care. These figures imply a total MR/DD population of about 3.5 million. Roughly 90 percent live at home and are usually cared for by parents or other close relatives. An estimated 350,000 MR/DD individuals live in staffed residential settings or supported living arrangements in their community.

Politicians are loath to yield control of the budgets for state agencies—even those for non-voters such as prisoners and the mentally retarded—but as governments ineluctably sink into red ink, they have to turn over agencies such as mental institutions to facilities management contractors like Res-Care. The latter do not increase the budgets but rather make a profit, if they are able, on the budget given them. Res-Care's GPM is 12.2 percent, up from 10.5 percent in 1991, reflecting the company's improved efficiency.

Current chairman Jim Fornear founded Res-Care in 1974 to operate the Whitney Young Job Corps Center in Shelbyville, Kentucky. Res-Care added other Job Corps contracts and later expanded into the operation and management of MR/DD facilities.

As of December 1993, Res-Care operated or managed 215 MR/DD facilities in nine states, serving approximately 2,700 residents. These facilities consist of two large state institutions managed by the company, ten larger private facilities, 18 clusters of group homes, and four supported living programs. The group-home clusters generally consist of 8 to 21 group homes with six to eight residents each. Revenues from this division were $83.7 million in 1993. Res-Care was recently approved to provide supported living services in New Mexico.

Res-Care also manages seven Job Corps Centers in three states and Puerto Rico for the Department of Labor. These centers can house nearly 1,900 students. Training services revenues for 1993 were $27.5 million.

Res-Care co-founded Home Care Affiliates (HCA) in 1986. HCA provides in-home nursing services and home infusion therapy. As of December 1993, Home Care Affiliates operated 49 home health agencies

RES-CARE, INC.

Chief Executive Officer:	Ronald G. Geary
Principal Location:	1300 Embassy Square Louisville, KY 40299
Telephone/Fax:	502-491-3464/502-491-8514
Satellite Locations:	Facilities in Kentucky, Florida, Tennessee, Indiana, Louisiana, West Virginia, Nebraska
Date Founded:	1974
Description of Business:	Provides residences and support to mentally retarded people.
# Employees Current:	3,900
# Employees Projected by 6/30/95:	Company withheld
Sales (Annualized) 1994:	$120,187,000
Gross Profit Margin (GPM):	12.2%
Selling Expenses/Sales:	not available
% Revenue Increase 1991–94:	+154.6%
% Change GPM 1991–94:	+16.2%
Total Debt/Net Worth:	78.1%
Net Profits Before Taxes:	$9,345,000
Operating Ratio:	7.8%
Net Profits per Employee:	$2,396
Traded On:	NASDAQ/RSCR
Principal Competitors:	State agencies and nonprofit organizations
# Potential Selling Sites:	Domestic: 1,500 facilities Foreign: 3,500 facilities
Problem Company Is Attempting to Solve:	There are approximately 3.5 million MR/DD people in the U.S. living with family members or in residential settings, excluding perhaps half again that number of homeless MR/DD, and the financial drain is becoming a serious issue.
Solution Company Is Conveying to Problem:	Res-Care provides residences and support services and manages facilities under contract to state agencies.

in Florida, Indiana, Tennessee, and Kentucky. Res-Care now owns 68 percent of HCA, and HCA's chairman and president each hold 16 percent. HCA generated $57.3 million in revenues during 1993.

In the past, mental retardation was treated like an illness, and people with MR/DD were housed in large state institutions. Lately, a more progressive, compassionate viewpoint has emerged. As recently as 1977 there were an estimated 150,000 MR/DD people living in state institutions; by 1992 this number had dropped to 78,000, and the decline is expected to continue. The service model now stresses active, customized programs for those with MR/DD. This includes greater independence, more rights, and increased integration into the community. Downsizing of large institutions should result in increased demand for companies such as Res-Care that are able to provide group-home and supported living arrangements.

Over the past five years, funding for community-based MR/DD services has been growing at an annual rate of 13 percent compared to 6 percent for the traditional state institutions. The efficient private operators have an opportunity to attract some of these funds by providing services for the states.

Consolidation in the industry favors the larger, multistate companies such as Res-Care. Smaller operators face a number of challenges: administrative and operational demands; complex state and federal regulations and standards for care that make compliance difficult (mandatory licenser surveys are conducted each year by the states and by the Health Care Financing Administration); high turnover among the direct-care staff; and sometimes difficult clients, making everyday operations a challenging task. Overworked smaller operators may either exit the business or lose their contracts when they run into problems renewed. Res-Care, a proven operator, will grow by acquisitions as well as by taking over the management of agencies from states.

RESEARCH MANAGEMENT CONSULTANTS, INC.

Women like Raydean Acevedo are changing the way the consulting business is conducted in the United States. Shoehorned in by the 8(a) minority contract, they are building important corporations that principally hire women consultants who walk in to the hot spots that old-line government contractors cannot deal with and, like a new broom, sweep out the trouble. Research Management Consultants, Inc. (RMCI) is that kind of firm. It has not only won every award available to it, but it is building a caring and sensitive employee base that reorders the priorities of wealth, career, and character in an important way.

Acevedo has steered RMCI into one of the fastest-growing companies in the United States. The company tackles large, tough assignments for the FAA, the U.S. Department of the Navy, and government contractors including the Raytheon Corp., EG & G, and the Reed Group, a specialist in gathering data in the medical and insurance industries. Acevedo is an on-site, hands-on manager who flies to each of the companies' job sites once every two or three weeks. She says she has yet to take a two-week vacation. However, she loves what she does and is dedicated to her staff. She makes it a point to make herself visible to all her employees and is committed to ensuring that they are working in an environment in which they are comfortable.

A big part of RMCI's success, Acevedo believes, is a highly trained and educated staff of professionals, most with advanced degrees, and an organization structured for maximum response to client needs. Unlike the multilayered government and corporate organizations that RMCI typically serves, she explains, the company functions under a compact, two-level structure comprising the technical consulting team and a division director. Acevedo focuses on overall operating direction.

Her staff is diverse both in terms of technical capabilities and background. While this diversity poses challenges, Acevedo says, it also gives her a good perspective in the final decision-making process and is the source of her company's strength. Acevedo's staff of 240 is 60 percent female, with a liberal sprinkling of African Americans, Asian Americans, and Hispanics. Revenue is growing more than 33 percent per year and employee growth at about 20 percent.

The company is decentralized geographically for maximum proximity to client sites. Although RMCI is based in Camarillo, California and does its accounting there, four of its six divisions are located in McLean

RESEARCH MANAGEMENT CONSULTANTS, INC.

Chief Executive Officer:	Raydean Acevedo
Principal Location:	601 Daily Dr. Camarillo, CA 93010
Telephone/Fax:	805-987-5538/805-987-2808
Satellite Locations:	Norfolk and McLean, VA; San Diego and Bakersfield, CA; Atlanta, GA; Denver, CO; Washington, D.C.
Date Founded:	1987
Description of Business:	Provides scientific and technical consulting services to government agencies and technology-driven corporations.
# Employees Current:	240
# Employees Projected by 6/30/95:	300
Sales (Annualized) 1994:	$25 million
Gross Profit Margin (GPM):	Company is privately-held and not required to make its financial statements public.
Selling Expenses/Sales:	not available
% Sales Increase 1991–94:	not available
% Change GPM 1991–94:	not available
Total Debt/Net Worth:	not available
Net Profits Before Taxes:	not available
Net Profits per Employee:	not available
Principal Competitors:	Bolt, Beranek & Newman, Anderson Consulting, EDS, Perot Systems, Inc.
# Potential Selling Sites:	Domestic: 1,000 Foreign: 1,000
Problem Company Is Attempting to Solve:	Solves technology-based problems for government agencies, such as the FAA and its corporate contractors.
Solution Company Is Conveying to Problem:	CEO Raydean Acevedo hired the best people she could find and sends them on-site to the locus of their clients' problems.

and Norfolk, Virginia, handy to Washington, D.C., with another division in Denver and branches in San Diego and Bakersfield, California; Atlanta; and Washington, D.C.

Reed Group President Dr. Presley Reed applauds Acevedo's strategy of client service, describing RMCI as "the most customer-oriented firm" he has dealt with—a quality he believes contributed to the success of a tailored software program the company developed that allows his employees to reference complex national disability data for use in their medical and insurance work.[1] RMCI has also received more formal recognition. The company was named the FAA's Woman Owned Business Enterprise of the Year in 1990—three years after its start-up—and again in 1991, marking the first time a company had won the award in consecutive years.

RMCI's decentralization applies to new business development as well as to customer service. For government and corporate contracts alike, new work is secured through personal contact rather than from advertising.

Community involvement is an important element in the mission statement at RMCI. "My parents taught me that giving to my community, making the world a truly better place, was the mark of an achiever. Now that RMCI and I are in a position to act as role models and to add value to our communities, we do it," Acevedo says.

---

[1] David G. Rouguilo, "Profiles," *Hispanic Business*, No. 130, June 1993, p. 124.

ROPER INDUSTRIES, INC.

President Ronald Reagan may have pulled off the biggest leveraged buyout of all time. He created a $400 billion deficit but opened up approximately two dozen markets for U.S. companies to sell their products and services. The rise of democracy in Eastern Europe was the payoff: Reagan's arms buildup broke the Soviet's financial ability and the Wall came tumbling down. Russia, the greatest emerging market of all time, needs just about every product and service the United States produces. It needs virtually everything that U.S. companies manufacture, and it has the raw materials in sufficient supply to backstop its credit. One of these raw materials is oil; Russia has the potential to become the world's largest oil producer if the right equipment is in place to pump it out of the ground.

We might expect to see Ingersoll-Rand, Cooper Industries, and Dresser installing their compressors alongside the Russian oil and gas rigs. But Roper Industries, Inc., has stolen a page from their books and won a $350-million, seven-year contract with GAZPROM, Russia's gas production and distribution agency.

Roper wasn't in the compressor business until 1992, when it purchased Compressor Controls Corp. (CCC) for $35 million. Talk about the right purchase at the right time.

Its contract with GAZPROM has CCC installing its advanced turbo compressor and turbine controls on GAZPROM's vast pipeline system. CCC achieved all of the objectives required under its first-year contract, delivering $46.6 million in equipment and training services during calendar year 1993. GAZPROM also met its commitments.

CCC's performance is even more noteworthy in light of the obstacles the company overcame to take advantage of an outstanding opportunity halfway around the world. CCC quadrupled its output to produce and ship control systems for 471 turbo compressors at 35 GAZPROM stations, established a Moscow office as a base of operations, arranged for training of 100 Russian engineers at CCC's headquarters in Des Moines, and oversaw the controls' installation at the initial stations.

Fiscal year 1993 was also a banner year for sales in other Roper operations, resulting from the successful introduction of new products, greater penetration of core markets, expansion into new domestic and foreign markets, and economic recovery in the United States. Earnings were sharply higher as a result of continuing gains in productivity and efficiency that strengthened operating margins.

ROPER INDUSTRIES, INC.

Chief Executive Officer:	Derrick N. Key
Principal Location:	160 Ben Burton Rd. Bogart, GA 30622
Telephone/Fax:	706-369-7170/706-353-6496
Satellite Locations:	Des Moines, IA; Portland, OR; Dallas, TX; Richmond, CA; Bury St. Edmunds, United Kingdom
Date Founded:	1981
Description of Business:	A capital equipment manufacturer of pumps, motors, and compressors—with a following in Russia.
# Employees Current:	688
# Employees Projected by 6/30/95:	Company withheld
Sales (Annualized) 1994:	$146,369,000
Gross Profit Margin (GPM):	51.0%
Selling Expenses/Sales:	30.2%
% Sales Increase 1991–94	+195.1%
% Change GPM 1991–94:	+20.5%
Total Debt/Net Worth:	47.3%
Net Profits Before Taxes:	$32,149,000
Operating Ratio:	22.0%
Net Profits per Employee:	$46,728
Traded On:	NASDAQ/ROPR
Principal Competitors:	Cooper Industries, Dressor, The Durion Company, Ingersoll-Rand, Gorman-Rupp
# Potential Selling Sites:	Domestic: 200 Foreign: 400
Problem Company Is Attempting to Solve:	Oil and gas field pumping equipment must be located in remote, hazardous places on land or at sea. The equipment must be kept running continuously. This is particularly true in Russia.
Solution Company Is Conveying to Problem:	Roper produces heavy-duty oil and gas field compressors and pumps, and it has managed to gain customers in Russia.

Roper Pump was a strong sales and earnings contributor. It increased its sales and bookings by 17 and 18 percent, respectively, principally on rising demand for its progressive cavity pump and mud motors used in horizontal drilling for oil and gas and higher sales to the power-generation and diesel locomotive industries.

The amazing group of companies that make up Roper was assembled by G. L. Ohrstrom & Co., a New York-based acquisition fund whose partners keep their heads under the hood, quietly building value through strategic acquisitions. The proxy statement indicates that a number of G. L. Ohrstrom principals are active Roper stockholders and board members, providing reassurance to anyone investing in or dealing with Roper.

RYKA, INC.

Ryka is a small but rapidly growing company that makes athletic shoes for women. The company's social conscience reflects the experiences and beliefs of its owner and CEO, Sheri Poe, a rape survivor who struggled long and hard to recover. When Poe began a program of aerobic exercise as part of her therapy, she was plagued with back problems that led her to take a closer look at her footwear. She discovered that most women's athletic shoes are shrunken versions of men's styles that don't take into consideration the differences in women's bodies, and she began to envision a shoe designed solely for a woman. Ryka made the vision a reality. Her company was brought public in 1986.

Poe always wanted to do more than make great shoes; she wanted her company to have "soul" and to reflect her concerns. In late 1992 Poe created the Ryka ROSE (Regaining One's Self-Esteem) Foundation, a nonprofit organization committed to helping end violence against women. The company announced that it would contribute 7 percent of its future pretax profits to the ROSE Foundation.

But profits have just recently come to Ryka. It eeked out a $106,000 profit in the first quarter of 1994 versus a $296,000 loss in 1993. The turnaround was due to improvement in GPM, from 24.7 percent in 1993 to 30.9 percent in 1994. The industry average is 35 percent—a goal Ryka surely aspires to.

Without sufficient capital—Ryka owes $3.90 for each $1 in equity —the company has had to pay very high capital costs. Interest rates have approached 20 percent. Interest expenses contributed $700,000 to the loss in 1993.

Sheri Poe will find the capital for her company. And she will develop several more distribution channels to ramp sales faster. Poe has had to overcome bigger problems in her past than improving her cash flow. It's not a bad investment policy to select entrepreneurs who have picked themselves off the canvas a time or two and jumped back into the ring. Poe is that kind of entrepreneur.

RYKA, INC.

Chief Executive Officer:	Sheri Poe
Principal Location:	249 Ocean Way Norwood, MA 02062
Telephone/Fax:	617-762-9900/617-762-7952
Satellite Locations:	none
Date Founded:	1987
Description of Business:	Designs, produces, and markets women's athletic shoes; founder has become a spokesperson for the campaign to end violence toward women.
# Employees Current:	27
# Employees Projected by 6/30/95:	31
Sales (Annualized) 1993:	$14,438,000
Gross Profit Margin (GPM):	30.9%
Selling Expenses/Sales:	13.1%
% Sales Increase 1991–93:	+180.9%
% Change GPM 1991–93:	+6.5%
Total Debt/Net Worth:	390.3%
Net Profits Before Taxes:	$(3,026,000)
Operating Ratio:	deficit
Net Profits per Employee:	not available
Traded On:	NASDAQ/RYKA
Principal Competitors:	Nike, Reebok, L.A. Gear
# Potential Selling Sites:	Domestic: 10,000 Foreign: 30,000
Problem Company Is Attempting to Solve:	Most mass-marketed women's sneakers are scaled-down versions of men's shoes. However, women's feet, hips, bone dimensions, and centers of balance differ dramatically from men's.
Solution Company Is Conveying to Problem:	Engineering and designing athletic shoes specifically for women and marketing them with the message that consumers can do well for themselves while doing good for others.

SENTINEL SYSTEMS, INC.

I magine bringing the power of the integrated circuit to the home security market," says Sentinel Systems' CEO, George R. Young. "You get home security plus the automation of a hundred functions." Young proceeds to list a few: turn on lights remotely before you get home; arm your system from your car or office if you forgot to set it before you left; instantly turn on all lights if you hear a suspicious noise; monitor sound in your home or office from a remote location; automatically dial emergency numbers; open or close your garage or gate from your house, car, or yard; turn off AC power to your garage door opener when away for added security; protect computers from hackers and viruses by keeping them offline when the computer is not in use; power up/down or reboot remotely; remotely access up to 256 computers and peripherals over one shared line; monitor breathing of infants while they sleep; monitor the elderly when they are left alone.

These and dozens of other functions are currently marketed by Sentinel in the Southeastern United States as well as numerous foreign countries at a price of less than $1,000 per home. Sentinel offers the most advanced home security and control systems currently available in the marketplace. Its system is able to perform all the functions of any other residential security system while offering features no other system has. The system can be connected to any conventional sensor, such as glass-break detectors, motion detectors, smoke detectors, door and window contacts, and medical emergency devices. Its 16-zone control panel, which is expandable to 80 zones, operates not only from the standard wall-mounted hardwired keypad but also from any Touch-Tone phone or from an optional wireless keypad. Using a keypad or phone, the user can perform any function the system offers. Sentinel's security alarm system is one of the first to operate from any touch-tone telephone and from a wireless interface.

When an alarm is activated, the vast majority of security systems require the homeowner to go to a keypad and read a small liquid crystal display (LCD) to find out the alarm's type and location. But Sentinel's system *talks*. A unique digitized voice system reassures the homeowner by giving the status of the system. The system can tell the homeowner if children have gone out the back door, if there is a fire and where it is located, or even if the gate to the pool has been opened—all while continuously relaying this information to the central monitoring station to take appropriate action. This voice feature makes the system vastly

SENTINEL SYSTEMS, INC.

Chief Executive Officer:	George R. Young
Principal Location:	2713 Magruder Blvd. Hampton, VA 23666
Telephone/Fax:	804-766-0200/804-766-2379
Satellite Locations:	none
Date Founded:	1985
Description of Business:	A leading distributor of home alarm and automation systems.
# Employees Current:	31
# Employees Projected by 6/30/95:	65
Sales (Annualized) 1994:	$12,000,000
Gross Profit Margin (GPM):	The company is privately-held and therefore not required to make its financial statement public.
Selling Expenses/Sales:	not available
% Sales Increase 1991–94:	+150.0%
% Change GPM 1991–94:	not available
Total Debt/Net Worth:	not available
Net Profits Before Taxes:	More than $1 million
Net Profits per Employee:	Approx. $33,000
Principal Competitors:	Wells Fargo, ADT, Honeywell, Sentrol
# Potential Selling Sites:	Domestic: 15 million Foreign: 60 million
Problem Company Is Attempting to Solve:	The increase in burglaries, break-ins, theft, arson, and crimes to property, and the need to monitor elderly people in need of assistance and children who are home alone.
Solution Company Is Conveying to Problem:	Inexpensive home alarm and home automation systems assessible by voice and vision, and very user-friendly.

more user-friendly, particularly for people uncomfortable with high-tech equipment. To accomplish all of these tasks, the system has a 200-word vocabulary (available in English, Spanish, or Italian) and a four-word description for each security zone.

Young started Sentinel Systems following a long (31 year) and accomplished career at NASA, where he headed the Mission Application Section. His brother and advisor, Frank, built Econ-O-Lodge into a major lodging chain. Young was also an advisor on the Lunar Orbital Project, and he helped select the Apollo satellite's landing site on the moon. Sentinel Systems is another of Young's missions.

Nagging nabobs frequently say, "If we can put a man on the moon, why can't we . . . do something or other?" In Sentinel you have a CEO who did head up a group of people that put a man on the moon. Now, Young is taking a bite out of crime.

SHAMAN PHARMACEUTICALS, INC.

Seeking medicines from plants dates back to 1673, when the Society of Apothecaries founded the Chelsea Physic Garden in London as a botanical garden and resource for medicines. At the end of the twentieth century, the garden still serves as a pathfinder for new drugs and also as a reminder of modern medicine's debt to the plant world.

Today a handful of companies and organizations look for leads for new medicines from plants. One of the most aggressive is Shaman Pharmaceuticals, Inc. Shaman targets plants used by indigenous peoples for medicinal purposes. If the same plant is used for the same purpose in three different countries, then Shaman will investigate it.

Lisa Conte, Shaman's founder and CEO, says, "We have focused our search for drug leads among shamans of the tropical forests because they do not keep written records of their medicinal plant knowledge. As a consequence they are more likely to use a plant extract from a single plant species or variety for a single disease, rather than extracts from mixtures of plants, which tend to be used in cultures with written records."[1]

The number of different tribes around the world makes it impossible to record or otherwise preserve more than a tiny percentage of their knowledge. And, since 1900, 90 of Brazil's 270 Indian tribes have completely disappeared, while scores more have lost their land to developers or abandoned their ways. More than two-thirds of the remaining tribes have populations of fewer than 1,000. Some might disappear before anyone notices.

Shaman currently has two products in clinical trials: Provir, an oral product for the treatment of respiratory viral infections; and Virend, a topical antiviral product for the treatment of herpes. Shaman is also developing a broad-spectrum systemic antifungal product. Through 1993, the company screened approximately 470 plants yielding 290 active extracts. From these extracts it has targeted for study 10 chemically unique and biologically potent compounds that it believes exhibit previously undiscovered activity.

Assuming FDA approval by 1996, revenues could begin by 1997. Shaman has roughly $50 million in cash and is losing $4 million per quarter. So the race against time is on.

---

[1] June Grindley, "The Natural Approach to Pharmaceuticals," *Scrip Magazine*, December 1993.

SHAMAN PHARMACEUTICALS, INC.

Chief Executive Officer:	Lisa Conte
Principal Location:	213 E. Grand Ave. South San Francisco, CA 94080
Telephone/Fax:	415-952-7070/415-873-8367
Satellite Locations:	none
Date Founded:	1990
Description of Business:	An ethnobiotanical-based pharmaceutical company seeking to find curative compounds from South American rain forests.
# Employees Current:	97
# Employees Projected by 6/30/95:	Company withheld
Sales (Annualized) 1994:	None expected for at least 3 years
Gross Profit Margin (GPM):	not available
Selling Expenses/Sales:	not available
% Sales Increase 1991–94:	not available
% Change GPM 1991–94:	not available
Total Debt/Net Worth:	not available
Net Profits Before Taxes:	not available
Net Profits per Employee:	not available
Traded On:	NASDAQ/SHMN
Principal Competitors:	All pharmaceutical companies
# Potential Selling Sites:	Domestic: Millions of people Foreign: Millions of people
Problem Company Is Attempting to Solve:	Diseases not susceptible to treatment with conventional or genetically engineered pharmaceuticals.
Solution Company Is Conveying to Problem:	Seeks out native plants in South American rain forests that may provide new medicinal drugs.

Conventional pharmaceutical and health and beauty aids companies were begun in a manner comparable to Shaman. Warner-Lambert's top-selling Chiclets chewing gum derives from a plant. Aspirin, tea, quinine, and dozens of other pharmaceuticals, medicinals, foods, and herbs were discovered in forests. Is there more to be discovered in the rain forests? Shaman and its employees and investors believe there is.

SRX, INC.

George Custer took his last stand on the same week in 1877 that Alexander Graham Bell got his telephone to work. Custer was full of hubris. Bell was full of challenge. No invention has ever come near the power of the telephone to change how we live. Many generals have acted as foolish as Custer since 1877. But there has been only one Bell. Billions of dollars, yen, and ringitt have been made improving the basic telephone. One hundred and five years later, entrepreneurs are still at it. SRX's target market encompasses companies seeking an integrated communications platform that provides the complete call-management scenario: from inbound/outbound calling to fax to computer-telephone integration (CTI) applications. SRX customers are in industries as diverse as finance, medicine, law, education, publishing, automotive, high-tech, government, utilities, real estate, and food and beverage.

The SRX Vision family of voice and data communications products provides a complete call scenario at more than 5,000 locations, offering feature-rich call-management systems that enable the user to track calls with its client/server systems.

SRX has always been nimble enough to be innovative and fast-moving enough to be the first to bring the latest innovations to smaller organizations. Small to midsize organizations are demanding an integrated voice and data communications platform to bring about increased productivity: a platform that combines voice and data at the applications level, with an open architecture, a graphical user interface (GUI), and a complete call-management capability, thus enabling true computer telephone integration. In 1994 SRX offered a true telecommunications breakthrough, OmniWorks, which provides a complete call scenario for small to midsize businesses—affordably—for the first time.

Because OmniWorks offers the same features as larger integrated systems, but at an affordable price, smaller companies can take advantage of consolidated voice technologies from a single multi-application platform. OmniWorks seamlessly meshes inbound and outbound call management, interactive voice response (IVR), fax, voice messaging, CTI, and private branch exchange (PBX) capabilities to streamline operations, promote customer satisfaction, and boost cash flow.

The OmniWorks outbound functions are just as impressive. Because of previous technological limitations, call centers segregated into

SRX, INC.

Chief Executive Officer:	James Steenbergen
Principal Location:	3480 Lotus Dr. Plano, TX 75075
Telephone/Fax:	214-985-2600/214-985-2772
Satellite Locations:	none
Date Founded:	1983
Description of Business:	The company develops, markets, and supports systems that link the features of the telephone with PCs and workstations.
# Employees Current:	95
# Employees Projected by 6/30/95:	118
Sales (Annualized) 1994:	$20,000,000
Gross Profit Margin (GPM):	The company is privately-held and not required to make its financial statements public.
Selling Expenses/Sales:	not available
% Sales Increase 1991–94:	not available
% Change GPM 1991–94:	not available
Total Debt/Net Worth:	not available
Net Profits Before Taxes:	not available
Net Profits per Employee:	not available
Principal Competitors:	Rolm, Northern Telecom, AT&T, Aspect, Rockwell, Centigram, Octel
# Potential Selling Sites:	Domestic: 15,000 Foreign: 30,000
Problem Company Is Attempting to Solve:	Many large organizations use antiquated telecommunications equipment that keep customers on hold too long, billable costs are charged to the wrong accounts, and messages that should have been logged on the computer are lost.
Solution Company Is Conveying to Problem:	SRX has developed a line of integrated products that link the PC and the telephone to allow the PC to record all incoming telephone information.

inbound and outbound groupings were commonplace. With OmniWorks' call-blending capability, outbound telemarketing agents are free both to place and receive calls. OmniWorks also stretches personnel resources by abolishing wasted dialing time. Automatic dialing returns phone calls and distributes them, freeing up agents. It even filters out unproductive calls.

The venture capital fund that brought us Lotus Development Corp. and Compaq Computer Corp., Sevin-Rosen Partners, is the financial backer of SRX. Can SRX become Sevin-Rosen's third billion dollar company? We'll know in several years.

If the telemarketers who reach you this evening seem happier and more effusive, you can probably thank OmniWorks.

STORES AUTOMATED SYSTEMS, INC.

~~tores~~ Automated Systems, Inc., (SASI) designs, develops, manufactures, markets, and supports innovative, integrated point-of-sale (POS) systems. Leading retailers in a variety of market segments have come to appreciate the value SASI systems bring to their organizations.

SASI is likely to become the idiomatic equivalent for a society that failed to educate everyone in the 3-R's. The SASI system shows pictures of products to the POS computer which computes price, thus obviating the need for cashiers to know how the word "tomato" is spelled or how to multiply 5 tomatoes times 50 cents apiece. Sad, but unfortunately true; there is a need for SASI.

SASI pioneered the use of PC architecture at the point of sale and was engineering industry-standard components into super price/ performance products long before "plug and play" became a popular concept. Its approach to POS hardware remains unchanged. As a result, its POS systems continue to be easy to use and service as well as ideally suited to the retail environment.

The company's system, called the *Experience*, speeds up supermarket checkouts by displaying pictures of products for quick identification and price verification. Priced at about $8,000 a unit, the *Experience* can be programmed quickly by store personnel. A voice tells the cashiers when they have made a mistake, and they record sales by touching the product's picture.

Customers find the *Experience* entertaining and informative. It can be used to flash store announcements and promotions, and customers can even send classified ads on the store's E-mail. "We are still learning about the power and performance capabilities of the *Experience*," says Bernard Greenberg, SASI's co-founder and CEO. "We only sold about 7,000 units last year in a market that bought 240,000 units. We have only dipped our toe into the market."

What makes SASI different from its giant competitors is that the others sell electronic cash registers and SASI sells interactive systems. "We have 42 programmers on staff, and we are continually adding more," says Greenberg. "Our software is written in C++, which is difficult and complex to write. But the payoff comes in customizing the *Experience*. Our customers want their POS systems customized. We can show them how to do it. If they want to hook up their individual POS system to a local area network (LAN) or a wide area network (WAN) for

STORES AUTOMATED SYSTEMS, INC.

Chief Executive Officer:	Bernard Greenberg
Principal Location:	311 Sinclair St. Bristol, PA 19007
Telephone/Fax:	215-785-4321/215-785-5329
Satellite Locations:	none
Date Founded:	1984
Description of Business:	Develops, produces, markets, and supports point-of-sale electronic terminals customized to meet individual stores' needs.
# Employees Current:	227
# Employees Projected by 6/30/95:	250
Sales (Annualized) 1994:	$40,000,000
Gross Profit Margin (GPM):	The company is privately-held and therefore not required to make public its financial statements.
Selling Expenses/Sales:	not available
% Sales Increase 1991–94:	not available
% Change GPM 1991–94:	not available
Total Debt/Net Worth:	not available
Net Profits Before Taxes:	not available
Net Profits per Employee:	not available
Principal Competitors:	AT&T, NCR, Fujitsu/ICL, IBM
# Potential Selling Sites:	Domestic: 500,000 Foreign: 1,500,000
Problem Company Is Attempting to Solve:	Supermarkets incur excessive costs in cashier turnover and training and in control of prices within the store and the community.
Solution Company Is Conveying to Problem:	Provides hardware and software as a total solution, with CD-ROM visuals that capture non-bar-codable items such as fruit and vegetables, and easy-to-customize software to make price changes, control inventory, and capture customer data.

inventory ordering or price controls, it's easy. Try getting AT&T or IBM to put that feature into their electronic cash registers."

Shoppers have something to do at a SASI POS terminal. Because the system is interactive, they can enter messages into it while waiting. Typically the messages announce a bicycle for sale or the need for a babysitter. The information is flashed to screens throughout the store.

SASI is clearly the future of POS technology; the standard by which all checkout systems will be judged over the next quarter century. The company is building up cash at a remarkable rate, according to Greenberg. "We don't need to go public," he says. "We have no need for more money." There is no pressure from venture capital funds to go public; SASI bootstrapped itself all the way.

SUNRISE MEDICAL, INC.

When Richard Chandler started Sunrise Medical in 1984, he had a simple plan. He'd seen the demographics: The country was getting older; demand for wheelchairs, crutches, and bathroom aids for the aged and disabled could only grow. And no one company dominated the market. Moreover, some of the wheelchair companies were renting their products at rates that were obscene, which drew enmity toward them and created opportunity for entrepreneurs. So Chandler borrowed $4.5 million and acquired 24 small companies that made products for the disabled, hoping to create a miniconglomerate with national marketing clout and economy of scale.

Buying the companies was easy, but getting them to work together wasn't. Sales grew to $140 million a year, but profits shrank. Chandler sought advice from users of Sunrise's equipment which led to significant design changes. He took these with him to Japan, where he studied the manufacturing methods of Toyota, Matsushito, and others. Since then, his company has done for the wheelchair what Nike founder Phil Knight did for the running shoe. Sunrise Medical now controls 55 percent of the U.S. market in ultralight manual wheelchairs. Co-designed by disabled athletes, the company's chairs are custom-designed for each user and are more comfortable, more colorful, longer lasting, and 20 percent less expensive than conventional wheelchairs.

Chandler's vision is more altruistic than creating the wheelchair version of $120 basketball shoes. He wants to make an entire range of products that improve the disabled person's daily life, and he wants to make those products better, more cheaply, and more efficiently.

As an important element of its corporate culture, Sunrise founded a nonprofit foundation called Winners on Wheels (WOW), which it supports with people and money. WOW addresses the social and educational needs of children in wheelchairs and helps them reframe their environment.

Sunrise spends $5 million a year on R&D, creating 60 new products a year. The biggest triumph: a portable toilet that cost $600,000 to develop. Injection molded and made from lightweight composites, it's more comfortable than the conventional metal product, rust-free, and 20 percent cheaper.

As the U.S. population gets older and more of the disabled insist on integration into the active mainstream, Sunrise Medical's opportunities

SUNRISE MEDICAL, INC.

Chief Executive Officer:	Richard H. Chandler
Principal Location:	2355 Crenshaw Blvd. Torrance, CA 90501
Telephone/Fax:	310-328-8018/310-328-8184
Satellite Locations:	20 including Ontario, Canada; Somerset, PA; Langen, Germany; Stevens Pt., WI; Tokyo, Japan
Description of Business:	Designs, develops, manufactures, and markets products that allow the elderly and disabled to live at home and participate in their communities.
Date Founded:	1984
# Employees Current:	1,800
# Employees Projected by 6/30/95:	Company withheld
Sales (Annualized) 1994:	$384,105,000
Gross Profit Margin (GPM):	36.2%
Selling Expenses/Sales:	21.6%
% Sales Increase 1991–94:	+88.4%
% Change GPM 1991–94:	+5.5%
Total Debt/Net Worth:	75.4%
Net Profits Before Taxes:	$33,122,000
Operating Ratio:	8.6%
Net Profits per Employee:	$10,351
Traded On:	NYSE/SMD
Principal Competitors:	Everest & Jennings, Healthdyne Technologies, Respironics
# Potential Selling Sites:	Domestic: 1,000,000 Foreign: 2,500,000
Problem Company Is Attempting to Solve:	The lack of utilitarian products adapted to modern needs of the elderly and disabled.
Solution Company Is Conveying to Problem:	Sunrise offers ultra-light wheelchairs, co-designed by disabled athletes, that are more comfortable, colorful, longer-lasting, and 20 percent less expensive than conventional wheelchairs.

can only grow. Health-care reform will favor home and nursing-home care and will play into Sunrise's low-cost, customer-needs-driven strategy.

Chandler's trip to Japan gave him the vision to turn Sunrise into a company built for the 21st-century. He shut down or sold off the nonperformers, curtailed new acquisitions, and reorganized his workforce into self-directed teams. Sunrise adopted just-in-time manufacturing, keeping only the inventory needed for that day's production and shipping a product out as soon as it was finished.

Sunrise has some of the best numbers in the medical device market. Its GPM is 36.2 percent and it has risen 5.5 percent since 1991. Sales have increased by 88.4 percent over the last three years but overhead has been held to 21.6 percent of sales. Sunrise earns 8.6 percent on sales and is working down its leverage ratio which rose to 75.4 percent in 1994 from 25.7 percent in 1993, but that happened when Sunrise borrowed $130 million to make a bell-ringer acquisition.

In July 1993, Sunrise paid $130 million to acquire DeVilbiss Health Care ($95 million in sales), a leader in home respiratory products, which gave Sunrise a new core product to expand on. Sunrise also completed six other acquisitions in 1993 to round out the product lines in its three core divisions—recovery, rehabilitation, and respiratory products.

Still, size clearly is not the motivator at Sunrise Medical. The company is extremely active in the disabled community at home and abroad, organizing Winners On Wheels circles that train new leaders who return to their communities to help children with disabilities. Sunrise also sponsors 50 disabled athletes who compete in everything from track and field to tennis; they took 44 medals at the 1992 Paralympic Games in Barcelona. Employees at the company's Sopur subsidiary in Germany have aided disabled Croatians to leave their war-torn country. And Sunrise recycles its profits back to its various communities—stockholders and the disabled—never forgetting who validates its existence.

SWIFT TRANSPORTATION CO., INC.

With a portable computer in hand, the store manager at Liz Claiborne's Factory Outlet Store in Budagher, New Mexico, walks among the racks. Her input is immediately transmitted to the corporation's central computer facility, which calculates what the Budagher store sold last year, last month, and last week, makes other adjustments, then merges that information with other stores' stock information and transmits orders to the corporation's contract manufacturers in South East Asia. The garments are produced, picked, and packed, and each box is addressed separately per individual store location. Federal Express picks up the boxes, drives them to its plane, flies them to Memphis, where they are sorted, and delivers them two or three days later to Budagher and the other stores. No warehouse cost. Days of inventory costs eliminated. Bank financing minimized. Middlemen's profits, interest expenses, warehouse operating costs—all these historical costs have been swept away.

Swift Transportation Co., Inc., is a major beneficiary of this paradigm shift in the way products are brought to market. The short-to-medium-haul truckload carrier seeks out large "service-sensitive" customers—Anheuser-Busch, Campbell Soup, Fred Meyer, Guess Jeans, Kimberly Clark, Mervyn's, Pep Boys, Procter & Gamble, and Rubbermaid, among others—who regularly ship goods over established routes. ("Service-sensitive" is a polite term for screamers—those customers who attempt to terrorize the hauler with threats to sensitive areas of the hauler personnel's bodies if their shipments are lost or delayed.) Swift installed a computerized package tracking system a few years ago, and it faxes frequent reports to its customers to reassure and calm them.

The company, based in the West, has grown by acquiring smaller carriers. Swift entered the East by acquiring Cooper Motor Lines in 1988; in 1993 it acquired West's Best Freight System, Inc. (105 tractors). Swift owns its own tractors and trailers, the vast majority of them less than two years old, and it orders standardized tractors and trailers manufactured to its specifications to minimize spare parts inventory, hold down maintenance costs, and simplify driver training.

Drivers are the company's largest investment: Swift has around 2,500 drivers out of 3,300 total employees. The drivers must meet fairly high skills standards, and they are tested for drugs. The company operates

SWIFT TRANSPORTATION CO., INC.

Chief Executive Officer:	Jerry Moyes
Principal Location:	1705 Marietta Way Sparks, NV 89431
Telephone/Fax:	702-359-9031/702-352-6303
Satellite Locations:	Phoenix, AZ
Date Founded:	1966
Description of Business:	Short-to-medium haul truckload carrier
# Employees Current:	3,000
# Employees Projected by 6/30/95:	Company withheld
Sales (Annualized) 1994:	$276,982,000
Gross Profit Margin (GPM):	35.9%
Selling Expenses/Sales:	not available
% Sales Increase 1991–94:	+45.5%
% Change GPM 1991–94:	+64.7%
Total Debt/Net Worth:	66.2%
Net Profits Before Taxes:	$21,409,000
Operating Ratio:	7.7%
Net Profits per Employee:	$7,136
Traded On:	NASDAQ/SWIFT
Principal Competitors:	J. L. Hunt, Landmark, Werner Transportation
# Potential Selling Sites:	Domestic: 7,500 Foreign: not applicable
Problem Company Is Attempting to Solve:	As retailers have converted to just-in-time product ordering from manufacturers, and as the U.S. economy has fast-forwarded to overnight package delivery, there is a greater need for short-to-medium-haul truckload carriers that are highly accountable and professional.
Solution Company Is Conveying to Problem:	One-day product deliveries, in specialized containers if required, from manufacturers to customers.

two driver training schools, awards bonuses, makes its drivers company stockholders through a 401(k) pension plan, and provides health and life insurance.

Swift's insurance and claims costs are rising faster than sales: from $5 million in 1991 to $12 million in 1993; something for company management to watch carefully. Another concerning area is related-party transactions, of which there are eight, and they aggregate more than $3.5 million in annual payments by the company to the principal stockholder. The entrepreneurs of Quantum Companies generally look to their ownership for their principal reward.

Politicians bash the trucking industry as if it were their papal right. They tollgate it, tax it, and regulate it in three- to four-year cycles, perhaps because they believe voters hate truck drivers. Whether it's tougher standards on diesel fuel emissions or stiffer fines for blowing off a weight station, these costs add up. Swift's operating taxes and licenses are also growing faster than sales: from $8.5 million in 1991 to $13.3 million in 1993.

But Swift seems to be managing these and other overhead costs better than its competitors. On a GPM basis, Swift owns a 35.9 percent ratio versus 34.0 percent for an average of comparable companies. On a Profits per Employee basis, Swift outperforms the industry average by $7,136 to $6,259.* Its growth is somewhat constrained by its business plan—short-to-medium-haul, service-sensitive customers—but look for more acquisitions in contiguous regions to keep growth going.

---

* KLLM, Landstar, and Weatherford.

SYBASE, INC.

The transition from host-based, proprietary mainframe computing to distributed, client/server, relational database management systems (RDBMSs) is a major paradigm shift that began early this decade and is expected to continue for several years. This trend is being fueled by the availability of microprocessor-based, high-performance desktop computing, downsizing, and related business process re-engineering and the demands on enterprises to gain competitive advantages in the rapid delivery of products and services. Enterprise client/server software technology plays a leading role in this shift by facilitating competitive advantages and business differentiation through timely, flexible, economic access to information and increased productivity of business processes.

In 1993 Sybase became the second-largest independent supplier of enterprise client/server RDBMSs worldwide. The company's strategy is focused on market-share growth in its core geographic regions throughout the world; innovative leadership products and services built upon its core architecture; and strategic acquisitions (such as Gain Technology in late 1992, several foreign distributors in 1993, and OASIS Group PLC, a business process re-engineering consulting firm, in January 1994).

Perhaps the best way to understand the significance of Sybase is to look at your own company in terms of its information flow. How do sales come into the company? How are orders processed? How does production get triggered and how is it tracked? How are costs recorded and maintained? You begin to see that the flow of information *is* the flow of work. When a system such as Sybase is installed in an organization, it involves senior management in thinking about the flow of work/information. Needless to say, many companies that install and run Sybase software end up significantly more streamlined and more profitable.

Revenues reached a record $426.7 million in 1993, up 61 percent from 1992, which was up 65 percent from 1991. Revenue growth continued to be geographically broad-based and balanced: North American revenues reached $305.2 million, up 50 percent over 1992; international revenues were up 99 percent over 1992 to $121.5 million; international revenues equaled 28 percent of total revenues (32 percent in the fourth quarter of 1993) in comparison with 23 percent of total

SYBASE, INC.

Chief Executive Officer:	Mark B. Hoffman
Principal Location:	6475 Christie Ave. Emeryville, CA 94608
Telephone/Fax:	510-922-3500/510-658-9441
Satellite Locations:	Burlington, MA; Berkshire, United Kingdom; Maarsen, the Netherlands; plus 39 foreign sales offices in 10 countries
Date Founded:	1984
Description of Business:	Develops, markets, and supports client/server software products and services for integrated enterprise-wide information management systems.
# Employees Current:	3,600
# Employees Projected by 6/30/95:	4,500
Sales 1993:	$426,698,000
Gross Profit Margin (GPM):	82.5%
Selling Expense/Sales:	43.6%
% Sales Increase 1991–93:	+78.9%
% Change GPM 1991–93:	–3.8%
Total Debt/Net Worth:	2.0%
Net Profits Before Taxes:	$71,203,000
Operating Ratio:	16.7%
Net Profits per Employee:	$28,165
Traded On:	NASDAQ/SYBS
Principal Competitors:	The ASK Group, Informix, Oracle Systems, EDS
# Potential Selling Sites:	Domestic: 10,000 Foreign: 30,000
Problem Company Is Attempting to Solve:	Evolution of client/server networking environments raises questions about how information flows through corporations, which leads to the more critical issue of how work gets done.
Solution Company Is Conveying to Problem:	When Sybase installs its software, it provides hands-on consulting services to re-engineer the customer.

revenues in 1992. License fees increased 58 percent to $301.8 million in 1993, while services revenues equaled $124.9 million, a 70 percent increase over 1992.

Full-year operating margins of 16 percent of revenues generated record operating income of $69.5 million, an 85 percent increase over 1992; net income of $44.1 million was up 86 percent from 1992. Net income per share increased to $0.86 from $0.48 in 1992. Net income growth was accomplished during a year in which the company invested 16 percent of revenues, or $66.2 million, in product development and engineering, introduced its new System 10 family of products, and added nearly 900 employees for a total of 4,500.

Substantial improvement was also achieved on the company's balance sheet. Total cash and short-term cash investments increased by $63.2 million, or 84 percent, to $138.1 million; days sales outstanding in receivables declined to 66 days at December 31, 1993, from 87 at year-end 1992; and debt-to-total equity declined to a minimal 2 percent.

The excellent health of this rapidly growing company has not been lost on the stock market. Sybase sports a P/E ratio of 49.0x in mid-1994, much higher than Informix's 25.0x or Microsoft's 30.0x. Company management told me that it expects to add 900 new jobs by June 30, 1995, a 25 percent increase. But, that's not surprising; Sybase's number of personnel has grown from 558 people in 1989. When a company works with its customers as closely as does Sybase, its greatest asset is a highly skilled workforce.

SYNAPTIC PHARMACEUTICAL CORP.

L et's talk about heart. The heart of Synaptic Pharmaceutical's drug development effort is a proprietary technology called human target-based drug design, which uses copies of actual human drug targets as the basis for designing drugs.

The drug design process begins with the identification of a human drug target and the cloning of its corresponding gene. To build a human target-based drug design system, the gene for the drug target is inserted into a living cell, which then produces copies of the target. Detailed study of the target, including computerized modeling, yields a blueprint for drug synthesis. By testing prospective drugs with panels of human target-bearing cells, researchers can gauge the drug's affinity for the intended target—a measure of its effectiveness—and its reaction with unwanted targets—an indicator of side effects.

Synaptic Pharmaceutical's drug design program is directed at five areas of the nervous system: alpha-adrenergic receptors, which regulate blood pressure, digestion, muscle tension, and other functions; serotonin receptors, implicated in aberrations including anxiety, depression, migraines, and heart disease; neuropeptide receptors, which affect a wide variety of functions, including appetite, and which may be used to treat diabetes; transporters, which play a role in epilepsy and anxiety; and dopamine receptors, which are implicated in schizophrenia and Parkinson's disease.

The heart that drives Synaptic Pharmaceutical belongs to its CEO, Kathlene Mullinix. While she was at Columbia University, a molecular biologist and a neurobiologist approached her with an idea for a new company they wanted her to run, one that would seek out new drugs to modulate the nervous system without producing the unpleasant and sometimes dangerous side effects—such as weight gain, sexual dysfunction, and impaired motor function—brought on by existing drugs.

Mullinix and her team believed that through molecular biology they could clone the genes that act as neurotransmitter receptors and in that way develop disease-specific drugs that work on the nervous system, have long-lasting effects, and produce no side effects. "We presented our story without a business plan to Adler & Co. and Athena Venture Partners, an Israeli fund, and they agreed that we may have something. They put in the first round and have been terrific supporters ever since," Mullinix says.

SYNAPTIC PHARMACEUTICAL CORP.

Chief Executive Officer:	Kathlene Mullinix
Principal Location:	215 College Rd. Paramus, NJ 07652
Telephone/Fax:	201-261-1331/201-261-0623
Satellite Locations:	none
Date Founded:	1987
Description of Business:	Conducts research involving a chemical in the brain called serotonin.
# Employees Current:	80
# Employees Projected by 6/30/95:	Company withheld
Sales (Annualized) 1994:	No revenues expected for at least 3 years
Gross Profit Margin (GPM):	not available
Selling Expenses/Sales:	not available
% Sales Increase 1991–94:	not available
% Change GPM 1991–94:	not available
Total Debt/Net Worth:	not available
Net Profits Before Taxes:	not available
Operating Ratio:	deficit
Net Profits per Employee:	deficit
Principal Competitors:	Various research institutions and pharmaceutical companies
# Potential Selling Sites:	Domestic: 350,000 Foreign: 700,000
Problem Company Is Attempting to Solve:	Schizophrenia, anxiety, migraines, nausea, depression, and addiction may be caused by imbalances of serotonin in the brain; conventional psychiatric drugs often cause unpleasant side effects.
Solution Company Is Conveying to Problem:	Synaptic Pharmaceutical is attempting to locate and identify the many receptors of proteins that act as docking sites in brain cells, to determine which relate to which maladies and then clone them genetically in drug form.

One of the very few women to have launched a biotechnology company, Mullinix admits she had greater hurdles to overcome than would a man in a similar position. "The venture capitalists who put in the initial capital said, 'Kathy, you can't be president. We'll do a search for a president. But you can be senior vice president,'" she recalls. She didn't wish to block the investment, so Mullinix agreed and ran the company while the investors looked for a president. A year passed, and Mullinix asked the venture capitalists to name her president and CEO. "'Well,' they said, 'you can be president, but not CEO. We will search for a CEO.'" Another year went by, and they made her chief executive officer.

Mullinix has raised more than $30 million privately for Synaptic, including $12 million from Eli Lilly and Co.; part is venture capital, and the other part is a research and development strategic partnering agreement. "We intended to form several partnerships such as this one because the established drug companies have much to offer us with their manufacturing and marketing capabilities. The revenue stream from licensing royalties, we believe, will become a significant number," Mullinix says. The company's investors include 18 venture capital funds, along with Aetna Life and New York Life Insurance.

More scientists and more capital will soon be needed. Recent studies suggest that serotonin drugs may prevent a broader spectrum of maladies than previously imagined, including heart disease. Synaptic, if it succeeds, could become one of the fastest-growing pharmaceutical companies of all time.

SYNOPSYS, INC.

You might expect the leading toolmaker of the information revolution to sport a GPM of 86 percent and growth and revenues that have just about quadrupled in four years. That describes Synopsys.

While consumers around the world are most familiar with the information revolution through such end-use products as personal computers, video cameras, and CD-ROM players, the real focus of the revolution is the integrated circuits that make these products possible. The design of these increasingly complex silicon chips encompasses a large and highly competitive industry, and anything that makes the design process more efficient, more productive, and less costly is particularly valuable.

Synopsys designs, develops, markets, and supports high-level design-automation software for designers of integrated circuits and electronic systems. Synopsys's software represents the cutting edge in electronic design automation (EDA), and the company's primary software product has captured roughly 80 percent of the rapidly growing EDA synthesis market. With a substantial lead on its competitors, a rock-solid balance sheet, and a new software product line called DesignWare that leverages off the company's dominant market share, Synopsys will grow to $1 billion in sales by the turn of the century. What it cannot develop the company will surely acquire, with a P/E ratio above 50.0x. It recently acquired CADIS GmbH of Aachen, Germany for $4 million in stock, and in January 1994 it acquired Logic Modeling Corp. of Beaverton, Oregon for $100 million in stock.

To appreciate the importance of Synopsys's EDA software products, it is necessary to understand the evolution of the chip design process. When the first chips were designed in the 1960s and early 1970s, the process was entirely manual. At that time, a complex chip contained, at most, a few hundred logic gates, each made up of approximately four transistors. In the 1970s, the first generation of automated chip design technology supplanted the manual design process. Called automated optical pattern generation, this technology made it possible to shorten the design process and to increase the complexity of chips so they contained up to about 1,000 logic gates.

The second generation of EDA arrived in the late 1970s and early 1980s. Known as computer-aided engineering, it used automated placement and routing to allow the designer to work at a higher level of

SYNOPSYS, INC.

Chief Executive Officer:	Aart J. deGeus
Principal Location:	700 E. Middlefield Rd. Mountain View, CA 94043
Telephone/Fax:	415-962-5000/415-694-4396
Satellite Locations:	Taipei, Taiwan; Munich, Germany; Tokyo, Japan
Date Founded:	1986
Description of Business:	Develops, markets, and supports high-level design-automation software for designers of integrated circuits and electronic systems.
# Employees Current:	590
# Employees Projected by 6/30/95:	Company withheld
Sales (Annualized) 1994:	$137,323,000
Gross Profit Margin (GPM):	85.8%
Selling Expenses/Sales:	39.8%
% Sales Increase 1991–94:	+339.1%
% Change GPM 1991–94:	+4.9%
Total Debt/Net Worth:	40.4%
Net Profits Before Taxes:	$19,976,000
Operating Ratio:	14.5%
Net Profits per Employee:	$33,857
Traded On:	NASDAQ/SNPS
Principal Competitors:	Xilinx, AT&T, Altera, Quicklogic
# Potential Selling Sites:	Domestic: 150 Foreign: 150
Problem Company Is Attempting to Solve:	The need for tools for designing integrated circuits.
Solution Company Is Conveying to Problem:	Offers integrated circuit software to speed up integrated circuit design and reduce costly errors.

abstraction. This innovation allowed designers to produce chip designs containing several thousand logic gates, and to do so substantially faster than before.

Synopsys's synthesis software represents the third generation of chip design automation. First introduced in 1988 and currently in Version 3.1, this software allows for an even higher level of abstraction in the design process. As a result, the designer is able to work at the functional level while the software generates the necessary design specifics at the gate level. With Synopsys's synthesis software, chip designers are able to design chips with as many as a million gates. And compared with second-generation products, Synopsys's synthesis software produces chips with approximately 25 percent less area and 30 percent higher performance.

Synopsys's high-level design software products achieve three important goals. First, they allow the chip designer to synthesize the actual design by translating a functional specification into a system of logic gates. The company's three synthesis tools—the Design Compiler family, the HDL Compiler family, and the Design Analyzer—are the state of the art in advanced EDA synthesis. Second, Synopsys's software allows the designer to simulate both the functionality and the implementation of the design by using the VHDL System Simulator. Use of the simulator helps to dramatically shorten the design cycle by reducing the need for long and costly implementation trials. And third, the Synopsys Test Compiler family of software allows the designer to make a chip that is easily testable. With these tools, the designer can explore size and performance trade-offs quickly and inexpensively.

What does this mean in plain English? Designing an integrated circuit is like designing a traffic signal system for New York City using street maps and information on traffic flows. If you do the job with one error in the traffic signal at the 59th St. Bridge—Second Ave. and 59th—the entire East Side of Manhattan, plus most of Queens and most traffic to Laguardia Airport would be in a miserable condition. But you can't tell if you've got errors until you plug in the system; then, if you do, you have to find them and fix them. Synopsys reduces the error rate. All traffic signals work from the get-go.

Together, these products have helped to propel Synopsys to the forefront of the worldwide market for advanced EDA products, a market dominated by U.S. suppliers. Approximately 55 percent of the company's revenues come from domestic sources. Its international sales are divided fairly evenly between Europe and Japan/Asia. The company has entered into R&D strategic alliances with Hewlett-Packard and LSI Logic as well as Texas Instruments, with which it is working to improve test compiler software.

SYSTEMIX, INC.

ometimes entrepreneurial companies' darkest nights end with their brightest days. Operating with just $181,000 in cash in March 1991, SyStemix raised $38 million in an initial public offering six months later. One month later, the U.S. Patent Office granted the company a patent on the hematopoietic stem cell. Then, two months later, in December 1991, Sandoz, the Swiss pharmaceutical giant, bought 60 percent of SyStemix for $392 million. To find the source of this incredible run of good fortune, look no further than the company's Chief Executive Officer, Linda D. Sonntag. "My father escaped Nazi Germany in 1936 and emigrated to South Africa, where I was born and raised," Sonntag said. "He saw oppression and other images and events in South Africa that must have reminded my father of Germany, because he continually told us to prepare ourselves with the skills that will enable us to leave some day. Our passport was education."

A native of South Africa, Sonntag earned a Ph.D. from the University of Witwatersrand and studied at the Weizmann Institute in Israel. At the age of twenty-five, Sonntag was a Professor of Genetics. She did further postdoctoral work at the University of California, San Francisco with Dr. Herbert Boyer, the co-founder of Genentech, Inc., and the father of genetic engineering. Sonntag was given business responsibilities along with scientific duties at Agrigenetics Research Corp. "She learned fast," said David J. Padwa, Sonntag's boss at Agrigenetics. "Coming out of an R&D environment, Linda was negotiating contracts better than most nonscientific people ever dreamed they could do. We knew she would run her own company some day. It was just a matter of time," Padwa added.

"David Padwa trusted me with responsibilities beyond my skills at the time," Sonntag said. "He was a terrific mentor to me. He put opportunities in front of me."

The success of SyStemix bodes well for the eventual victory of scientists armed with genetic engineering skills in combat with autoimmune disorders and various cancers. The company's fundamental work is in using the body's own cells to fight disease. The immediate goal is to isolate a patient's stem cells and then grow them outside the body, where they can be coaxed into differentiating and/or being genetically modified with inserted genes. This technology ultimately aims to develop universal donor cells, enabling a cell-farming industry that will cryogenically bank cells for emergency needs. Presently, the company

SYSTEMIX, INC.

Chief Executive Officer:	Linda D. Sonntag
Principal Location:	3155 Porter Rd. Palo Alto, CA 94304
Telephone/Fax:	415-856-4901/415-813-5101
Satellite Locations:	Lyon, France
Date Founded:	1988
Description of Business:	A biotechnology company concentrating on developing universal donor cells to combat autoimmune disorders.
# Employees Current:	245
# Employees Projected by 6/30/95:	315
Sales (Annualized) 1994:	$6,703,000
Gross Profit Margin (GPM):	The company spent $31,142,000 in 1993 of which $22,969,000 was for R&D.
Selling Expense/Sales:	not available
% Sales Increase 1991–94:	not available
% Change GPM 1991–94:	not available
Total Debt/Net Worth:	15.4%
Net Profits Before Taxes:	$(23,127,000)
Operating Ratio:	deficit
Net Profits per Employee:	deficit
Traded On:	NASDAQ/STMX
Principal Competitors:	Research institutions and pharmaceutical companies including Amgen, Genetic Institute, Immunex Corp.
# Potential Selling Sites:	Domestic: 1,500,000 Foreign: 1,500,000
Problem Company Is Attempting to Solve:	Certain therapies destroy or injure the patient's systems.
Solution Company Is Conveying to Problem:	Purifying the parent cell of the blood immune system for transplantation or reintroduction into patients following their destructive therapies.

has a mouse model that is proving effective in investigating the pathogenesis of HIV infection. The company's mouse is the only animal model now available to study HIV infection in the setting of human organs.

Biotechnology is an industry in which women entrepreneurs are making enormous strides. It is knowledge-based, not asset-based. Its principal resource is scientific knowledge, and the business goal is to commercialize discoveries at the molecular level. There are 10 women-founded, women-run biotechnology companies and they are going to end up at the top because, as Sonntag told me, "I have to prove myself over and over again to the financial community." Sonntag tries harder than her male competitors, and this has led to SyStemix sitting on more cash than the competition. Sonntag takes nothing for granted. SyStemix is going to be at $150 million in revenues in five years, and you read it here first!

TECNOL MEDICAL PRODUCTS, INC.

Tecnol makes masks for use in laser surgery, with patented filters that screen out submicron-size particles of bacteria contained in the smoke and airborne diseased-tissue particles cast off by the lasers. Reacting to the tuberculosis scare, the company recently designed a snugger-fitting mask that filters out even more microscopic airborne particles. To guard against AIDS, the company makes a fluid-shield mask: a clear plastic shield attached to a mask that protects surgeons' and nurses' eyes from blood during surgery.

By specializing in these high-tech masks, Tecnol grew to sales of $71 million by 1991, when Goldman Sachs & Co. took the company public. Using the cash from that IPO to make acquisitions, Tecnol has become the industry leader in two additional niche markets: ice packs and patient safety restraints.

The worldwide face-mask market is estimated to be larger than $200 million and growing rapidly. Up until 1992, the U.S. hospital market for surgical face masks was growing at 10 percent per year and consisted primarily of generic, low-priced products (at 14 to 16 cents apiece). Since then, the rate of growth has doubled, and greater emphasis is placed on higher-quality, premium-priced masks (at 60 cents to $1.25 each) that afford better protection for a larger segment of health-care workers.

Tecnol is well positioned to benefit from the growth of higher-priced, premium-quality face masks. In 1988 the company introduced FluidShield, with a built-in breathable film. Protected by several U.S. patents, FluidShield is the only product on the market that completely protects the wearer from fluids such as blood, the transmitting medium of AIDS/HIV and hepatitis. In 1989 the product line was expanded with the introduction of a wraparound visor that protects the wearer's eyes from fluids. Recently the FDA approved the commercial release of Tecnol's newest products for protection against both blood-borne and airborne microorganisms. These premium masks afford better protection and sell for several times more than generic masks.

The U.S. hospital market for ice packs is relatively small at approximately $20 million per annum. However, the annual growth rate is 15 percent and increasing, driven by demographic trends (an aging population and higher levels of physical exertion heighten injuries). Tecnol is the leader, featuring 15 different styles, and it expects to increase market share with its proprietary Stay-Dry technology, which

TECNOL MEDICAL PRODUCTS, INC.

Chief Executive Officer:	Van Hubbard
Principal Location:	7201 Industrial Park Blvd. Fort Worth, TX 76180
Telephone/Fax:	817-577-6403/817-577-6599
Satellite Locations:	Del Rio, TX; Acuna, Mexico
Date Founded:	1977
Description of Business:	Designs, develops, manufactures, and markets disposable medical products including surgical masks, back supports, trauma pads, and more.
# Employees Current:	1,574
# Employees Projected by 6/30/95:	Company withheld
Sales (Annualized) 1994:	$95,418,000
Gross Profit Margin (GPM):	47.6%
Selling Expenses/Sales:	18.5%
% Sales Increase 1991–94:	+172.8%
% Change GPM 1991–94:	+2.0%
Total Debt/Net Worth:	42.1%
Net Profits Before Taxes:	$9,019,000
Operating Ratio:	9.5%
Net Profits per Employee:	$5,730
Traded On:	NASDAQ/TCNL
Principal Competitors:	3M, Johnson & Johnson, Bristol-Myers Squibb, Boehringer Mannheim GmbH
# Potential Selling Sites:	Domestic: 6,000 Foreign: 12,000
Problem Company Is Attempting to Solve:	Johnson & Johnson and 3M were ignoring the surgical mask market.
Solution Company Is Conveying to Problem:	Developed a line of innovative masks to meet customers' needs. Has grown through strategic acquisitions.

uses ordinary ice cubes and maintains a steady temperature longer but eliminates condensation and costs less than chemical gel-cooled packs.

The market for patient safety restraints is $25 million and growing. Tecnol is the market-share leader (40 percent) with the widest assortment of products in this category. Constructed of lightweight, ultrasonically bonded fabrics, Tecnol makes products that are stronger and more comfortable and require less labor to maintain than traditional canvas restraints.

The greatest growth opportunity lies in the orthopedic market, which is estimated to exceed $1 billion in sales. Tecnol manufactures and sells over 130 different products in this market, generating sales of $10.5 million last year. Its product line includes cervical collars, arm slings, splints, knee and shoulder immobilizers, and back supports. In 1992 it made strategic acquisitions to strengthen its market position with the purchase of Warm 'N Form (a line of moldable back supports) and Poly-Med Industries (a manufacturer of moldable splints). The strategy is to become a major player in this category through product expansion and innovative manufacturing techniques.

By finding overlooked, high-margin niches and building on them, Tecnol has created a rapidly growing, sustainable, and interesting company. Van Hubbard and Kirk Brunson, Tecnol's two senior officers, are in their mid-fifties and own 25 percent of Tecnol's common stock. They have a good 10 years of time and energy left to build a billion-dollar business that Johnson & Johnson might try to acquire.

TETRA TECH, INC.

I n tollgates, there are profits. Leave it to Congress to erect expensive tollgates in the environmental field. Fleet-footed entrepreneurs such as Li-San Hwang have found opportunities in helping large corporations and municipal governments clean up their spills and circumnavigate the tollgates.

Tetra Tech provides a wide range of services at government, industrial, and military sites nationwide, including remedial investigation/feasibility studies (RI/FS), risk assessments, design of remedial action plans and specifications, and cleanup oversight and implementation. Recently, major projects have included RI/FS work at manufactured gas plant sites for utility companies in California, Virginia, and New Jersey; RI/FS work at several municipal landfills for local governmental agencies in the Mid-Atlantic states; and commencement of work under a $32.5 million contract for hazardous-waste services at Tinker Air Force Base, with a task order to perform a Resource Conservation and Recovery Act of 1976 facility investigation.

New regulations are in place to control pollution from storm-water runoff, a problem that is estimated to contribute nearly 50 percent of the pollutants entering our nation's waterways. In 1993, Tetra Tech was awarded $44 million in EPA contracts covering nonpoint-source technical support, contaminated sediments, toxicity methods, industrial effluent guidelines, and watershed modeling. It also won surface-water contracts at the state and local levels for watershed/storm-water management and nonpoint-source support. New projects include a five-year, $5 million contract with Prince Georges County, Maryland, as well as contracts with counties and municipalities in six other states. Tetra Tech also received new task orders from Washington State to conduct water-quality surveys of the Columbia River and from Oregon to survey the Willamette River.

Groundwater contamination resulting from decades of fuel-storage-tank leaks, landfill leaching, and industrial-chemical releases is one of the most severe environmental problems in the United States. Tetra Tech's services include identifying sources of chemical contamination in groundwater, examining the nature and extent of groundwater contamination, analyzing the speed and direction of contaminant migration through the use of proprietary three-dimensional computer models, and designing and implementing groundwater remediation technologies. Between 1993 and 1994, the company pursued groundwater investiga-

TETRA TECH, INC.

Chief Executive Officer:	Li-San Hwang
Principal Location:	670 North Rosemead Blvd. Pasadena, CA 91107
Telephone/Fax:	818-449-6400/818-351-1188
Satellite Locations:	San Bernadino and Lafayette, CA; Christiana, DE; Sterling, VA
Date Founded:	1988
Description of Business:	Environmental cleanup and compliance.
# Employees Current:	607
# Employees Projected by 6/30/95:	Company withheld
Sales (Annualized) 1994:	$81,747,000
Gross Profit Margin (GPM):	25.1%
SG&A Expenses/Sales:	11.1%
% Sales Increase 1991–94:	+148.4%
% Change GPM 1991–94:	+21.3%
Total Debt/Net Worth:	39.6%
Net Profits Before Taxes:	$8,161,000
Operating Ratio:	17.7%
Net Profits per Employee:	$13,455
Traded On:	NASDAQ/WATR
Principal Competitors:	Dames & Moore, EMCON, TRC Companies, The Earth Technology Corp., Versar
# Potential Selling Sites:	Domestic: 3,500 Foreign: 10,000
Problem Company Is Attempting to Solve:	The need for industry to comply with stricter environmental laws.
Solution Company Is Conveying to Problem:	Provides engineering and consulting services to solve complex water contamination and other environmental problems.

tions at several sites for major pharmaceutical companies and provided similar services for chemical and manufacturing companies. It also conducted large-scale groundwater investigations at March Air Force Base and Vandenberg Air Force Base in California. Tetra Tech recently acquired Simon Hydro-Search, a Colorado-based water-management firm that will give it an array of private-sector clients to balance its government business.

And the list goes on. Tetra Tech management knows how to price its services, and it has control of overhead. Its ratio of SG&A Expenses to Revenues in 1994 was a low 11.1 percent. The company's GPM increased 21.3 percent from 1991 to 1994, an unusual achievement for a consulting company. But then, Tetra Tech is unusually well-positioned. Someone *has* to clean up the radioactive waste of earlier decades. Elves will not come to these sites on their tippy toes while we sleep. Tetra Tech wields the big broom in the post-nuclear age.

THERMO ELECTRON CORP.

Thermo Electron Corp. is 15 distinct companies, including 9 that are publicly held. Occasionally, one of the "pups" has offspring of their own—what securities analysts refer to as spin-offs. For instance, ThermoTrex Corp., which operates a military lab in San Diego and is 55 percent owned by Thermo Electron, recently spun out ThermoLace, Inc., by selling a 19 percent interest in a private placement to develop a hair-removal idea.

Thermo Electron began 38 years ago as an instrument maker, period. But CEO George Hatsopoulos views business as a solar system, with the parent at the core and new ventures revolving like planets around it. When one of the company's ventures began to show promise but required capital for R&D, Hatsopoulos sold new shares to the public to fund it. Rather than spin off peripheral companies, Thermo Electron continually spins out parts of its core. Moreover, it never uses the spin-offs to generate capital for itself, although it gives the "pups" access to capital and accounting, legal, and other corporate services. Thermo Electron is somewhat like a publicly held, high tech venture capital fund.

Environmental cleanup service is now the second-largest core business, following instruments. Thermo Remediation, Inc., was spun out of Thermo Process Systems in 1993 to provide cleanup of petroleum-contaminated soil from a national network of offices. The new spinout acquired a waste-fluids recycler later in the year to reclaim, process, and resell used motor oil.

The first offspring—and the first departure from Thermo Electron's long-standing emphasis on instruments and energy technology—was Thermedics, Inc., which was working on an artificial heart pump to keep cardiac patients alive while they wait for a transplant. After more than a decade of work, the artificial heart has been a lifeline for more than 100 trial patients.

As its spinouts have proliferated, Thermo's culture has changed. "When someone comes up with a bright idea," says John Wood, Chief Executive, "other workers ask: 'What else can we do with this?'"

For example, Tecoflex, a plastic made by Thermedics, was developed for use inside the heart device. But researchers realized that because it was biologically inert, it would also be useful to makers of other medical devices. Now used in such products as heart catheters, it brings in $4 million a year. But it doesn't stop there: Because Tecoflex can be cured

THERMO ELECTRON CORP.

Chief Executive Officer:	George N. Hatsopoulos
Principal Location:	81 Wyman St. Waltham, MA 02254
Telephone/Fax:	617-622-1000/617-622-1207
Satellite Locations:	Offices in most developed countries
Date Founded:	1956
Description of Business:	Identifies emerging societal problems and develops technological solutions in subsidiary companies, parts of which are spun off to the public to raise capital for R&D.
# Employees Current:	8,800
# Employees Projected by 6/30/95:	Company withheld
Sales (Annualized) 1994:	$1,3407,431,000
Gross Profit Margin (GPM):	37.5%
Selling Expenses/Sales:	22.4%
% Sales Increase 1991–94:	+162.3%
% Change GPM 1991–94:	–16.4%
Total Debt/Net Worth:	144.6%
Net Profits Before Taxes:	$148,837
Operating Ratio:	11.4%
Net Profits per Employee:	$16,913
Traded On:	NYSE/TMO
Principal Competitors:	Hewlett-Packard, Ensys Environmental Services, Loral General Instruments
# Potential Selling Sites:	Domestic: 1,500,000 Foreign: 3,000,000
Problem Company Is Attempting to Solve:	How does a successful company continue to remain entrepreneurial when it achieves $1 billion in sales?
Solution Company Is Conveying to Problem:	Thermo Electron spins out young subsidiaries to the public to raise capital; if their R&D pays off, employees are rewarded with personal wealth.

without heat, researchers figured it could be mixed with delicate oils and pharmaceuticals. One product, a perfume sample strip for magazines that has no smell until opened, has become a hit.

New products can come in a rush. After Thermedics found a way to test blood for the angina drug nitroglycerin, David Fine, a company researcher, began tinkering with devices that could sniff traces of explosives made from the chemical. Now, Thermedics (54 percent owned) sells bomb detectors to police and to airports in Europe and the Middle East. The technology has been further modified to sniff out cocaine, methamphetamines, and heroin.

Managers who come to Thermo from other companies are sometimes surprised by their new freedom. In a *Wall Street Journal* article, Thomas Corcoran, who joined Thermo Power Corp. from Carrier Corp. when his refrigeration unit was acquired, recalled "the three or four levels of bureaucracy we had to go through to get a capital project approved. And as a small business inside a big company, we were always the last in line." At Thermo, Corcoran noted, he gets quick clearance for worthy projects.[1]

All in all, the parent company and its subsidiaries have made about 70 acquisitions over the years. But not all of Thermo's acquisitions have worked out. A small metal-plating company bought a few years ago went sour, costing $18 million and more than a year to fix, and an environmental engineering company purchased in 1988 drained $6 million. Thermo has also had its share of technological dead ends. One was a 1960s effort to build a plutonium-fueled, steam-driven implantable artificial heart.

Right now, Thermo's hottest prospect may be the hair remover. While others have tried unsuccessfully to use lasers this way, ThermoTrex researchers invented and patented a method using a proprietary skin preparation and a special laser. Thermo claims it is fast, painless, and generally superior to electrolysis, in which an electrified needle must be inserted in each follicle. Clinical trials have just begun, and the method will need FDA approval.

The technique's potential persuaded Thermo to create ThermoLase, which in March raised $15.2 million in a private offering of a 19 percent stake. With ThermoTrex, Hatsopoulos says he hopes to create a new crucible of start-ups, and he is convinced the spinout strategy can make it happen: "There's no better way to stimulate creativity than to see the guy next to you get $500,000 in options for a great idea."

---

[1] "Thermo Electron Uses an Unusual Strategy to Create Products," John R. Wille, *Wall Street Journal*, August 5, 1993, p. A-1.

3COM CORP.

3Com Corporation pioneered the networking industry. The company evolved from a supplier of discrete networking products to a supplier of local-area networking systems (LANs) and enterprise networking systems. Today 3Com is a leading independent global data networking (GDN) company offering customers a broad range of networking solutions, including routers, hubs, and adapters for Ethernet, Token Ring, and fiber distributed data interface (FDDI) networks. The company's products and systems are distributed and serviced worldwide through 3Com and its partners—principally systems integrators, value-added resellers, national resellers and dealers, distributors, and original equipment manufacturers.

3Com's name is derived from its focus on computer communications compatibility. With its long-standing focus on multivendor interoperability, the company has been a leader in defining, shaping, and promoting the growth of a networking infrastructure that transmits data to all parts of the world as quickly and efficiently as today's most effective telephone networks make voice connections. Underlying this commitment is a focus on simplicity in the way 3Com designs and manufactures products, as well as in the way it works with customers; scalability of products to allow customers to purchase only those networking components that meet their networking requirements today, with the assurance that 3Com has cost-effective migration and upgrade paths for systems as networking needs change; and value in providing high performance with low cost of total networking ownership.

In fiscal 1991 the company took significant steps to refocus on the emerging GDN environment, including exiting the workgroup server and network operating system business. During fiscal 1992, 3Com rebuilt its product portfolio, retrained its sales force to focus on selling connectivity products and solutions, and expanded its global presence. The acquisition of the data networking products business of United Kingdom-based BICC Group PLC in January 1992 strengthened 3Com's position in the growing structured wiring hub market, enhanced its other data networking product offerings, and expanded its worldwide market coverage. That year the company also established "parts banks" in Europe and Singapore and service centers in the United Kingdom, Australia, Japan, and China to improve its customer service capabilities.

During fiscal 1993, 3Com furthered its commitment to GDN with the introduction of key new platforms for its adapter, hub, and internetworking

3COM CORP.

Chief Executive Officer:	Eric A. Benhamou
Principal Location:	5400 Bayfront Plaza Santa Clara, CA 95052
Telephone/Fax:	408-764-5000/408-764-5001
Satellite Locations:	Northboro, MA; Blanchardstown, Ireland
Date Founded:	1979
Description of Business:	Develops, produces, sells, and supports global data networking systems.
# Employees Current:	1,971
# Employees Projected by 6/30/95:	Company withheld
Sales (Annualized) 1994:	$752,990,000
Gross Profit Margin (GPM):	50.5%
Selling Expenses/Sales:	22.2%
% Sales Increase 1991–94:	+182.2%
% Change GPM 1991–94:	+4.1%
Total Debt/Net Worth:	62.7%
Net Profits Before Taxes:	$12,665,000
Operating Ratio:	1.7%
Net Profits per Employee:	$6,426
Traded On:	NASDAQ/COMS
Principal Competitors:	Cisco, Lannet, Cabletron, Bay Networks, Inc.
# Potential Selling Sites:	Domestic: 15,000 Foreign: 45,000
Problem Company Is Attempting to Solve:	Need to adapt PCs to growing requirements of the networking environment.
Solution Company Is Conveying to Problem:	Offers a broad range of networking solutions to a worldwide customer base.

product portfolios. The company believes that these platforms, alone or in combination, address the current and anticipated networking requirements of its worldwide customer base. In January 1993 3Com acquired Star-Tek, Inc., a Massachusetts-based technological innovator, to further enhance its Token Ring technology base. Additionally, the company completed and began full-scale operations at its 60,000-square-foot manufacturing facility in Ireland, opened seven new sales offices throughout the world, and launched the Network Technical Services Alliance, a commitment among 33 networking vendors to provide the resources and cooperation necessary to resolve multivendor technical support problems.

Intensifying its acquisition strategy, 3Com acquired Synernetics, Inc., in January 1994 and assumed all outstanding Synernetics stock options. The purchase price: $104.0 million plus $3.3 million of stock options. Synernetics develops, manufactures, and markets LAN hardware and software. In February 1994 the company acquired Centrum Communications, Inc., and assumed all outstanding Centrum stock options for approximately $36.0 million. Centrum develops, manufactures, and markets remote access products and technology. After making these 1994 acquisitions, 3Com's cash on hand was more than $81 million and its funded debt rose by a mere $500,000.

3Com was funded with approximately $18 million provided by the Mayfield Fund and other venture capital funds. Mayfield is the creation of the late Tommy Davis, the first venture capitalist, along with his former partner, Arthur Rock, who set roots on Sand Hill Road in Menlo Park, California, in the shadow of Stanford University. Davis gave Intel its seed capital. 3Com was founded by Robert M. Metcalfe, the principal inventor of Ethernet, while he was at Xerox Palo Alto Research Center in the early 1970s. Metcalfe, it might be said, is the founder of the public utilities system for computer users, opening the way for millions of firms and emancipating millions of entrepreneurs to contribute, collaborate, and communicate with other users.

3Com's continual growth is testament to the fact that it persists in making a valuable commercial statement. Its increasing GPM indicates that 3Com is not being hammered by the competition. It is a gatekeeper company in the true sense of the word: collecting tolls from others, rarely paying them.

THREE-FIVE SYSTEMS, INC.

D emand creates its own supply," goes the old adage. And if you have invested in the supplier, what a lovely place to be. In the rush to bring new hand-held PCs and telecommunications products to the market, Three-Five Systems, Inc., has become one of the most important producers of liquid crystal display (LCD) and light-emitting diode (LED) displays. An indication of the ferocious demand for the company's manufacturing capability: Its stock price soared 900 percent in the 12 months ending in April 1994. Still, its LCDs and LEDs are in very short supply.

Three-Five raised $25 million in fresh capital in April 1994 to expand its primary manufacturing facility in Manila and to build a new manufacturing and R&D center in Tempe, Arizona. The new Tempe facility will manufacture LCD glass in an automated factory.

The value-added that Three-Five brings to an original equipment manufacturer (OEM) is its ability to problem-solve rapidly. Because it focuses on display technology, Three-Five is contacted by OEMs that need a certain kind of display and need it quickly and in quantity. For example, a cellular-telephone OEM customer asked the company to design a thinner display with more graphics and a different appearance for its next-generation product line. Three-Five did the design work within a few weeks, fully costed it in-house, and gave the customer a price 20 percent below that of the original product line. Three-Five knows its costs because it generally keeps the work in-house.

Three-Five is not the kind of company that will explode to $1 billion in sales over the next three years, then flame out while it searches for new products or new markets. It has neither the marketing plan nor the sales force. David R. Buchanan, the company's CEO and co-founder, says, "If you want to understand what the potential is for this company, look at everything that has a user interface, and that's our potential. And it's staggering. That's why we can't quantify it. With respect to our customers, I believe that we will become a major supplier of services to a small number of very large customers. Take the customers we have now, and as they grow and each gives us $20 million of revenues, we'll be a half-billion-dollar company."

One of the reasons companies such as Three-Five, IEC Electronics, Inc., Quality Technologies Corp., and other contract manufacturing companies are succeeding so handsomely is the trend among modern managers to focus on what they do well and outsource what they don't

THREE-FIVE SYSTEMS, INC.

Chief Executive Officer:	David R. Buchanan
Principal Location:	10230 South 50th Place Phoenix, AZ 85044
Telephone/Fax:	602-496-0035/602-496-0168
Satellite Locations:	Manila, Philippines
Date Founded:	1990
Description of Business:	Designs, develops, and manufactures user-interface devices for information-display functions.
# Employees Current:	141
# Employees Projected by 6/30/95:	Company withheld
Sales 1993:	$38,002,000
Gross Profit Margin (GPM):	29.7
Selling Expenses/Sales:	10.1
% Sales Increase 1991–93:	+103.2%
% Change GPM 1991–93:	+32.6%
Total Debt/Net Worth:	21.7%
Net Profits Before Taxes:	$6,173,000
Operating Ratio:	16.2%
Net Profits per Employee:	$43,780
Traded On:	ASE/TFS
Principal Competitors:	Rohm Company Ltd., Philips Components B.V., Stanley Electric, Ltd., Optrex Corp., Hewlett-Packard, Quality Technologies Corp.
# Potential Selling Sites:	Domestic: 50 Foreign: 30
Problem Company Is Attempting to Solve:	Explosive growth in hand-held telecommunications devices has created a need for information displays.
Solution Company Is Conveying to Problem:	Manufactures LED and LCD display devices for cellular phones, home alarm systems, bar-code readers, and consumer electronics.

do well. Many telecommunications and computer companies excel at systems design and marketing, but not at manufacturing.

Buchanan says, "The major challenge in the three industries we serve—telecommunications, medical electronics, and office automation—is the advancement of technology. Technological change is leaping forward on a monthly basis compared with what used to be every three to five years. So our customers need to remain at the forefront of these changes; and by outsourcing the manufacturing to us, they can change direction on a dime. That is the critical need that we serve."

It would be impossible to bring new designs to customers this quickly without computer-assisted design, or CAD, software. Emerging technologies, including laser sintering and free-form fabrication, will build in hours almost anything a CAD system can dream up. CAD puts the engineer's information in the right form; the new rapid prototyping technologies will transform ideas to prototypes with no chips left over. These faster and cheaper methods will likely still not satisfy the customers, who will want mass production in units of one in real time.

Three-Five sports a nifty P/E ratio of 47.0x in mid-1994, which indicates a strong stock market following. Behind that support is confidence in the company's future earnings growth. And behind that is a reputation among OEMs, particularly in the wireless communications market, that Three-Five can deliver the lightest weight, smallest size devices for the lowest cost.

TRANSMEDIA NETWORK, INC.

Clubs are going to become an increasingly important marketing channel on the American economic stage, because Americans love to join clubs. We love to be part of groups, to be members, to be included. The first person to notice this yearning was Alexis de Tocqueville, who visited America in 1832 and wrote about what he saw[1]:

America is a nation of joiners.

The inhabitant of the United States learns from birth that he must rely on himself to combat the ills and trials of life; he is restless and defiant in his outlook toward the authority of society and appeals to its power only when he cannot do without it. The beginnings of this attitude first appear at school, where the children, even in their games, submit to rules settled by themselves and punish offenses which they have defined themselves. . . . Where enjoyment is concerned, people associate to make festivities grander and more orderly. Finally, associations are formed to combat exclusively moral troubles; intemperance is fought in common. Public security, trade and industry, and morals and religion all provide the aims for associations in the United States. There is no end which the human is capable of attaining by the free action of the collective power of individuals.

The right of association being recognized, citizens can use it in different ways. . . . It counts its supporters and involves them in its cause; these supporters get to know one another, and numbers increase zeal. An association unites the energies of divergent minds and vigorously directs them toward a clearly indicated goal.

What was true in 1832 is true today. "Numbers increase zeal" and the zeal is expressed in loyalty to the club whose purpose it is to spread the gospel of the product or the service to the many. Televangelists call it "seeding the faith," and their clubs have millions of zealots as faithful members.

Transmedia Network, Inc., is in the club-creating business. It issues and markets a private restaurant charge card, called the Restaurant Card, that entitles its holders to a 25 percent savings when dining at restaurants that participate in its program. Restaurants that join the Transmedia Network program benefit on two fronts: advance financing and additional diners. The company provides financing in exchange for

---

[1] Tocqueville, Alexis de, *Democracy in America*, Harper & Row, New York, 1969, pp. 189–190.

TRANSMEDIA NETWORK, INC.

Chief Executive Officer:	Melvin Chasen
Principal Location:	11900 Biscayne Blvd. North Miami, FL 33181
Telephone/Fax:	305-892-3340/305-892-3317
Satellite Location:	New York
Date Founded:	1983
Description of Business:	Issues a membership card entitling holders to a 25 percent discount on meals in participating restaurants.
# Employees Current:	61
# Employees Projected by 6/30/95:	Company withheld
Sales (Annualized) 1994:	$43,675,000
Gross Profit Margin (GPM):	39.2%
Selling Expenses/Sales:	27.8%
% Sales Increase 1991–94:	+318.3%
% Change GPM 1991–94:	+2.9%
Total Debt/Net Worth:	41.9%
Net Profits Before Taxes:	$5,490,000
Operating Ratio:	12.6%
Net Profits per Employee:	$90,000
Traded On:	NASDAQ/TMNI
Principal Competitors:	American Express, Citicorp, MasterCard, Visa
# Potential Selling Sites:	Domestic: 50,000 Foreign: 150,000
Problem Company Is Attempting to Solve:	Restaurants need capital and diners.
Solution Company Is Conveying to Problem:	Developed the concept of a membership club for restaurants that offers discounts to diners.

approximately twice the amount in food and beverage credits (rights to receive), which are then charged to card-holding members who patronize the restaurants. Transmedia derives its income from (a) the difference between its cost for the food and beverage credits and the proceeds from card members' charges, (b) annual membership fees paid up front, and (c) franchise fees for sales of the Transmedia concept to others.

Americans are joiners; Americans love a discount. Given those two premises, Melvin Chasen came up with his first idea: Market a discount dining card. That would make everyone happy except the restaurants. To win their cooperation, Chasen came up with his next neat idea: Use Transmedia's up-front membership fees to lend money to restaurants (obviously an inducement to accept the card) for refurbishment or working capital. The restaurants repay Transmedia with credits for food and beverages, thus permitting them to conserve cash flow. Even after selling meals at a discount, the restaurants still earn decent profits.

Two-audience companies are fascinating. As they build cash flow, they develop multimarket cash flow channels such as magazines and product catalogs. Transmedia is very small, with years of growth ahead of it. It is currently in only 2,000 restaurants with a mere 180,000 cardholders, primarily in New York and South Florida. It is franchising California and other markets.

Indeed, once a club or association kicks into high gear, it not only increases the company's persistency ratio but it begins to generate a considerable amount of cash flow for the company through multiple marketing channels. The fun of running a club-based company adjunctively is to try to implement multiple cash flow generating marketing channels, each of which is providing channels of float.

Recognizing this adjunctive market, a few years ago American Express, the mother of all club companies, developed its own product catalog, thus earning a healthy markup on products, made by others, that it began to offer in its catalog. American Express doesn't make these products nor does it inventory these products. Heaven forbid, for that would be a serious misuse of float. And do you think that American Express gives away its catalog pages? Don't bet on it. If a manufacturer wants its product seen by 30 million privileged consumers, they have to pay American Express for catalog space. More up-front cash. More float. Look for Transmedia to begin ancillary cash flow channels such as its own magazine with hundreds of advertising pages and its own product catalog. The PC can manage millions of names and addresses of club members and their eating out habits. Thus, overhead at Transmedia is negligible, and should remain so.

TRESP ASSOCIATES, INC.

TRESP Associates, Inc., is a facilities-management company with a simple and elegant operating strategy: When a government agency or a large corporation is unable to operate a plant, subsidiary, or division profitably or efficiently, TRESP offers to manage the operation using the available people and equipment; it is paid the agency's or division's budget. If it produces the desired results and saves some of the money it is paid, the savings represent profit. A facilities-management company in the information industry can take on several similar jobs simultaneously, selling off incremental equipment, laying off incremental personnel, and showing some huge profits.

Electronic Data Systems Corp. (EDS), Ross Perot's venture, is the granddaddy of facilities management. Lillian B. Handy, founder and CEO of TRESP, has her eye fixed on building an EDS clone. Rather than bid one-shot consulting contracts, TRESP manages entire operations and facilities for government agencies and corporations. The bulk of the contracts are in connectivity and networking environments, one of the fastest-growing industries in the country.

TRESP's facilities-management (and other) contracts include the following:

- For the Department of Defense: Developing and managing the Defense Applied Information Technology Center (testing and prototyping information technologies). This contract involves installing, maintaining, and administering a 200-node Ethernet local area network (LAN) utilizing VAX 11/780, DEC Micro VAXII, Gould 6050, Elxsi 6400, Pyramid 98x, SUN Workstations, IBM and compatible PCs, Apple Macintosh, Wang, and Xerox Workstations, and mainframe, mini, and PC-based software, including FORTRAN, C, C++, BASIC, COBOL, HyperSearch, UNIX, Ethernet, dBase II, and Clipper.
- For the Department of Energy: Designing, acquiring, installing, and maintaining a campuswide fiber-optic LAN serving Morgantown, West Virginia; Oak Ridge, Tennessee; Laramie, Wyoming; and Washington, D.C. This contract involves designing the network architecture to permit substantial growth for future collateral services such as fiber distributed data interface (FDDI) and integrated services digital network (ISDN); installing a transmission system of over 40 miles of inside and outside

TRESP ASSOCIATES, INC.

Chief Executive Officer:	Lillian B. Handy
Principal Location:	4900 Seminary Rd. Alexandria, VA 22311
Telephone/Fax:	703-845-9400/703-671-3492
Satellite Locations:	Oak Ridge, TN
Date Founded:	1981
Description of Business:	Manages the data-processing operation for the federal government.
# Employees Current:	195
# Employees Projected by 6/30/95:	250
Sales (Annualized) 1994:	$16,000,000
Gross Profit Margin (GPM):	The company is privately-held and not required to publish its financial statements.
Selling Expenses/Sales:	not available
% Sales Increase 1991–94:	not available
% Change GPM 1991–94:	not available
Total Debt/Net Worth:	not available
Net Profits Before Taxes:	not available
Net Profits per Employee:	not available
Principal Competitors:	NetFRAME, Cambridge Technology Partners, various other consulting firms
# Potential Selling Sites:	Domestic: 150 Foreign: not applicable
Problem Company Is Attempting to Solve:	The federal government and its hundreds of agencies frequently lack the expertise to carry out the functions assigned to them by Congress.
Solution Company Is Conveying to Problem:	Offers high-quality, high-tech consulting, fairly priced.

distribution cable; and procuring and installing a LAN using a fiber-optic backbone and 3Com's 3+ Open Network Operating System, which serves 800 users on the primary network.

- For IBM: Providing support for the Federal Aviation Administration's Advanced Automation Systems in Rockville, Maryland.
- For the office of the Secretary of Defense: Managing the Defense Applied Information Technology Center, where TRESP tests and prototypes information technologies utilizing VAX 11/780, SUN Workstations, and a variety of sophisticated computer systems.

CEO Lillian Handy has built a highly successful business, one that will endure for years to come. "I'm not the technical person," she told *Minority Business Entrepreneur* magazine, adding, "Technical people usually don't make good managers. Likewise, managers don't often make good technical people. It's very difficult to combine the two." A company will fail most often, she said, "because they don't manage."[1]

Ms. Handy is projecting a 30 percent increase in personnel over the next year. This could be indicative of another revenue leap, well in excess of 30 percent, since the name of the game in facilities management is to leverage skilled people and useful assets.

---

[1] Jeanie M. Barnett, "Unlimited Ceiling," *Minority Business Entrepreneur*, Vol. 7, No. 5, Sept.-Oct. 1990.

VIVRA, INC.

ccording to data from the Health Care Finance Administration, the number of patients who require chronic kidney dialysis grew from approximately 60,000 in 1982 to approximately 157,000 in 1992, representing a compound annual growth rate of approximately 9 percent. Most chronic patients obtain treatment at a freestanding dialysis facility or at a hospital. As of December 1992, approximately 82 percent of chronic dialysis patients were receiving treatment at outpatient facilities (including 30 percent at hospital-based centers) and 18 percent at home.

Dialysis treatments are generally given by means of an "artificial kidney" machine, which pumps the patient's blood through a filter to remove toxic substances and then returns the cleansed blood to the patient's body. Typically, dialysis for the chronic patient is performed three times a week for approximately four hours per treatment; normally it must continue for the patient's lifetime. Vivra's dialysis facilities are designed specifically for outpatient hemodialysis. They typically contain a large dialysis treatment area, nurses' stations, a patient weigh-in area, examination rooms, water treatment space, staff work areas, offices, and a kitchen, lobby, supply room, and staff lounge.

By late 1993, Vivra owned and operated 138 independent dialysis facilities under the name Community Dialysis Centers, with a total capacity of 2,268 licensed stations. Of the 138 facilities, 111 are located in leased premises and 27 in buildings owned by the company. Vivra also serves inpatients with acute kidney disorders at general hospitals in the vicinity of its outpatient facilities. In addition, where appropriate, it provides training, supplies, and on-call support services to facilitate the implementation of home hemodialysis and intradialytic parenteral nutrition (IDPN).

As required by Medicare regulations, each facility is supervised by a medical director, a licensed physician in private practice who is directly responsible for the quality of patient care. A unit administrator, generally a registered nurse, supervises the day-to-day operation of each facility and the staff. The staff consists of registered nurses, medical technicians, nurses' aides, a unit clerk, and certain part-time employees, including a social worker, a registered dietitian, and a machine repair technician. The number of personnel at each facility is adjusted according to the number of patients receiving treatment. Medicare and Medicaid pay for

VIVRA, INC.

Chief Executive Officer:	Kent J. Thiry
Principal Location:	400 Primrose Burlingame, CA 94010
Telephone/Fax:	415-348-8200/415-375-7550
Satellite Locations:	Numerous, particularly in California, Florida, Georgia, and Texas
Date Founded:	1973
Description of Business:	Owns and operates dialysis centers and recently expanded into ambulatory service centers and rehabilitation therapy.
# Employees Current:	2,740
# Employees Projected by 6/30/95:	Company withheld
Sales (Annualized) 1994:	$225,377,000
Gross Profit Margin (GPM):	31.1%
Selling Expenses/Sales:	9.0%
% Sales Increase 1991–94:	+84.5%
% Change GPM 1991–94:	-0-
Total Debt/Net Worth:	14.9%
Net Profits Before Taxes:	$43,804,000
Operating Ratio:	19.4%
Net Profits per Employee:	$15,986
Traded On:	NYSE/V
Principal Competitors:	National Medical Care, American HealthCorp, Inc.
# Potential Selling Sites:	Domestic: 35,000 Foreign: 70,000
Problem Company Is Attempting to Solve:	Lack of suffcent facilities for treatment of chronic kidney failure.
Solution Company Is Conveying to Problem:	Operates 138 independent dialysis facilities and is expanding into new treatment areas.

70 percent of each treatment, and a secondary carrier, or the patient's hospital, Veteran's Administration, or state kidney associations pay the balance.

In 1991 Vivra established Associated Health Services to provide IDPN pharmacy and support services to its dialysis patients. The company opened its first pharmacy the following year and also began providing IDPN therapy services to third-party dialysis patients as well as its own patients. In 1993 the company initiated mail order delivery of oral medications for dialysis and transplant patients from its Southern California pharmacy.

In March 1992 Vivra acquired Health Advantage, Inc., a provider of diabetes management services to general hospital staff, patients, and personal physicians. Centers are established pursuant to contracts with the hospitals. The goals of the centers are to assist the patients and their families to understand, control, and adapt to the disease and achieve a reasonably satisfactory lifestyle. The emphasis is on patient education and aggressive medical management in cooperation with the attending physicians and hospital staff. Quality assurance and utilization review procedures have been developed on the basis of the American Diabetes Association's national standards of care. The company works closely with each hospital's quality assurance coordinators and utilization review committees to tailor these procedures to the requirements of each hospital. It plans to expand its diabetes management services into additional states.

Vivra also established Surgical Partners of America in February 1992 to acquire, develop, and operate ambulatory surgery centers. Ambulatory, or outpatient, surgery has gained increasing acceptance in recent years as an alternative to surgery in acute-care hospitals. Industry sources estimate that by 1995 as much as 60 percent of all surgeries in the United States will be conducted on an outpatient basis.

The stock market is sanguine about the future earnings growth potential of Vivra, giving it a P/E ratio of 18.0x in mid-1994 and a market value-to-revenues ratio of approximately 2:1. The connectivity hardware and software Quantum Companies trade at P/E ratios twice Vivra's on average, and the problem they solve may someday vanish or shrink when all computers are linked. But kidney failure and diabetes seem to be constants.

VIVUS

Alejandro Zaffaroni invented the birth control pill, which more than any other invention or development in the history of civilization, has given women the capacity to make choices about their lives. His first company, Syntex, benefited from the commercial success of the pill throughout the 1970s. To house his future inventions, Zaffaroni founded Alza Corp. in the mid-70s, but no sustainable medical inventions came about. Until now. The problem of male sexual impotence may be solved by the MUSE (Medicated Urethral System for Erection), an Alza invention.

There have been numerous attempts to correct erectile dysfunction by urologists-turned-entrepreneur, including imbedding receivers under the epidermis of the penis and putting transmitters in garage door opener-type gadgets. But erections were occurring when they were not supposed to. Upjohn is working on an injection therapy, Syntex on a topical solution, and Johnson & Johnson on an injection therapy. The present system—implanting a football-inflator-like device in the man's lower stomach and pumping hot air into the penis prior to sexual intercourse—is unpleasant, cumbersome, and, worst of all, not reversible. Thus, if the cause of his impotence is one day solved, he must continue using the pump.

Dr. Virgil A. Place invented the MUSE while he worked for Alza, and the patents are in Alza's name. But he left Alza to launch Vivus with $35 million of venture capital provided by The Mayfield Fund, Domain Associates, and Institutional Venture Partners. Alza had little choice but to license Vivus and take back some shares of stock and a future royalty stream. The venture capitalists hired Leland F. Wilson, former Vice President-Marketing of Gene Labs Technologies, to run Vivus. Following FDA approval of Phase I clinical trials, an underwriter was found to raise $30 million from the public, valuing Vivus at $154 million—several years before revenues will hit the cash register.

The MUSE is easy to use with minimal instruction, unlike injection therapy which requires precise injection into a corpora cavernosa. MUSE is noninvasive and painless. It utilizes a small, easily carried, disposable applicator that can be discreetly applied and is easily integrated into the normal sexual life of the patient; administration takes less than a minute. The MUSE therapy mimics the normal vasoactive process, producing an erection that is more natural than those resulting from vacuum constriction devices or surgical implants.

VIVUS

Chief Executive Officer:	Leland F. Wilson
Principal Location:	545 Middlefield Rd. Menlo Park, CA 94025
Telephone/Fax:	415-325-5511/415-325-5546
Satellite Locations:	none
Date Founded:	1991
Description of Business:	A leader in the development of advanced therapeutic systems for the treatment of erectile dysfunction.
# Employees Current:	25
# Employees Projected by 6/30/95:	39
Sales (Annualized) 1994:	none
Gross Profit Margin (GPM):	The company has not been permitted by the FDA to begin selling its product yet.
Selling Expenses/Sales:	not available
% Sales Increase 1991–94:	not available
% Change GPM 1991–94:	not available
Total Debt/Net Worth:	5.5%
Net Profits Before Taxes:	$(7,775,000)
Net Profits per Employee:	deficit
Operating Ratio:	deficit
Traded On:	NASDAQ/VVUS
Principal Competitors:	Upjohn, Johnson & Johnson, Syntex
# Potential Selling Sites:	Domestic: 7,000,000 Foreign: 7,000,000
Problem Company Is Attempting to Solve:	Male sexual impotence of approximately 10 percent of the adult male population.
Solution Company Is Conveying to Problem:	A painless, easy-to-administer therapy.

The system is substantially narrower than a standard urethral catheter. A patient urinates, shakes the penis to remove excess urine, inserts the MUSE approximately three centimeters into the urethra, releases the medication—alprostadil—and then rolls the penis between the hands for 10 seconds to distribute the medication.

The pharmacological agent dissolves in the small amount of urine that remains in the urethra. After absorption, it moves across the adjacent tissue and into the erectile bodies. An erection is produced within 15 minutes of administration and lasts approximately 30 to 60 minutes.

In clinical trials to date, the MUSE has been utilized to treat more than 800 men at more than 25 study sites in the United States. Additional trials are under way and scheduled through 1994.

Vivus estimates that over 10 percent of adult males in the United States suffer from some degree of erectile dysfunction. They also believe that, because it is a discreet, easily administered therapy, the MUSE may increase the number of men who will seek and receive medical treatment for erectile dysfunction.

Although the price for the company's products has not been established, management anticipates it to be a competitive, cost-effective therapy. The quality of life for many people, particularly older couples, is certain to be enhanced by Vivus. And its irony is that it began with birth control.

WALL DATA INC.

Named for John R. Wall, its founder and chief software developer, but run since 1988 by James Simpson, formerly CEO of Qume Corp. and before that, Durango Systems, Inc., Wall Data Inc. is a *tollgate* company. That is, if you pay it a "toll," through purchasing its *Rumba* software, your many PCs can access information and files that reside in any host mainframe or minicomputer. The PCs can be running Windows, OS/2, VAX, or operating in the Macintosh environment. Other competitive software of this genre, known as emulators, can do the same thing; but many of the magazines that review software give *Rumba* first place.

The product is boundaryless. It will work as easily in Bora Bora as in Seattle. In fact, approximately one-third of Wall Data's sales in 1994 were foreign, and the percentage is growing. The company has installed *Rumba* on more than 500,000 PCs at 3,000 customer sites. And with 50 million PCs tied to networks, Wall Data has merely nicked the tip off of the iceberg.

The company's efficiency is improving. Its GPM rose nearly 3 percent from 1991 to 1994, and its Net Profits per Employee are $28,642. The employee head count is fairly high for two reasons: (1) it takes quite a few programmers, working in the C and C++ languages, to link any computer with any other computer—micro, mini, or mainframe; and (2) in a market where a cacophony of claims for interconnectivity draws out the truth, Wall Data has to put a lot of foot soldiers on the street to tell its story to prospective customers. Of its 388 employees, 250 are in sales, marketing, and customer support; 100 are in product development. That's appropriate for a high-growth company.

Wall Data also sells through national distributors, software retailers, value-added resellers, and original equipment manufacturers (OEMs). The company is spending 42 cents of every sales dollar on selling and supporting its product. If it could find ways to make multiple sales with one sales call—perhaps by licensing foreign marketing partners—this ratio could drop into the more appropriate twenties.

To sustain its growth, Wall Data must follow *Rumba* with a hot product. Simpson thinks he's got it with *Salsa*, which is supposed to enable faster development of easy-to-use applications by less technical users. *Salsa* is based on a new data modeling methodology called Semantic Object Modeling, which is intended to enable end-users to

WALL DATA INC.

Chief Executive Officer:	James Simpson
Principal Location:	17769 NE 78th Place Redmond, WA 98052
Telephone/Fax:	206-814-9255/206-814-4300
Satellite Locations:	Middlesex, United Kingdom; Cedex, France; Munich, Germany; Toronto, Ontario, Canada
Date Founded:	1982
Description of Business:	Develops, markets, and supports Windows-based connectivity software products to enable PCs to communicate with mainframes and minicomputers in local and wide area networks.
# Employees Current:	388
# Employees Projected by 6/30/95:	Company withheld
Sales (Annualized) 1994:	$71,686,000
Gross Profit Margin (GPM):	84.7%
Selling Expenses/Sales:	42.3%
% Sales Increase 1991–94:	+490.9%
% Change GPM 1991–94:	2.7%
Total Debt/Net Worth:	13.3%
Net Profits Before Taxes:	$11,113,000
Operating Ratio:	15.5%
Net Profits per Employee:	$28,642
Traded On:	NASDAQ/WALL
Principal Competitors:	Microsoft, Novell, DCA, Elcon Technology, Attachmate
# Potential Selling Sites:	Domestic: 50,000 Foreign: 250,000
Problem Company Is Attempting to Solve:	Much of the corporate world's data reside on mainframes and minicomputers while the people who need to access it sit in front of PCs.
Solution Company Is Conveying to Problem:	The company's *Rumba* emulator products is easy to install, easy to use, and gives the PC user instantaneous access to the host computer.

quickly create, use, and modify their own database applications without having to be trained in data modeling techniques.

A less costly strategy, perhaps, and one that Wall Data can easily afford, would be to make a symbiotic acquisition. The company has cash and short-term investments on March 31, 1994 of $49 million.

Another positive attribute of Wall Data is that its CEO, James Simpson, is having his third at bat. He got on base with Qume and Durango, but didn't drive in many runs. Very experienced this time up, Simpson is expected to hit a grand slam home run. The stock market thinks he will. Wall Data commands a P/E ratio of 42.0x, higher than every other software Quantum Company except Davidson Associates (85.0x), Synopsys (55.0x), Ascend Communications (48.0x), and PARCPlace Systems (47.0x).

WHOLE FOODS MARKET, INC.

U p until the late 1930s, chemical pest control was dominated by such compounds as nicotine, arsenic, sulfur, oil, and soaps, and was also heavily dependent on various nonchemical practices such as crop rotation, burning or plowing of crop refuse, and the use of resistant crop varieties. These methods were imperfect, and consumers accepted some pest damage in the final products.

Then came dichlorodiphenyl-trichloroethane, or DDT, with its broad-spectrum insecticidal properties. DDT was so effective that farmers used it on just about everything, and consumers became accustomed to foods without pest damage. Although DDT was banned in the United States in the early 1970s, it is still used in many countries that export food to this country.

In the 1980s, a number of agriculture-oriented genetic engineering firms were launched with the mission of altering soil and seeds genetically to enable crops to resist pests without pesticides. There have been some, but not many, successes in the agri-genetics fields, most of them on Wall Street rather than Main Street.

Meanwhile, the number of deaths due to cancer continues to grow, and scholars from Rachel Carson (*Silent Spring*) to Ronald Capes, founder of Cetus Corp., attribute the problem to pesticide residue. Cancer deaths in the United States at the turn of the present century were less than 1 percent. Today cancer is the country's leading killer.

This fact seems to have been lost on all of the major supermarket chains in the country, but not on entrepreneurs like John Mackey, founder and CEO of Whole Foods Market, Inc., the nation's largest chain of natural foods supermarkets.

Natural foods can be defined as those that are minimally processed, largely or completely free of artificial ingredients, preservatives, and other non-naturally occurring chemicals, and in general as near to their whole, natural state as possible. According to *The Natural Foods Merchandiser*, a leading trade publication for the industry, natural foods sales have grown at an average rate of about 11.6 percent per year since 1987, reaching over $5.6 billion in 1993. This growth has been propelled by several factors, including increasing consumer concern over the purity and safety of food; environmental concerns; and healthier eating patterns. While production costs are higher for organic and natural food

WHOLE FOODS MARKET, INC.

Chief Executive Officer:	John Mackey
Principal Location:	2525 Wallingwood Dr. Austin, TX 78746
Telephone/Fax:	512-328-7541/512-328-5482
Satellite Locations:	Numerous locations throughout the country
Date Founded:	1980
Description of Business:	Owns and operates the nation's largest chain of natural foods supermarkets.
# Employees Current:	4,150
# Employees Projected by 6/30/95:	Company withheld
Sales (Annualized) 1994:	$367,368,000
Gross Profit Margin (GPM):	32.6%
SG&A Expenses/Sales:	3.5%
% Sales Increase 1991–94:	+212.5%
% Change GPM 1991–94:	+2.5%
Total Debt/Net Worth:	32.8%
Net Profits Before Taxes:	$9,890,000
Operating Ratio:	2.7%
Net Profits per Employee:	$2,383
Traded On:	NASDAQ/WFMI
Principal Competitors:	Wild Oats, Harry's Farmers Market, Greenfield Foods
# Potential Selling Sites:	Domestic: 70 million Foreign: 140 million
Problem Company Is Attempting to Solve:	Supected correlation between use of pesticides on foods and increased U.S. cancer rate.
Solution Company Is Conveying to Problem:	Sells natural foods that are free of pesticide residues and artificial ingredients which are healthier for consumers.

products, Whole Foods believes that a significant segment of the population values high-quality natural food and is willing to pay higher prices for such food items.

Whole Foods' strategy is to bring the consumer into its stores on the promise of healthfulness. To compete with conventional supermarkets, it offers 10,000 items in addition to pesticide-free produce.

The natural foods industry is highly fragmented and is characterized by a large number of independently owned stores. According to the June 1992 issue of *The Natural Foods Merchandiser*, there were 5,540 independent natural food stores in the United States in 1991 (representing $3.15 billion of the industry's sales), only 195 of which were larger than 5,000 square feet. Yet these 195 stores accounted for over $750 million of the total sales volume in the industry. In the past, most natural and health food stores provided only a limited selection of products, but natural foods supermarkets now provide a complete grocery shopping alternative to conventional supermarkets. Whole Foods believes that apart from its own stores, there are fewer than 30 other natural foods stores in the United States that are larger than 10,000 square feet and that, therefore, there are excellent opportunities for the supermarket-size format to gain market share in the industry. Whole Foods also believes that the growth of larger supermarket-size natural foods stores has increased consumer awareness of and demand for natural foods.

The company has achieved higher store sales per gross square foot, at $490 for fiscal 1994, than most other traditional supermarkets or food retailers, and all of the company's stores that are more than six months old are profitable. Whole Foods attributes its success to its ability to differentiate itself from other retailers competing for consumers' food dollars by tailoring its product mix, service standards, and store environment to satisfy the needs of the natural foods shopper and to appeal to the broader market of quality-oriented consumers. (The company targets consumers aged 25 to 50 who are better educated and more affluent than the populace as a whole.) One-stop shopping, quality standards, competitive pricing, and a tailored product mix are all key to its success.

Like many of the new and highly successful retailers of the 1990s, Whole Foods makes all its employees stockholders. Is it any wonder that this company's stock has a higher P/E ratio than most high-tech companies?

WHOLESOME & HEARTY FOODS, INC.

The stock market loves Wholesome & Hearty Foods, putting a P/E ratio on the quasi-health-care company of 67.0x in mid-1994. And why not? Its GPM grew 16.4 percent from 1991 to 1994, suggesting minimal price sensitivity and excellent cost control. Sales have grown nearly five times over the last four years, while the ratio of SG&A Expenses to Sales has moved up modestly from 25.7 percent four years ago to 32.3 percent in 1994. The company earned 19.8 percent on annualized 1994 sales, and $33,807 per employee, substantially greater ratios than its competitors. Someone's minding the store in Portland.

That someone is Paul F. Wenner, founder and Chief Executive Officer, who publishes a Mission Statement (something every company needs to do) for his employees, clients, and stockholders. It reads as follows:

> Wholesome & Hearty Foods pursues visionary ideas that are helping to sustain the health and integrity of our planet. We are committed to offering convenient, gourmet, whole-food choices to the world.
>
> Our objective is to develop products that are timely, yet futuristic; products that are made with compassion and a caring consciousness for the earth's fragile resources. We believe in the importance of producing only "earth-wise" products for all present and future generations.
>
> Wholesome & Hearty Foods values its employees. They are the very soul of our company. We know our continuing success depends upon respecting every individual's uniqueness and recognizing each person's contributions.
>
> We strive to promote harmony in the world by working to develop our dream of a healthy and balanced planet.

Wenner insists that the company is an active member of its community, rather than a cold, insensitive corporation. It promotes energy conservation, reading, and fighting hunger. Wholesome & Hearty Foods leads with its heart, a fundamental of many Quantum Companies. The company "adopted" a class of second graders at Buckman School in Portland. "We've begun focusing some of our community relations efforts on this dynamic and innovative learning institution," says Wenner. "In the past, we helped fund the construction of a playground structure and this year donated money to buy books. To grow, we need good food, and that's what Wholesome & Hearty is all about. We also need food for the mind . . . and nothing is more nutritious for the mind than books," says Wenner.

WHOLESOME & HEARTY FOODS, INC.

Chief Executive Officer:	Paul F. Wenner
Principal Location:	2422 SE Hawthorne Blvd. Portland, OR 97214
Telephone/Fax:	503-238-0109/503-232-6485
Satellite Locations:	None
Date Founded:	1985
Description of Business:	Provides a line of food products that includes a variety of frozen, meatless items that are soy-free, cholesterol-free, and low in fat.
# Employees Current:	101
# Employees Projected by 6/30/95:	120
Sales (Annualized) 1994:	$15,025,000
Gross Profit Margin (GPM):	53.4%
Selling Expenses/Sales:	32.3%
% Sales Increase 1991–94:	+466.2%
% Change GPM 1991–94:	+16.3%
Total Debt/Net Worth:	9.7%
Net Profits Before Taxes:	$2,975,000
Operating Ratio:	19.8%
Net Profits per Employee:	$33,807
Traded On:	NASDAQ/WHFI
Principal Competitors:	Worthington Foods, Pillsbury, Con Agra, Imagine Foods
# Potential Selling Sites:	Domestic: 200,000 Foreign: not applicable
Problem Company Is Attempting to Solve:	The number of people who "will not eat anything that has a mother" is growing dramatically. Someone has got to feed them.
Solution Company Is Conveying to Problem:	Wholesome & Hearty Foods produces meat-free, soy-free, fat-free products such as the "gardenVegan," a 3.4-ounce patty containing 190 calories, no artificial additives, and 16 grams of protein.

Founded in 1985, Wholesome & Hearty Foods is an innovator in the manufacturing and marketing of frozen, meatless, soy-free food products. The company distributes its garden products to more than 17,000 food service outlets throughout the United States, Canada, and abroad, including restaurants such as TGI Friday's, Hard Rock Cafe, Marie Calender's, and Red Robin International; corporate and industrial cafeterias; university dining halls; as well as hotels, schools, warehouse stores, hospitals, airlines, and sports arenas. Retail customers include more than 4,800 grocery and specialty food stores and more than 3,000 natural food stores.

If you think your business is tough, try the business of getting shelf-facings in a supermarket for a new product line that doesn't advertise on national T.V. It is frightfully difficult. Supermarket managers have limited real estate and they are not inclined to carve out two feet for "healthy" foods when the high-in-fat, high-in-cholesterol stuff sells so well. It is necessary to pay slotting allowances or offer other forms of incentive. Wenner is big on saving the planet; but he can afford to because he's winning the war in the store.

The Wholesome & Hearty product line includes the gardenSausage, gardenMexi, gardenVeggie, gardenSteak, and gardenVegan. The company also offers Original and Vanilla almondMylk, a dairy-free and soy-free alternative to milk, and almondCheeze, a lactose-free cheese alternative in four flavors.

Customers know that a percentage of their dollar goes back into useful charities, principally to heal the environment. When will Wholesome & Hearty Foods attract major competition? And will it have the street smarts to defend itself? We shall see.

WORK/FAMILY DIRECTIONS

Rising health-care costs are driven by behavioral or lifestyle risks. Corporations are bearing the burden for health-care costs, thus they are looking at behavioral issues—alcoholism, eating disorders, drugs, nutrition, divorce. Extensive studies of 20,000 employees at Control Data and Steelcase Corporation show that the greater the numbers of behavior risk factors, the higher the cost of health care. Corporations are becoming aware of this correlation, but only about one in ten are doing something about it. Fran Sussner Rogers saw the need to reduce behavioral risks for corporate employees more than 10 years ago. Her discovery came by accident.

When Rogers's first child developed asthma, she had to begin working at home part time. As a result, she was pressured and then written off by the educational consulting firm she worked for.

"I knew I could be a good mother and get my work done, but the company didn't," she says. So she began her own consulting business from home, counseling individuals and companies on resolving conflicts between work and family. The business allowed her more flexibility and control over her life than she had ever had before, as well as the opportunity to work on issues she cared about deeply.

Work/Family Directions creates and manages dependent-care programs for more than 100 companies, including IBM, AT&T, and American Express. Services range from advice on where to find appropriate day care and elder care to a counselor-staffed telephone consulting service that helps parents motivate their children, solve learning problems, and select schools. Work/Family also trains managers to be sensitive to family issues and conducts research on the changing demographics of the labor force.

"The market for helping employees deal with family issues is pretty big, and it's untapped," Rogers says. Indeed, only about 7,000 of the 78,000 U.S. companies with more than 100 workers offer employees some form of child-care support such as referral services for day care, on-site day care, or after-school programs, according to the Families and Work Institute, a New York research and consulting firm. Yet child care is a pressing need for many employees. In a 1991–1992 study of 10 companies conducted by the institute, 33 percent of employees reported difficulty locating child care.

Child care is just one segment of the market, however. Experts in work and family issues say that the need for elder care will explode in

WORK/FAMILY DIRECTIONS

Chief Executive Officer:	Fran Sussner Rogers
Principal Location:	930 Commonwealth Ave. Boston, MA 02215
Telephone/Fax:	617-278-4000/617-566-2806
Satellite Locations:	none
Date Founded:	1983
Description of Business:	Consults with companies to put together work-family programs.
# Employees Current:	312
# Employees Projected by 6/30/95:	330
Sales (Annualized) 1994:	40,000,000
Gross Profit Margin (GPM):	Company is privately-held and not required to make its financial statements public.
Selling Expenses/Sales:	not available
% Sales Increase 1991–94:	not available
% Change GPM 1991–94:	not available
Total Debt/Net Worth:	not available
Net Profits Before Taxes:	not available
Net Profits per Employee:	not available
Principal Competitors:	not available
# Potential Selling Sites:	Domestic: 2,500 Foreign: not applicable
Problem Company Is Attempting to Solve:	Women are a rising percentage of the workforce, but they have unique stressors that they bring to the workplace.
Solution Company Is Conveying to Problem:	Works with corporations to adapt to worker needs by introducing dependent-care programs and part-time hours for those with parenting responsibilities.

the next decade. About 10 percent of employees today are responsible for an aging relative, says Dana Friedman, Co-president of the Families and Work Institute. Based on employee expectations in companies she's surveyed, that figure will jump to 40 percent by 1997. "It is going to be huge," Friedman says. "And we find that there's a more significant work impact from elder care than child care because it's not just [finding] a place to put your elderly relative—it's medical, and legal, and health and in-home [services], and transportation."

Work/Family Directions' first big client was IBM, which asked Rogers to develop a nationwide day-care referral service for its employees. With start-up funds from IBM, Rogers set up a team and a database. Soon other Fortune 500 companies knocked on her door. The business, which Rogers moved out of her house and into an office building when her children were five and two, now has offices in San Francisco and Chicago, has grown from 8 employees and $2 million in revenues in 1985 to 240 employees and nearly $40 million in revenues in 1993. Rogers and her staff work with more than 90 companies a year.

Rogers developed the confidence to start a business from her mother, who shared responsibilities with her father in a small upholstery business that the couple ran. "They would process the day's request at dinner and the emphasis was always on customer service," Rogers says. "The other great influence in my life was Eleanor Roosevelt. My family revered her as someone who could make a difference. She visited my home town when I was six years old, and she left an indelible impression on me."

Of her company's success Rogers says, "We've always said we started out as a mission that became a business. Now we're a business with a mission. The desire to get rich or produce a big, successful company was not the goal," says Rogers. "It's just a wonderful by-product of doing wonderful work."

WORKSTATION TECHNOLOGIES, INC.

The dominant factor driving the PC revolution is the force of creativity and specialization that Adam Smith identified two centuries ago as the economic engine we know as entrepreneurship. Digital wireless mobile communications—sending data upline or downline from the road to the home office, to a branch, or to a vendor—has made the laptop and palmtop computer business a $39 billion industry, according to Frost & Sullivan. When *video* is added to the laptop and to the palmtop, yet another industry is created; another degree of specialization; another handful of entrepreneurs digging through the low point of the "S" curve known as the tunnel.

Workstation Technologies, Inc. is the clear leader in the very important race to produce *video on demand*. The trophy is wealth at the Microsoft level—more than $20 billion—for the company that licenses this technology to the telephone carriers and to Hollywood. Only Workstation can send a color picture over standard analog telephone lines. This gives it a significant lead over the competition, some of whom are well-funded and charging hard.

Its other products include black and white color video codecs, software, cameras, and related products for the Macintosh, PC, and PS/2 operating environments. When integrated into a modular host architecture, these products deliver high-quality video conferencing on a desktop computer, at the lowest price point in the market. "We've evolved without venture capital," says Workstation's co-founder and CEO, Chris Miner, a Norwich, New York native. "OEM (original equipment manufacturers) customers paying upfront with orders and strategic alliances have been our funding sources."

One of Workstation's well-heeled competitors is Voyant Corp. Jim Wilson founded Voyant Corp. two years ago to develop a digital video wireless mobile computer. He brought Bruce Smith, the former CEO of Nomadic Systems, Inc., and Network Equipment Technology Corp., to run the company. Together they raised venture capital from Nazem Corp., Cirrus Logic, Inc. (a Quantum Company), and Cable & Wireless PLC.

"We believe we have the engineering team to bring video to the palmtop," says Smith. "This may not be the biggest market for mobile digital video. But it's the job of the entrepreneur to find the lowest hanging fruit. And movies on demand will be the first market, before mobile digital video adopts a serious following."

WORKSTATION TECHNOLOGIES, INC.

Chief Executive Officer:	Christopher D. Miner
Principal Location:	18010 Sky Park Circle Irvine, CA 92714
Telephone/Fax:	714-250-8983/714-250-8969
Satellite Locations:	none
Date Founded:	1989
Description of Business:	Developed the technology to enable media and telecommunications companies to send color video over standard analog telephone lines.
# Employees Current:	35
# Employees Projected by 6/30/95:	50
Sales (Annualized) 1994:	$10,000,000
Gross Profit Margin (GPM):	The company is privately-held and not required to make public its financial statements.
Selling Expenses/Sales:	not available
% Sales Increase 1991–94:	not available
% Change GPM 1991–94:	not available
Total Debt/Net Worth:	not available
Net Profits Before Taxes:	not available
Net Profits per Employee:	not available
Principal Competitors:	Innovasys, Inc., Voyant, Intel, Apple, Hewlett-Packard
# Potential Selling Sites:	Domestic: 30 million Foreign: 60 million
Problem the Company Is Attempting to Solve:	There are a number of significant problems that could be mitigated by mobile wireless video communication, perhaps the largest of which are credit card fraud, kidnapping and child abuse, death due to misdiagnosing and anaphylactic reaction to drugs, and the crimes of burglary and armed robbery.
Solution Company Is Conveying to Problem:	Deliver high-quality video conferencing on a desktop computer, at low cost.

Whereas Voyant designed the principal chip to bring video from the sender or caller, through the laptop/palmtop and up to the screen, Innovasys, Inc., in St. Louis, Missouri, run by Malaysian-born Yit K. Lee, has begun at the palmtop level and is working on compressing video signals to its small screen. Innovasys shipped $20 million of Handbit palmtop computers in the last 12 months, and Lee says, "We hope to have developed a video chip and be in production by late 1995." Lee is less optimistic about video on demand. "It uses too much memory; and it takes about 30 minutes to download a full-length movie." This barrier persuades Lee to take Innovasys into industrial rather than consumer channels.

Smith sees the consumer carrying a small box. "It will be full-featured, with voice, caller i.d., data, and video," says Smith. "It will have a small camera, keyboard, and telephone handset. It will be ubiquitous." Voyant is Smith's third launch, and the day I interviewed him at Voyant's offices in Fremont, he was wearing a backbrace. "These lift-offs get heavier with age," he joked. Smith has the credentials to attract serious amounts of capital, enabling him to operate in what he calls "a sphere of confidence, driven by the approbation of the marketplace."

Workstation Technologies, Voyant, or Innovasys. Which one will the fountain bless?

XILINX, INC.

In 1985, Xilinx introduced a new type of programmable logic device that forever changed the landscape of the custom integrated circuit (IC) market. Xilinx's invention of field programmable gate arrays (FPGAs) has resulted in one of the fastest growing segments in the semiconductor arena. According to *Dataquest*, Xilinx maintains a 72 percent share of the FPGA market, which is expected to grow from $117 million in 1990 to $688 million in 1995. The recent acquisition of start-up Plus Logic Inc. expands the potential market for Xilinx products to $1.1 billion in 1995. Field programmable gate arrays are standard ICs programmed by system designers to meet the unique logic requirements of most electronic systems. Logic circuits provide the characteristics that differentiate one system from another. Xilinx holds numerous patents on its proprietary Logic Cell™ Array (LCA) technology and its XACT™ development system software, which programs the LCA devices. Xilinx's customers, including IBM, Siemens, Sharp, AT&T, Ericsson, Fujitsu, and Hewlett Packard, have endorsed the production worthiness of its FPGAs, while benefiting from the significant time-to-market savings these novel devices provide.

To visualize the Xilinx FPGA, picture a blank slate that can be drawn on by the system designer at her facility to implement a set of digital logic functions required by the customer. She has everything in the FPGA slate to create a new design in a mere few hours. She has never worked with anything so efficient.

Xilinx has continued to improve its offerings in the six years since it introduced its first product. With its newest third-generation family, Xilinx has increased the density and speed of its devices by a factor of four. The company also has made its software easier to use. The introduction of X-Blox synthesis software in November 1991 created a new standard for FPGA synthesis tools. Not only are tedious gate-level design methods eliminated with X-Blox, but the powerful tool allows designers to increase chip utilization and performance. Xilinx FPGAs and the XACT development system software have set a new standard for digital logic in electronic systems.

Xilinx enjoys an installed base of more than 11,000 software sites. About half of these sites are in North America, with a quarter in Europe and most of the remainder in Japan. Xilinx's goal is to increase its

XILINX, INC.

Chief Executive Officer:	Bernard V. Vonderschmitt
Principal Location:	2100 Logic Dr. San Jose, CA 95124
Telephone/Fax:	408-559-7778/408-559-7114
Satellite Locations:	Edinburgh, Scotland; Tokyo, Japan; Hong Kong; Munich, Germany; Surrey, U.K.; Jouy en Josas Celes, France
Date Founded:	1984
Description of Business:	Designs, develops, and markets CMOS programmable logic integrated circuits.
# Employees Current:	732
# Employees Projected by 6/30/95:	950
Sales 1994:	$256,448,000
Gross Profit Margin (GPM):	61.5%
Selling Expenses/Sales:	22.7%
% Sales Increase 1992–94:	+262.7%
% Change GPM 1992–94:	+9.5%
Total Debt/Net Worth:	30.8%
Operating Ratio:	26.3%
Net Profits Before Taxes:	$67,436,000
Net Profits per Employee:	$97,875
Traded On:	NASDAQ/XLNX
Principal Competitors:	Altera, AT&T, Cypress Semiconductor, Motorola, Quicklogic
# Potential Selling Sites:	Domestic: 30,000 Foreign: 60,000
Problem Company Is Attempting to Solve:	Logic circuits provide the characteristics that differentiate one electronic system from another. If logic circuits are programmed while they are being manufactured the manufacturing cost drops, and the time-to-market will fall dramatically.
Solution Company Is Conveying to Problem:	Produces programmable logic ICs and licenses its technology to others and subcontracts its manufacturing.

installed base of software sites to 25,000 over the next two years. Xilinx has shipped well over 11 million LCA devices to more than 3,500 companies worldwide.

To reach its broad customer base, Xilinx has established a worldwide sales network that includes 10 direct sales offices, 128 locations for manufacturers, representatives, and 7 distributors. This network operates throughout North America and in 24 countries in Europe and Asia.

Xilinx is one of the fabless semiconductor companies. (See Atmel for definition.) From its inception, the company decided its FPGAs would be manufactured using readily available, well-proven semiconductor process technology. This would enable it to focus on design, architecture, and market development, rather than on process. A long-term manufacturing agreement with Seiko Epson gives Xilinx access to one of the world's most advanced complementary metal oxide semiconductor (CMOS) fabrication facilities. Xilinx added Yamaha in 1991 as a second foundry. Today, Xilinx LCA devices are manufactured in at least three separate facilities on a contract basis; a tenet of the virtual corporation: minimize the investment in brick and mortar.

The numbers tell the story of a remarkable, well-managed company. Net Profits per Employee are a smashing $97,875. GPM is 61.5 percent and rising. Net Worth is $173 million, and cash plus marketable securities aggregates $115.6 million. These numbers are at March 31, 1994. If you vector the company's net profits growth out five years at 40 percent per annum, it will earn $310 million after taxes in the year 2000 and have more than $1 billion in cash on hand; all in 15 years.

XIRCOM, INC.

Today's portable computers are ideal tools for executives, workers, and students on the go. They offer the speed and power of desktop PCs in a small, light, battery-powered machine. Since 1991 their numbers in worldwide business use have grown from 11 to 18.5 million and are projected to swell to 37 million units in 1997. But portable PCs are only as valuable as the information they can reach, information that is usually stored on local area networks (LANs). Xircom is expert at providing network access for the growing army of nomadic computer users.

In 1989 Xircom pioneered the use of personal computers' parallel port to connect portable PCs to LANs, creating a new market: laptop-to-LAN connectivity. Today Xircom leads this market with a broad family of Pocket LAN Adapters and PCMCIA-compliant CreditCard LAN adapters that work with virtually all portable PCs and networks. In 1993, Xircom dominated the parallel-port LAN adapter market with an 82 percent share and led the emerging PCMCIA-compliant LAN adapter market with a 49 percent share.

Its newest product, the Xircom Netwave, connects portable PCs to LANs via radio transmissions. With Netwave, users can roam freely within offices while maintaining seamless access to the network. Xircom's new Ethernet+Modem products are the first in the industry to combine an Ethernet LAN adapter and a high-speed data/fax modem, eliminating the need for two cards.

Xircom addresses two growth trends in the mobile connectivity industry: business users' increased reliance on portable PCs and their need to connect those PCs to networks. The worldwide installed base of portable PCs used in business applications, primarily notebooks and subnotebooks, is projected to grow at a compound annual rate of 22 percent through 1997. The percentage of these portable PCs connected to networks is projected to double during the same period. Xircom addresses parallel-port and PCMCIA card connections between portable PCs and LANs, which currently account for 80 percent of the market. (The other 20 percent are connected through docking stations.) Xircom sells its products primarily through national and international distributors, supported by sales and service organizations in the United States, Europe, and Hong Kong. International sales constituted 43 percent of total sales for fiscal 1993.

XIRCOM, INC.

Chief Executive Officer:	Dirk I. Gathers
Principal Location:	26025 Mureau Rd. Calabrass, CA 91302
Telephone/Fax:	818-878-7600/818-878-7630
Satellite Locations:	Antwerp, Belgium; Hong Kong
Date Founded:	1983
Description of Business:	Leading provider of products for connecting laptop computers to LANs.
# Employees Current:	193
# Employees Projected by 6/30/95:	Company withheld
Sales (Annualized) 1994:	$88,418,000
Gross Profit Margin (GPM):	53.7%
Selling Expenses/Sales:	20.8%
% Sales Increase 1991–94:	+335.9%
% Change GPM 1991 94:	+4.5%
Total Debt/Net Worth:	18.6%
Net Profits Before Taxes:	$15,819,000
Operating Ratio:	19.2%
Net Profits per Employee:	$81,964
Traded On:	NASDAQ/XIRC
Principal Competitors:	Toshiba, NEC, Texas Instruments, Megahertz
# Potential Selling Sites:	Domestic: 250 Foreign: 350
Problem Company Is Attempting to Solve:	Connectivity—keeping traveling business executives in touch with their offices.
Solution Company Is Conveying to Problem:	Developed a family of products that connect laptop/palmtop users with their LANs.

To say the market for connectivity products is competitive is like saying boxing is a contact sport. The mobile connectivity market is brutally tough, and the parameters are constantly changing as the technology makes quantum leaps in product simplicity and cost reduction.

The ultimate in mobile connectivity is wireless wide area networking, or wireless WAN. In the future it will be possible to easily and economically connect to an office network from just about anywhere—in a taxi or at a sidewalk cafe. True location independence. As digital cellular networks come online, performance, reliability, and cost will all be improved. And future cellular modems will take advantage of these advances to offer ubiquitous network connections. The emergence of wireless WANs will also likely coincide with advancements in "personal digital assistants," or PDAs. Wireless WAN solutions will enable these new generations of mobile pen-based and palmtop computers to become the real personal communication and productivity enhancing tools that they were designed to be. International Data Corp. estimates that more than 4 million PDAs will be in use by 1996.

This elegantly managed company richly deserves a P/E ratio in the Ascend, Cambridge Technology Partners, PARCPlace Systems area. Xircom addresses an exploding market. Its sales grew 213.0 percent over the last four years. Its GPM is 53.7 percent and rising. Profits per Employee are $81,964, placing it in the top 10 of all Quantum Companies, and producing an Operating Ratio of 19.2 percent. The company's P/E ratio? An uncomplimentary 20.0x. The reasons for this dichotomy are several, but an obvious one is that it takes five words ("laptop-to-LAN-connectivity-devices") to explain what Xircom does for a living, and stock buyers like simpler stories. Another is location: NASDAQ tables are too long to fit on one page *and* the prices of Xilinx, Xircom, and Zebra Technologies—three of the most exciting Quantum Companies—are carried over and buried next to coffee futures. Notably these three companies have P/E ratios in the low 20s. They richly deserve more.

ZEBRA TECHNOLOGIES CORP.

Zebra Technologies Corp. was founded in 1969 by Edward L. Kaplan, 51, and Gerald Cless, 54, who pooled their resources ($500 apiece) to form what was then called Data Specialties, Inc. In 1986, having located a niche in the bar-code labeling field, they changed the name of the company to Zebra.

Zebra's products include a broad line of computerized demand bar-code printers, specialty bar-code labeling/ticketing material (including adhesives), and ink ribbons. The company's equipment and supplies are designed to be operated at the user's location to produce bar-coded labels in extremely time-sensitive and physically demanding production environments.

Zebra's machines range in price from $1,600 to $10,000, and after the sale-in, there are years of follow-on supplies to sell the customer. Zebra's labels can be applied to any surface, such as plastic, metal sheeting, and textiles. They are used in U.S. Steel's mills, affixed to coils of steel at a temperature of 400° F, and they are used to label a unique library of DNA samples at Los Alamos National Laboratory, which are stored at –110° F and are then repeatedly thawed and restored. Zebra also creates high-security black-on-black bar-codes that are readable only by machine.

One of Zebra's customers, Pillowtex Corp., regards Zebra as "our insurance policy." Pillowtex sells $200 million worth of bedding products annually, and much of that goes to Kmart, which fines its manufacturers $5 per carton for every carton that has an unreadable inventory label. With up to 400 bedding cartons per trailer without proper labeling, the Kmart fine could be punitive without proper labeling.

Kaplan and crew turn out some elegant numbers, by the way. Net Profits per Employee of $82,266 places the company among the top 10 Quantum Companies in this important category. GPM is 49.8 percent and has been rising, notwithstanding that the customer base is so cheap they've been seen looking for dimes in the parking lots. And Zebra's Operating Ratio is a stunning 32.6 percent. Zebra's P/E ratio is the only disappointing number associated with this company: 24.0x in mid-1994.

Industry analysts foresee the $2 billion bar-code products industry growing approximately 18 percent per annum through the rest of the decade. That augers well for Zebra.

ZEBRA TECHNOLOGIES CORP.

Chief Executive Officer:	Edward L. Kaplan
Principal Location:	333 Corporate Woods Pkwy. Vernon Hills, IL 60601
Telephone/Fax:	708-634-6700/708-913-8766
Satellite Locations:	Preston, United Kingdom
Date Founded:	1969
Description of Business:	Designs, develops, manufactures, sells, and supports a broad line of bar-code labeling and ticket printing systems for industry and government.
# Employees Current:	330
# Employees Projected by 6/30/95:	Company withheld
Sales 1993:	$87,456,000
Gross Profit Margin (GPM):	49.8%
Selling Expenses/Sales:	10.5%
% Sales Increase 1991–93:	+91.7%
% Change GPM 1991–93:	+2.8%
Total Debt/Net Worth:	26.5%
Net Profit Before Taxes:	$28,468,000
Operating Ratio:	32.6%
Net Profits per Employee:	$82,266
Traded On:	NASDAQ/ZBRA
# Potential Selling Sites:	Domestic: 10,000 Foreign: 25,000
Problem Company Is Attempting to Solve:	Need for industrial bar-code labeling systems for virtually any surface.
Solution Company Is Conveying to Problem:	Design bar-code labeling systems for manufacturers of myriad products, from pillows to rolled steel, helping them lower manufacturing costs with improved production controls.

ZIA METALLURGICAL PROCESSES, INC.

The most efficient plant built by U.S. Steel or any other steel maker using conventional production methods has capital costs of $7,500 per ton for every ton it ships out. A steel mill built using Zia Metallurgical's method will cost from $300 to $500 million to construct. Each ton of special bar quality (SBQ) steel will cost $300 per ton, and each ton of finished steel (thin slab) will cost $500. The capital cost savings ranges from 1/15 to 1/25 of U.S. Steel's capital costs for its most efficient mill. As for operating costs, a Zia Metallurgical plant costs 40 percent less than a conventional U.S. Steel plant to operate.

If you built a Zia steel mill next door to a Nucor mini-mill, the capital costs to produce the same SBQ would be 25 percent less at the Zia plant—$300 vs. $400 per ton. And given constant raw material costs, the Zia operating costs would be 20 to 40 percent less than Nucor's. The favorite steel mill of the stock market, Nucor sports a P/E ratio of 43.0x in mid-1994.

"Now which steel mill will the emerging countries want to build?," asks Ed Bottinelli, Zia's CEO. "They do not have scrap metal; thus mini-mills are out. If it's between a traditional integrated steel mill and a Zia steel mill, Zia will become the dominant steel mill of the twenty-first century." Currently there is a working prototype in Pennsylvania and a Kobe Steel plant in Japan built using Zia's original patents, developed 16 years ago. Zia's first full-scale plant will go up in Puerto Rico in 1995.

The process works like this: Zia has developed and patented a steelmaking process capable of converting iron ore and iron-bearing metallurgical wastes directly into high-quality steel products. The process utilizes a proprietary design rotary hearth furnace to convert iron-bearing materials, palletized with coal or other forms of carbon, into a carbon-containing direct reduced iron (DRI). This DRI is fed, hot from the rotary hearth furnace, into a patented Zia All-Purpose Vessel (ZAV), where it is melted and refined into high-quality steel.

A specially designed turret with three independent arms, each supporting a separate ZAV, comprises the heart of the melt shop. No overhead cranes are required to transport molten metal from the smelting/refining operation to the ladle metallurgy station, then to the caster and back to the smelting/refining point. The molten steel is contained in the ZAV throughout the operations, eliminating the possibility of steel contamination by nonmetallic inclusions occasioned

ZIA METALLURGICAL PROCESSES, INC.

Chief Executive Officer:	N. Edward Bottinelli
Principal Location:	5344 Alpha Rd. Dallas, TX 75240
Telephone/Fax:	214-980-7700/214-233-8213
Satellite Locations:	The company's first plant is under construction in Puerto Rico.
Date Founded:	1992
Description of Business:	Designed and developed a unique, proprietary, and substantially less expensive means of producing steel.
# Employees Current:	8
# Employees Projected by 6/30/95:	12
Sales 1993:	none
Gross Profit Margin (GPM):	The company is privately-held and therefore not required to make its financial statements public.
Selling Expenses/Sales:	not available
% Sales Increase 1991–93:	not available
% Change GPM 1991–93:	not available
Total Debt/Net Worth:	not available
Net Profit Before Taxes:	not available
Net Profits per Employee:	not available
Principal Competitors:	Nucor, U.S. Steel, Kobe, Bethlehem, LTV Weirton
# Potential Selling Sites:	Domestic: 25 Foreign: 75
Problem Company Is Attempting to Solve:	The steel industry is plagued by environmental, quality, financial, and overcapacity problems. Mini-mills, so popular a decade ago, are running out of their raw material, scrap metal.
Solution Company Is Conveying to Problem:	Zia Metallurgical developed a steelmaking process that is less expensive and produces a higher-quality material in an environmentally friendly manner.

by exposure to ambient air during metal transfer into ladles. The result is very clean, low-carbon generic steel that can be alloyed to produce virtually any desired grade, from stainless steel to common structural steel.

Almost any reasonable source of iron oxide can be used as DRI feedstock: The dust from existing blast furnaces and basic oxygen furnaces, scale from steel rolling operations, red mud from bauxite operations, waste from copper mining operations, and other iron-bearing metallurgical wastes can all serve as iron oxides for DRI in this process.

The required carbon can also come from various sources. Blast furnace dust, for example, contains a significant amount of carbon. While not all carbon sources are suitably reactive to serve as a reductant in the DRI process, there is a wide range to choose from.

The Zia steelmaking technology has taken well-known, currently employed steelmaking practices and refined them into a simple and easily controlled direct steelmaking process. Iron oxides and carbon are transformed directly into high-quality steel without the intermediate ironmaking step. Coke plants and blast furnaces, with their extremely high capital costs and environmental problems, are completely by-passed. Steel is directly produced in an environmentally friendly manner, with no undesirable by-products left for disposal. All water is either recirculated or evaporated in the rotary hearth furnace or by the cooling of slag. Any dust collected is put right back to use in the process, as is scale from steel rolling operations. Slag is processed to recover metallics and is sold as aggregate. Nothing remains for landfill disposal in any form other than the normal office paper, miscellaneous carton and supply packaging, and the domestic sewage and wastewater from the offices and change houses. (Zia will treat wastewater and use it for maintaining landscaping.)

To put a fine point on it, if a Zia plant can sell steel to the automobile industry in the United States or South East Asia or Europe for 30 percent less than an integrated mill or mini-mill, is Zia going to get the business? You bet it is.

PART THREE

INDEXES

GEOGRAPHIC INDEX

COMPANY INDEX

INDUSTRY INDEX